Ariel —
Hope your Best
Rob Armstrong

Daddy 3.0
A Comedy of Errors

A Novel

ROB ARMSTRONG

Gear Press
Philadelphia

Copyright © 2016 Rob Armstrong
All rights reserved.

ISBN: 0997588101
ISBN 13: 9780997588101
Library of Congress Control Number: 2016941536
Gear Press, Wayne, PA

To Jen, Lena, and Debby for the motivation, inspiration, and support.

ABOUT THE AUTHOR

Rob Armstrong mines comedy from his own life as a stay-at-home dad.

After graduating from the Wharton School of Business, he worked in communication finance, before taking an "early retirement" to look after his two daughters.

Armstrong lives with his wife and daughters in the Greater Philadelphia area. He has served as treasurer of the local PTA and as an elected member of the school board.

The characters and events in this book are fictitious. Any similarity to real persons, living or dead, is coincidental and not intended by the author.

All rights reserved. In accordance with the US Copyright Act of 1976, the scanning, uploading, and electronic showing of any part of this book without the permission of the publisher constitutes unlawful piracy and theft of the author's intellectual property. If you would like to use material from this book (other than for review purposes), prior written permission must be obtained by contacting the publisher at editor@gearpress.org.

Thank you for your support of the author's rights.

Gear Press

Philadelphia

www.gearpress.org

CONTENTS

Daddy 3.0
A Comedy of Errors

1

DON'T EAT THE SAND

My attitude about most everything was lousy. This negativity placed me on the wrong side of Supermom. Supermom was everything I was not. She was a walking checklist of desirable qualities: tall, skinny, tan, blond, blue eyed, and attractive. She wore stylish clothes, hailed from a well-heeled family from Connecticut, was married to a rising-star orthopedic surgeon, had graduated from Harvard with a degree in English, was an avid skier and tennis player, was a great cook, and was fluent in French. Her five-year plan, after her son and daughter, ages four and three, reached school age, was to start and run a charitable foundation directed toward issues of poverty among women in sub-Saharan Africa. Supermom was the rare person who required no more than four hours of sleep a night, and she was able to utilize the extra hours each day for things such as keeping up correspondence with a seemingly endless list of people who often vis-ited her. She was also the type of stay-at-home parent who would actually do rainy-day activities with her kids, such as painting, clay sculpting, and messy glue projects with feathers and glitter. Before the park incident, I had been on cordial terms with her, placing her in the category of being otherworldly—like a two-dimensional superhero character, ready to take on the world and never requiring a potty break.

Supermom was slow in meeting us that day, but she did unfortunately come. It was late afternoon, and the twins were fighting over a broken sand scoop. I said several times, "Claire. Maude. Can you play nicely and share?" Unfortunately, three-year-olds have short memories. My patience ran thin. Around me were packed kids, moms, and nannies, all of us trapped in a hot asphalt park, not yet ready to return to our cramped Upper East Side apartments. At any point in time, at least one kid could be heard crying or screaming. I had nowhere else to take the girls that didn't cost money. In Manhattan, circling the block cost five bucks. I had an hour to kill until Liz finished up at the hospital and we could go to our Friday dinner at Mandarin Deli. She had been working a boatload of hours since starting her surgical fellowship at the Hospital for Special Surgery on July 1. It was one of those days—a crab-apple day. The problem was that now most every day was a crab-apple day.

The novelty of being a stay-at-home dad had worn off. I was still looking for work but had few job leads. That day, I had received another rejection call from another second interview. While I was feeling sorry for myself, a grimy boy, maybe four, peed in the sandpit. I looked around for his keeper, but no one seemed to be with the kid. The kid pissed for about five seconds before other people started to notice. The sandpit cleared. "Whose kid is this?" I shouted. "He can't do that here."

Ignoring me, he finished his business. Suddenly, a grandmotherly woman pushed through the crowd that had formed and screamed at the kid in a language with many hard consonants. She tugged at his arm and dragged him away. Eventually, kids began to settle back into the sandpit, keeping clear of the area of drainage until it dried. I suggested to my girls that they move on to the jungle gym. I got no argument.

My friend Good Heart had finally gotten to the park with her daughter, Sammie. "Some kid just peed in the sand pit. Do you believe it?"

"Our pediatrician told us to avoid the sand boxes in the parks. Rats play in them at night," Good Heart said. "Do you let your twins play in the sand?"

"Not now, I'm not." Good Heart had a gap-tooth smile, which she hoped to rectify as soon as her husband completed his medical fellowship and they could afford cosmetic dental work.

I lost sight of Claire and Maude, as they blended into the swarm of kids on the jungle gym, despite having distinctive curly blond hair. No matter what I was doing in the park, I instinctively looked for the kids every thirty seconds. The thought of not knowing where the kids were scared me. Good Heart understood my need to chase after the kids. I was learning that it was rare to have a full conversation with another adult.

Maude and Claire were hidden beneath the jungle gym, arguing with a slightly older kid over a bike with training wheels. Maude was straddling it, demonstrating her imagined ownership of it. She pulled against the boy's grip on the handle bar. Her loyal sister yelled, "Our bike."

I said, "This bike doesn't belong to you. You have to ask him for a turn if you want to ride it."

Maude kept pulling on the bike. She was not going to yield. The little boy started to stutter-cry.

"Can they have a turn for a little bit, please?" I asked.

"It mine," he wailed.

Fearing a confrontation with my spunky little Maude, I bent down to speak to the boy, thinking he might be more reasonable than my own child. "My kids are younger than you and don't understand what it means to share. Can you be a big boy and show them how sharing is done?"

As soon as I said it, I knew I had screwed up. I had failed to heed the prime directive of parenting: do not impose your parenting style on another person's kid.

"That's my son's bike," a woman yelled. "And don't you lecture my boy."

"Sorry."

"I don't want 'sorry.' Just get your kids away."

"You don't have to be nasty. Everybody knows that when you bring a toy to the park, you kinda of have to be willing to share it."

Second mistake. Do not impose your parenting style on other parents.

What followed was a verbal volley that not only started to draw the attention of those around us, but also caused me to say, "Don't curse in front of the kids. It's just a bike. Let me buy you and your son an ice cream. No hard feelings."

Third and fourth mistakes, simultaneously—don't tell a person who has clearly gone off the deep end to stop cursing, and never say "no hard feelings" to soften a situation.

She cursed not only in English, but also in Spanish. She was so complete in her litany of expletives that surely none was left out in either language. Her final threat upon leaving was that I should never come back to the park again or her boyfriend would tear my arm off and beat me senseless with it.

In an instant, I became the buzz of the park. Fortunately, since I was a guy, I'd be forgiven for not knowing the rules of park etiquette. Stay-at-home dads get a lot of free passes in the world of moms.

Good Heart and I met back up at the swings. Our kids swung as we talked. Good Heart had been dragged from the bowels of the Midwest by her spouse, who was in his second year of a three-year oncology fellowship at the prestigious Memorial Sloan Kettering Cancer Center. (Reader note: try saying Memorial Sloan Kettering Cancer Center while gargling with mouthwash.) Good Heart was a tall woman, big boned, but not heavy, who still held the athletic physique of her time in college basketball ten years earlier. Her long, dirty-blond hair was forever in a ponytail, while her typical attire drew heavily from her collection of exercise clothes. Her narrow eyes and thin lips gave the trace impression of melancholy, which was tied to her open and freely discussed desire to be back home, with a tight network of family and friends. She was six months into her second pregnancy; the twenty-week ultrasound had hinted that it might be a boy.

"Rough day, Nick?" she said.

"I've got to learn to keep my mouth shut."

"Especially in New York. What were you thinking?"

"I didn't say anything bad. That woman was a nut job."

"But even if she's wrong, just keep apologizing. You've got to think about the safety of your girls."

"Things didn't get that bad. She was just blowing off steam. Normal people don't go postal."

"You don't know that in New York," she said.

Good Heart was dramatic. Her world was filled with lurking fears. I just knew she was a "defensive driver," even though I had never been in a car with her.

Just then, Nifty-Fifty Wife and Supermom joined us in the swing-set corral. Nifty-Fifty Wife's daughter, Sofia, was asleep in her stroller. Supermom's kids, Mitch Jr. and Hillary, circled the crowded set of swings, waiting for a turn. Mitch Jr. was not a patient little cowboy type.

"Where are you coming from?" Good Heart said.

"Mitch Jr. wanted to watch the feeding of the sea lions over at the Central Park Zoo," Supermom said.

Good Heart seemed disappointed. "You should've called me to go. Sammie's been asking for Hillary all day."

"I called you, but it rang and rang," Supermom said.

"I've got a lot of cell phone problems in this city. I never had these issues back home. What service do you guys use?" Good Heart said.

I loved the "I tried to call you, but you didn't get it" excuse. It was the modern equivalent of "the check is in the mail." Supermom was clever— my guess was that she didn't want to be with Good Heart at the zoo. Supermom tended to hang with the well-dressed, "sophisticated" moms. Good Heart was a hick from armpit junction.

After stalking the swings for several minutes, Mitch Jr. made his move and tugged on Claire's swing chain, hoping to slow her. "It's my turn," he said. Mitch Jr. was about a year older than the girls. And he was a little snot.

Claire tumbled from the low swing and hit the rubber playground mat below. It was a slow-motion fall. It didn't seem too bad—more drama than actual pain. She starting crying, holding her elbow.

I bent down and kissed her elbow. "Are you okay, Claire Bear?"

"Mitch Jr., can we be a little gentler?" I asked. Again, I failed to heed the prime directive of parenting.

Maude stopped swinging. She shoved Mitch Jr. to the ground as he tried to climb into Claire's empty swing.

"Maude just pushed Mitch Jr." Supermom said.

Her regal holier-than-thou tone pissed me off. "Pushing happens with little kids. Don't you think he kind of deserved it a little bit?" I said.

Maybe I should have delivered my response with humor. Or maybe I could have been more charming that day. More sleep the night before might have helped me to be more patient and tactful. Or maybe I should have been as uptight and neurotic as Supermom and admonished Maude for her defense of her sister. Any of these actions might have averted her newfound displeasure of me. I noticed the soft clench of her jaw and the slight narrowing of her eyes after I spoke. I had screwed up big time.

"Mitch Jr., please apologize to Claire. We do not ever put our hands on other people in anger," Supermom said. "Say you're sorry,"

Mitch Jr. mumbled an apology and again climbed onto the swing.

Good Heart spoke. "It's been a long day for everybody. The kids must be getting their late-afternoon grumpies. I certainly could use a nap and a snack."

Good Heart was becoming a dependable apologist for me. Whenever I did something boneheaded, she seemed to know when I needed a lifeline. I guess she felt sorry for me because I sucked at the whole stay-at-home parent thing. Supermom smiled at Good Heart. She helped Hillary into the swing that had been abandoned by Maude. I roped my arms around the girls so that no more altercations could occur.

Nifty-Fifty Wife concurred with her English-as-a-second-language skill. "This time of day is very hard for the little ones. Today, I am thankful that Sofia take a nap in the stroller. Matías do not like it when Sofia acts bratty with no nap." I had not spent a lot of time with Nifty-Fifty Wife. She seemed to be part of Supermom's orbit of stay-at-home women. She was married to a neuroradiologist who was in the middle of his second fellowship. They were from South America. I forget which country.

Supermom said, "Mitch Sr. likes the kids bathed and fed before he sees them. But most nights it doesn't matter, because he's in the OR late and misses them altogether."

To break the awkwardness I had created, I fumbled into the conversation. "I'm lucky that Liz is a snake charmer with the kids. She's able to change their mood pretty quickly, so the night goes smoothly. If she gets home early enough, she even gives them their bath." Why I felt the compulsive need to chat up my spouse, while they were running down their husbands, I'll never know, but Supermom's haughty vibe affected me.

"Does she do the cooking too?" Nifty-Fifty Wife said.

"She's too busy. She and Mitch are in the same program and have the same crazy schedule. I do the cooking, the cleaning, and the dragging of kids to activities and playdates," I said. Truth be told, my cooking consisted of boiling pasta and nuking canned pasta sauce. As for cleaning correctly—forget about it.

"I thought you had nanny. You make program of web things or something?" Nifty-Fifty Wife said.

"Back in San Francisco, I was a senior programmer."

The economy had turned crummy. The web start-up company that I had worked for had had more fun pretending to be a company than actually being a company that cared about profits. Any economist will tell you that a firm that provides three meals a day, fat salaries, and endless hours of free play to recharge employee morale, without actually having any sales, is not destined to stay in business very long. It was a lot of fun while the $20 million of venture funding lasted. I had had a good time, even if my stock options were now worthless. It didn't make sense to rattle around Silicon Valley like the Ghost of Christmas Past while Liz had a place at a top-notch program.

"So you don't have a job?" Nifty-Fifty Wife said.

It was embarrassing to be a guy without a job. I had thought staying home with the kids would be a part-time gig. Getting a job in New York seemed like a cool idea, but after a few months of hunting during a hiring slump, I discovered the number of job openings to be about the same as the number of hairs on my bald head. It seemed that the dot-com companies had finally decided to be prudent and control expenses. Go figure.

"He's one of us," Good Heart said.

"You're like that guy from the movie *Mr. Mom*," Nifty-Fifty Wife said.

I didn't like when someone made the *Mr. Mom* crack. But I did like the movie. Nifty-Fifty Wife made me uncomfortable about being the only guy from the building who was home with the kids. I felt like a screw-up when people realized I was no longer the breadwinner.

Until we had come to New York, the childcare issue had been very manageable. Most of Liz's immediate family lived in the Bay Area. Liz's homemaker mom had watched the kids during the day. At night, if both of us had been late coming home, Liz's nearby cousin had picked up the slack. We had been able to avoid the whole nanny-versus-daycare issue. As soon as we had moved to New York and Liz had hit the floors of the hospital for her one-year surgical fellowship, we had lost our safety nets. We had been forced to figure out the childcare strategy in a hurry.

There had been several facts to consider:

1. I was unemployable until the job market was taken off its respirator.
2. Liz's surgical fellowship was more than a full-time commitment.
3. Fellows don't make a lot of money.
4. Fellows don't make a lot of money.
5. We had no friends or family in New York that could help full-time with the kids.
6. Due to the abovementioned salary cap, the nanny option was out.
7. Daycare was a budget stretch since we could not count on significant financial help from either set of our tightwad parents. Liz's parents especially would not help, since they had not yet recovered from the shock that their daughter had chosen to marry me. They still held a grudge over my arrest for rappelling down a wall during college graduation. (I had wanted to impress Liz and march with her in the ceremony. One would think her parents would have been touched by such an act of devotion.)

The conclusion had been clear: logic dictated that until I was able to get a job in my field, I would watch the kids. The only problem with this childcare solution was that that the caregiver—me—was not in tune with kids. I was an only child and had never babysat for kids growing up. We all know that only children tend to be self-centered. And I had never found the kids of others to be particularly interesting or amusing.

As a kid, I had not liked growing up. As far as I'm concerned, growing up sucks and if you liked it, something is wrong with you. After our twins were born, nobody, including Liz, really had any big expectations that I would be an extraordinary parent. I never got up with the kids in the middle of the night. Because Liz breastfed them, she was already up, right? Liz was always with the twins on weekends or, if not, would get a babysitter to help out. I rarely was alone with the twins.

Pretty much, I had coasted through the first three years of child rearing. It had been quietly understood that I was the primary breadwinner. No one had ever penalized me for not being around. I had been the fun-time parent, coasting in for story time after their bath.

"This is just temporary. I'm looking for a job," I said.

Supermom said, "I love being home with the kids. My career is fine on hold. I'll never regret the time."

All the moms nodded.

"It makes such a difference in a child's development. It certainly beats a nanny or the daycare option," Supermom said.

"I've heard of so many problems with nannies," Nifty-Fifty Wife said.

"Like what? Not many people I know have nannies," Good Heart said.

"You see it in the park. Nannies ignore the kids and talk on their cell phones," Nifty-Fifty Wife said. "Or they let the kids cry in their strollers while they run personal errands. Back home, a friend of mine got a nanny cam and found out that her nanny left her daughter in the crib for hours so she could keep up with her soaps."

"And, what about when the nanny leaves abruptly to go to another family? Kids get upset. And you have to take time off from work," Supermom said.

"And forget about getting an au pair. It's like raising another child. Or you've got worse problems if she's skinny and pretty," Good Heart said.

"There are lots of good nannies. It's just the bad ones that stand out," I said.

"When you start working again, we will watch your nanny," Nifty-Fifty Wife said.

"And maybe Liz could slow down a little at the hospital and help out some more too," Supermom said.

I almost told Supermom to grow a hump and die. It amazed me how little support successful women got. Liz was competing in the macho zone with a wolf pack of orthopedic surgeons. Supermom's husband, Mitch Sr., was one of the alpha wolves, and he was a platinum-plated asshole. You could bet that none of Liz's male colleagues were berating each other over who was spending more time with his or her kids.

This time, I kept myself somewhat in check, but I probably should have done a better job. I didn't want to totally piss off Supermom twice in the same day. She could put a choke hold on my social network for Claire and Maude. Except for my friend Wolfie, whose kids were slightly older than mine, we didn't know anybody in New York. The families of other medical fellows were our only source for playdates. Plus, we all lived in the same building, and Supermom was the president of the family association. And everybody seemed to idolize her. When I went back to work, I wanted the girls to still have friends. So I made nice—but with a little twist of lemon.

"Your hubby is really good with the kids. You're lucky," I said.

No one except Supermom seemed to get my sarcasm. I knew she had because she validated my comment with too much enthusiasm.

"Mitch Sr. is a dear. The kids just love when he's around. They just forget about me as soon as he's home. *Daddy* this and *Daddy* that. I couldn't ask more from him."

Except for Good Heart, I don't think any of the stay-at-home moms in the family association had any real comfort with me. I was a male interloper into their world, and awkward in my new role. I should have done many things better that day.

2

THE GREEN WATERS OF MANDARIN DELI

Liz was irritable again.

Surgical fellowship was performing a personality transplant on her. While understandable, it was no less annoying or difficult to deal with. Her work hours were even longer than they had been in residency. Her hours of sleep were even fewer. When we met Liz for dinner later that afternoon, she had gotten up at 4:00 a.m. to keep up on her medical journals, before prerounding at 6:00 a.m. at the hospital, prior to performing a series of knee replacements. As a fellow, she had been paired with a particularly brutal attending physician this month, and her OR schedule was grueling. She was not as much fun to be around as she used to be.

She clucked. Nothing seemed to be appealing on the menu. The twins were bickering over who had collected the most chopsticks from the table.

"Please be nice; Mommy is trying to read the menu."

I came to the rescue. "Go check out the fish and turtles while we order."

Mandarin Deli was the home of the kid-magnet, green-water aquarium. It was the foulest tub of water any sea creature had ever swum in. Visibility in the tank was perhaps two inches.

"Daddy, I want wonton and rice," Maude said. She clumsily tumbled out of her seat. Silverware clattered to the floor. Claire followed her.

A few months ago, the twins had decided they would only eat white food.

"We've got to find a new place for Chinese. I'm tired of this menu," Liz said. "And it smells like dog in here. You order something for you and the girls. I'll eat cereal or something at home."

Liz had started the habit of giving me the business over going to Mandarin Deli every Friday, but she had offered no alternatives. It was a hospital hangout. It was the type of place that could only survive in the stale retail space between three East Side hospitals. Workers could get Jewish deli and subs, as well as kung pao chicken, around the clock. The best thing about it was that it was cheap. Plus, I could get white food for the girls. Rice. Pork dumplings. Lo mein. Wonton soup. Sometimes cooked shrimp in a garlic butter sauce.

"Sorry, babe," I said. This was my new mantra. "But this place works for the girls. Keep it simple. Get a steamed vegetable dish over rice. You'll feel better after you eat."

"I don't like eating junky food after a long day. It's just not fun for me going to restaurants anymore. The girls aren't good at eating out," Liz said. "And we really can't afford it anymore."

Liz used to just roll with stuff, and she had had lower food standards. At Berkeley, she had loved to get cheap Indian and Chinese food from sidewalk trucks and had rarely gotten sick. Whenever I had joined her, the same food had run through me like the Union General Sherman through Atlanta. Liz had a cast-iron stomach, impervious to spice and grease. Surgical residency and fellowship had definitely put a strain on her intestinal tract. Hopefully, in a year, when the fellowship would end, and she would have better hours and more sleep, her disposition would also improve. I wanted my happy Liz back. We used to have so much fun, before the kids.

I nodded. It was easier to agree with her than to defend the limp and greasy food of Mandarin Deli. I was not big on cooking at home, because, basically, I was lazy. As a distraction, I told her about the park, including

Supermom's comment that she should slow down at the hospital in order to have more time for the twins.

"She's being bitchy because Mitch believes I have a shot at getting a good recommendation from John Warner for the Hunter Clinic. Whoever gets in with Warner gets the job with the practice," Liz said.

Dr. John Warner was the head of surgery at the Hospital for Special Surgery (HSS), arguably the most prestigious orthopedic surgical program in the country. As the chief, Warner was connected with all the private orthopedic practices in the Northeast. The Hunter Clinic on Long Island was one of the more lucrative practices in the country, and one of the hip- and knee-replacement specialists was about to retire. A position there was coveted. We would need a U-Haul truck to carry home her annual income if she landed that job. In the meantime, we lived as poor grad students, soaking up whatever meager perks the hospital ecosystem kicked off.

My earnings potential sucked wind in the current slow job market. "Are you thinking we should stay on the East Coast after your fellowship?"

"Maybe."

I wished to return to my native soil in San Francisco, but I decided not to push my agenda for the moment. Life was not working out for me in New York City as I had hoped. But maybe the tech job market would pick up on the East Coast.

"Do you think you have any shot at winning Warner over?"

"Sure, but Mitch is a very charming and qualified weasel," Liz said.

I agreed. Mitch was the typical smug doctor type. He fit the stereotype of a surgeon, holding a high opinion of himself and a firm belief that he belonged at the top of the food chain. "I'm hoping Supermom only mildly hates me, but after today, that seems ambitious. Her coven of stay-at-home moms could give me and the girls the brush-off."

"Since when did you care about crap like that?" Liz seemed amused.

"Well, it matters now that I'm home full-time with the girls."

"Only since the beginning of July. You'll get another great job, and we'll get a nanny."

"Not so simple. The job market is a crushed beer can right now. New York has nothing. Nobody is putting up any start-up money anymore. The companies already in business are not hiring webmasters or programmers until things get better."

"What about your buddy at that start-up, selling comic books online?" Liz said.

"Morris wants me to come in to talk, but I don't think they're serious."

"You'll find something, eventually. Just hang in there, sweetheart." Liz stroked my hand.

Claire and Maude had pushed chairs over to the aquarium while Liz and I had been talking. Now, they were standing on them. Their greasy fingers pressed against the glass. Harried waiters scowled at them. I thought to go over and supervise the girls, but I was tired and spent from the heat of being outside all afternoon. My hope was that they would just be mildly annoying and no one would say anything to me. Liz usually let the girls do what they wanted anyway.

We ordered. As always, fussing over the menu was an empty ritual, because Liz and I got the same dishes every week. Kung pao chicken. Sweet and sour shrimp. Garlic string beans. Starters included steam dumplings and hot and sour soup. The girls got a selection of white food, most of which would not be eaten; it would be brought home so that it could rot in our refrigerator, to be thrown out next Friday with fresh replacements.

As we waited for our food, Liz went to say hello to a few of her surgical buddies at a neighboring table. Maude returned from the fish tank. She held a fist-sized turtle in her hand.

I remained calm, trying not to draw attention. "Maude, honey, we gotta put it back."

"But, Daddy, it looks sick. Can Mommy make it better?" Maude said. She pushed the algae-smelling turtle near my face.

The turtle was limp. Too limp. Actually, it was dead. Taking it from her, I quickly wrapped it in a napkin and hid it behind the green teapot on the table. I didn't want Maude to take the blame for killing the turtle. My plan was to throw it away as we left—maybe flush it down the toilet in the men's restroom.

"Did something happen to the turtle? Did you drop it?"

She shook her head. "Daddy, why in napkin?"

"I thought it might be cold. Let's just let it sleep for now." From the kids' diaper bag, I pulled out waterless soap and squirted her hands with it. "You can't take stuff out of the tank."

Maude nodded as she stared at the napkin ball that held the turtle. Meanwhile, Claire's arm was elbow deep in the tank. She was trying to catch some of the more lethargic goldfish. I grabbed another napkin and went to the front of the restaurant after her. Too late. The manager finally noticed. He shook his finger at Claire and shouted out a litany of angry words in what I assumed was Mandarin.

"Look, I'm sorry. She's a little kid." I pulled Claire from both the chair and the tank.

The manager mumbled something again. He snapped the tank lid closed. "You no do that here. Child stay with parent at all time."

An older waiter passing by spoke to the manager. The waiter pointed to Maude. The manager frowned. "He tell me that you little one took out one my turtle."

A few weeks earlier, before the manager loathed us, he had shared with me and the girls that the turtles were special to him. They had been a gift from his wife for their twenty-fifth wedding anniversary. In China, turtles represent longevity. I feared he would totally freak out if he knew that the turtle was dead. God only knew what he might do. Maybe call the police. I wasn't totally sure if Maude was to blame. It could have been dead before she had put her hand into the tank. "No turtle. She was just playing with a rock and put it back. I'm very sorry. We'll sit down now. I'm sure the turtle is just hiding somewhere." I guided the kids to the table and hoped that the manager had bought my lame explanation.

He hadn't. Twenty minutes after reentering the kitchen, he returned with two beefy cooks, a fish net, and a flashlight.

During the twenty minutes that the manager had been in the kitchen, dinner had progressed like a theme park of calamity. Liz had returned to the table as soon as our greasy food had arrived. The kid's burned through the remaining sanity that Liz and I had for the day. Claire spilled her soda, thereby summoning a pit crew of waiters who replaced the tablecloth, brought more soda, and blotted the floor with towels. Maude, not to be outdone, chose to annoy us by dipping her steamed dumplings in her water glass, in order to wash off the duck sauce. "Yuck," she said, "No brown stuff." She succeeded twice before knocking over the glass of water, which thankfully did not fall to the floor as it had done last week.

The conversation that Liz had just had with her surgical buddies had not improved her mood. Upon returning, she told me that the OR schedules were getting changed again, and she and several other fellows were going to wind up with more early and late times for their operations over the next few weeks. She said something about hospital renovations causing the change in the OR schedules. I wasn't sure exactly what she was talking about.

I often zone out when the talk of anything related to healthcare comes up. It doesn't appeal to me. And sometimes Liz nails me on my lack of recall. It's a little embarrassing. It makes me lose husband points with Liz. Lately, I've been losing a lot of points.

Upon reaching the fish tank, the taller cook rolled up his sleeves and pushed his hand deep into the tank. He groped around the bottom, feeling for what I imagine was a turtle. The other cook pointed the flashlight into the tank. He motioned at possible places where a turtle could be. The manager held the net. He squinted and pressed his face against the glass. I hoped the murky water would help keep my secret until we were able to leave, but the kids were eating slowly.

Two of the turtles were found. Only one seemed to be missing. The manager held up three fingers and said something to the taller cook. The taller cook disappeared into the kitchen.

I motioned for the check.

"What's going on over there?" Liz said. Surrounding tables were snickering at the unfolding sideshow.

"You don't wanna know."

Liz shook her head. "Nick, I don't what to be embarrassed again. Half the surgical fellows are here."

"Maude pulled a dead turtle out of the tank," I said.

Liz raised her hands above her head. Her eyes bugged out. "Why can't you watch these kids a little better? What else are you doing? Something is always going wrong."

"What was I supposed to do? I panicked and hid the dead turtle in my napkin," I said.

Liz rose. My guess was that she wanted no part of the impending retribution. "Girls, Mommy has got to run to the hospital for a bit. I'll be home soon for reads and kisses." And she left. If Liz had been a cartoon character, a trail of smoke would have been the only trace left behind.

The check came, and I hurried to pay it. As I pulled cash from my wallet (a faster form of payment), two waiters cleared the table. The napkin with the dead turtle was collected before I was able to stash it in the diaper bag during our exit. The turtle rolled out of the napkin and slid across the tile floor in front of everyone.

After the police citation, our eating privileges at Mandarin Deli were permanently revoked.

3

I HATE PUPPETS

The day after the turtle incident, I struggled to push the double stroller along First Avenue, fighting a bent front wheel. Liz was working another Saturday morning. I was rushing to meet Wolfie and his kids for a triathlon of puppet theater, swim lessons, and brunch at the tip of the Upper East Side in Yorkville. Puppets and swim lessons were at the Asphalt Green complex, while brunch would be across the street at Eli's Vinegar Factory—a place I would not leave without buying imported white beans, matzo ball soup, white-cheddar macaroni and cheese, and crusty french bread.

The 9:00 a.m. puppet show was on the verge of starting, and I hoped that Wolfie had bought extra tickets. The shows often sold out. I thought to call him, but Claire, my youngest by ten minutes, was trying to get my attention. The sun canopy of the stroller, coupled with the steady hum of traffic, muffled her words, "Doo-cho-baa!"

I leaned closer, while still walking a brisk pace, as the stroller kept pulling to the right. One of the wheels was wobbling. My words of inquiry only elicited frustrated grunts and sobs. Maude, the dominant twin, joined her sister in a sympathy protest by screaming "Daddy" repeatedly. After an impromptu game of twenty questions, I discovered that Claire had dropped her security blanket. I turned and saw that it had fallen along the curb, several storefronts behind us. It was three minutes before the show, and I sprinted toward the blanket, while keeping a watchful eye on the kids.

Claire's security blanket was called Doo-cho-baa. Once pink wool, a gift knitted by my mother, the blanket was now a matted rose gray, which, despite repeated handwashings by Liz, always had the appearance of a cleaning rag. At least once a week, it would get twisted in the wheels of the stroller and collect more street grime. The origin of the name I did not know. My guess was that it was a mispronunciation of a word or words by Claire when she was two. I was careful to not mispronounce its name.

Doo-cho-baa was rarely out of her reach. Once, it was lost at a resort while on vacation in Florida. For three days, back home, Claire wandered about the apartment sniveling. Finally, I called the concierge and offered a bounty of one hundred dollars for the return of Doo-cho-baa. It arrived via FedEx shortly thereafter, smelling faintly of bacon.

After returning to the twins, I jogged the final two blocks to Asphalt Green. Asphalt Green was a five-acre health, fitness, and sports center that included Manhattan's only Olympic-sized pool. With a hurried motion, I opened the door nearest the auditorium and dragged the stroller backward for better control.

I saw Wolfie in the lobby, waving a handful of tickets. "Doo-cho-baa fell out of the stroller." Wolfie rolled his eyes. His kids, Alden and Carly, excitedly greeted the twins.

Physically, Chuck Wolfe and I were opposites. Wolfie was fit and skinny and had curly blond hair, while I was fat—or just burly if you asked my mom—with more hair in my trimmed goatee than on my pale head. We had been freshman roommates at Berkeley sixteen years earlier. Wolfie had majored in French; I had studied computer science. Today, I wore faded baggy jeans and a sweatshirt emblazoned with a yin-yang symbol. Wolfie, while often choosing to wear exercise clothes during the week, wore his typical weekend outfit of khakis and a thin monochromatic cotton shirt.

The show was starting. Wolfie motioned his five-year-old son toward the show door. Alden grabbed the tickets from his dad and pushed them into the clown mouth of the ticket collector's painted box. Claire and Maude voiced disapproval for not being able to handle their tickets, as I hurriedly left their stroller among nearly three dozen others in a corner of the lobby. Carly, as always, soothed the twins by playing the role of big sister—she was eight. "You can do it next time. Come. Let's sit in the front, under the stage." The four kids pushed through a cluster of families that were still trying to divine the best possible seats, as the lights dimmed.

I avoided the bleacher seating and found a place on the floor near the kids. Wolfie slid beside me with a sigh. "Do you think this show will be more or less lame than the one from last week?"

I agreed. Threadbare puppets, off-key singing, and performers with nervous ticks are hard to relish. "At least the kids are quiet for an hour." I turned to look at the crowd of a hundred and recognized another West Coast expat from Berkeley undergrad. He caught my glance and returned a nod. I nudged Wolfie, and he smiled up at Miles Brenton as well. Neither of us was very fond of him at school.

Wolfie continued. "You know, there aren't many places to bring kids on the weekends. Mostly, the options are the parks, the zoo, or the natural history museum. If I take Alden and Carly anywhere else, it costs a small fortune. Even here, we get banged eight bucks a head for this sock-puppet show and then more money for the swim lessons and brunch."

"It adds up real fast," I said. I missed getting a paycheck.

Dancing rats with Brooklyn accents opened *The Pied Piper of Hamelin*— as Pappy's Puppet Playhouse had performed it for twenty-three seasons. The rest of the show was a jumble of muffled dialogue and jerky movements. Despite all the changes in the field of modern child psychology and the resultant movement to more child-centered rearing, the puppet playhouse kept the traditional ending of the story: all the children of the town marched into the sealed cave and never returned to their parents. A few kids in the audience cried; most just watched the curtain fall with puzzled looks. I knew that at the very least, Claire would sulk all day and then refuse to go to sleep that night.

I made a mental note to pay more attention to the content of the show and not talk to Wolfie so much. The next time I would find an excuse to pull the kids out when the story turned ugly. Light applause greeted the puppeteers as they emerged from behind the plywood sides of their performance booth.

We collected the kids as the audience thinned. Maude mouthed the word "poopy" to me as she tugged at her pull-up. "Why didn't you say something, honey? Remember to tell me when you have to go."

"The show was too scary, Daddy."

Reaching for her hand, I signaled Wolfie to watch Claire as I went to change Maude. After fetching the backpack from the stroller, I reached the men's locker room. Maude was too big for the baby-changing station's table. I grabbed a handful of thin workout towels and made a makeshift station on the floor—several feet from the urinals and toilets.

The locker room was full. Saturday-morning workout routines were finishing. I tried not to make eye contact with anyone. Many of the men were clearly annoyed by the presence of a three-year-old girl and her toilet-training mishap. Usually Maude showed little embarrassment in such situations, but today she was clearly uncomfortable.

"It's okay, honey. Accidents happen. You've been doing really well lately."

Maude looked over my shoulder. A familiar voice came from an area near the urinals. "Nick Owen. How's it goin'?" It was Miles Brenton.

I collected the soiled pull-up and put it into a gallon ziplock bag for public disposal. I wished I hadn't made eye contact with Miles earlier at the show. "Right now, a little messy; otherwise, okay." Maude scrambled to her feet and struggled with the faucets of the sink. I tossed the plastic bag into the trash. "I'd shake your hand, but I don't think you'd appreciate that," I said.

Miles Brenton half smiled. He wore a peach oxford shirt, khaki pants, and a blue blazer over a painfully thin frame. "What are you doin' now?" He followed me to the sink to wash his hands. "Last I heard, you were doing a start-up to help people find better parking spaces or something. But not in New York, right?"

Actually, it was a website that tried to help commuters locate a partner for carpooling in major cities around the country, combined with a dating service. "We ran out of money and went belly-up. Now I'm home with the kids," I said.

"Some harsh trajectory my friend—did you ever wind up marrying that girl Liz from school?" Miles said.

"Yes, after graduation. She just started a medical fellowship in orthopedic surgery."

"Not a bad gig, marrying a doctor. Now you can loaf around the house, just you and the hot nanny, home all day?"

I shook my head. "Not quite. Medical fellows make squat. We never had a nanny. So until I can find another job, I'm Mr. Mom." I hated that term. Unfortunately, it summed up my situation in two syllables.

Miles hesitated before speaking. I could sense the political correctness filter turning on. "I think that's just great. More men should step up to the plate. Maybe in a couple of years, once I have enough fuck-you money, I might move to Connecticut and do the same thing. Of course, I'll have a nanny or something." He leaned toward me. "You're not cleaning toilets, scrubbing the dishes, and making dinner are you?"

"Unfortunately, I'm currently full service," I said.

With more enthusiasm than required, Miles said, "I love it. Former egghead and master of the web is now superdad. I guess that makes you like a Daddy 2.0, a husband that's willing to pitch in and split the load with the missus, fifty-fifty on taking care of the kids." He checked his watch. "I've gotta run, pal. It was good seeing you again. I'm taking the wife and kids to Barneys for lunch."

I forgot what Miles eventually wound up doing after college. I'm sure his career didn't include diplomacy and tact as part of its skill set.

Maude was getting restless. She began peeking under the stalls of the toilets.

I found Wolfie and the kids poolside, just before the start of the swim lesson. Digging into my backpack, I pulled out swimsuits and goggles. Maude didn't like the swimsuits. "I want the pink one, Daddy." Maude was my verbal child. Claire agreed with her sister, but I couldn't understand what she said next, something about clowns with cheese.

Sometimes I had a hard time understanding her words. "Wear them and we'll get a treat after lunch, maybe something with white chocolate."

Begrudgingly, the girls allowed me to put on swim diapers under their suits. The rule of the pool was for kids to wear them if they weren't potty trained. The twins chose to go limp in my lap, making the process stretch even longer. Passive resistance was an effective weapon for them. "Go with Carly and Alden. Uncle Wolfie and I will be right here on the bleachers watching."

"Do you promise not to leave?" Claire gave me a hug. The creepy feelings from the puppet show were no doubt still active in her head. Impatiently, Maude pulled her sister from my lap.

"Maude is one tough biscuit," Wolfie said. "You're in big trouble come the teen years."

"I agree. She's a lot like her mother, only shorter."

"At least Liz channels her energy into her work and spares you."

Claire looked back for me as their teacher greeted them.

"The kids are still not used to me being around all the time," I said. "It was Liz's mom who spent more time with them than anybody."

"Not true. You were always good about keeping your weekends free."

"You're being too kind. I was a drive-by parent."

Claire timidly joined her sister in the water.

Wolfie said, "Unless you're punching the clock nine to five, nobody has good hours any more. I work late at the restaurant and sleep while the kids are in school. I only get kid duty when Emma has sessions with patients on Saturday." His wife was a psychiatrist.

"You're around at least some part of the day for them, every day. I never came even close to that. It's like I'm starting all over with the twins. They have a better relationship with Liz's mom. They want me to get a job again so they can have their grandmother back," I said.

"You don't know for sure that the kids prefer Liz's mom."

"Maude tells me every day, sometimes twice."

Chuck Wolfe was a minor celebrity of sorts. He was chef of *L'Usine de Nourriture*—the food factory—a French nouvelle restaurant that he and a business partner had opened a year earlier. His Zagat listing was impressive: "Some of the best bistro food this side of the park. Enjoy loud and fun dining at a wraparound butcher-block counter, where Wolfe and his crew cook for all to see. Come early to this Meatpacking District haunt, because waits often exceed an hour. The mantra here is 'First come, first served, but all leave sated.'"

Claire and Maude were holding onto the side of the pool and practicing their kicks. The teacher shouted approval.

"I must confess that I really suck at being a stay-at-home dad. I don't see anybody else running around Manhattan the way I do. All I do is rush, trying to fit everything in, and, in the process, piss off the kids and annoy Liz."

"Your problem is you have a short attention span and don't get enough sleep, because you stay up too late playing the video games you and your friends built. But even a sane, well-rested person would have a hard time with three-year-old twins."

"You'd think the kids would be better with me than with a nanny, but, instead, they complain and whine about everything I do. You saw how just putting on a swimsuit was an ordeal."

Maude splashed her sister. Claire screamed for her to stop.

Wolfie said, "Kids can be a real pain in the ass. I'm definitely not the best parent in the world, but you can't take everything so seriously. They're kids, not robots. They're not going to be everything you want. For instance, just because you like gourmet food, doesn't mean they're going to like it."

"Are you implying something, Chef Boyardee?"

"You're off the deep end with this 'white food' thing. At first, I thought it was funny. Obviously, I'm all about food, but three-year-olds do not have that fine a palette. Who cares where you get your mac and cheese? For them, it's salt, grease, and sugar."

"God only knows how the fixation on white food popped into their sweet, curly-locked heads. It started with wanting Annie's Organic Shells and White Cheddar, because they like the rabbit on the box. I wanted to respect their choices. I thought I was being an evolved male, letting the kids control some part of their lives. In Manhattan, finding the best of everything can become an addictive game pretty fast. At this point, I'm starting to think the kids are just messing with me."

"Colby has twin boys the same age as yours. He has the best philoso-phy on raising kids. Colby says that kids are like waves in the ocean: you can either ride the wave or get pulled down by the undertow."

"Colby is an asshole, so smug about being the cool dad."

"Maybe he is, but he does have a point," Wolfie said, "and he does always look like he's having fun with his kids."

As swim class was ending, Claire ran toward me crying. "Daddy, Maude splashin'! Daddy, Maude splashin'!"

Behind Claire, the swim teacher blew her whistle and warned against running. Claire was startled by the sharp noise and tripped. She slid across the tile floor. I considered it a minor tumble, only a little bit of blood on her lip. But a few seconds later, as I tried to comfort her, she un-leashed a screaming wail that halted movement in the indoor pool area. Her eyes were pinched shut as she bared her teeth. Tears mixed with snot. Everybody turned toward the source of the scream.

I waved my arm in the air. "Everything's okay. Just a fall; she's a little scared, that's all."

A few people were skeptical and shook their heads. I preferred to under-react when the kids got upset. I thought it was good modeling for them to remain calm in a crisis. I politely smiled at the other swim-class parents who gathered around us. Their faces of concern conveyed that they did not share a similar belief. Unlike me, they were not the daily witness to hyperbolic hysteria from their kids. A plump, red-haired mother of another kid in the class gathered Claire in her arms. She stroked Claire's hair. "Are you all right, sweet girl?" Claire's tears slowed, and she mumbled a response that nobody understood. "It'll be okay," the mom said as she rocked Claire to and fro. "Where's your mommy, sweetheart? You need your mommy now."

At that moment, I would have rather been kicked in the privates than listen to this strange woman soothe my child. Fortunately, the humiliation did not last long, as Claire soon recovered and wanted to leave. The other parents disbanded, awkwardly saying good-bye to me. I'd been nominated as the loser parent that Saturday.

It was time for more humiliation at Eli's Vinegar Factory.

4

THE CURSE OF WHITE FOOD

I had catalogued forty-one choices for white food. The most popular was pasta: no red sauce, butter applied in moderation. At least twice a week, I placed some sort of green vegetable, such as a broccoli floret or a string bean, on the twins' plates. It was usually whisked to the floor in less than nine seconds. Remaining vegetable options: tofu, cauliflower, jicama, and potatoes. To argue with the twins would have invited my fear of creating an eating disorder. It was somehow on my watch, not that of my mother-in-law's, when white food had eclipsed pizza and hot dogs.

New York City had too many places to buy food. It seemed that nearly every block had a supermarket, deli, or fine-food store. But not one carried all that I needed. Too many choices meant that I could indulge the fat guy inside me to hunt for the ultimate in white foods for my kids.

Each day meant another food venue.

Monday, after music class (and before nap time), I picked up two pounds of imported ricotta cheese at Grace's Market.

Tuesday, I would peruse the sumptuous fish display of the Upper East Side Citarella. The twins loved gray dover sole, with a light buttery coating of bread crumbs. They also ate shrimp cocktail, no sauce.

Wednesday I deemed pasta day. I would collect from Agata and Valentina fresh ravioli with cheese sauce, and, for later in the week, a white-cheese pizza and tortellini that could be warmed up quickly.

Thursday meant a West Side hike to Fairway Market for dairy products and vegetables. Weather permitting. Otherwise, I would go to the cavernous space of the Bridgemarket under the Queensboro Bridge. If I did make it to Fairway Market, I could find whitefish salad, sturgeon, and potato salad at nearby Zabar's that Liz loved too.

Dinner on Friday had been Mandarin Deli, but a new place was now required.

Saturday brunch on the East Side was its own religion. With kids, it was an ordeal: long waits for a table; crowded; no place to stash a stroller; antsy, hungry kids; and sporadic service. The restaurant at Eli's Vinegar Factory was all of the above, and no reservations were accepted, but the breadbasket with butter and jam could make up for a lot. I loved to eat the food in the restaurant upstairs as much as the gourmet food I could buy at the market downstairs. The bread was baked on-site in the renovated kitchens of the brick-and-timber building, where a vinegar and mustard factory had once operated.

From our table, I noticed Doug, the weekend manager, an acquaintance from a Monday music class with the girls. Doug had a three-year-old son and a wife who was a corporate lawyer. We were friendly to each other since caregiver dads were a rarity on the East Side.

Doug was lanky, with closely shaved hair. He came to our round table in the child-screaming section. "The usual, I suppose: scrambled egg whites?" he said with a chuckle. "Where's Dr. Frankenstein this afternoon?"

Doug could be a little annoying.

"Liz will be here soon." She had hoped to finish up her medical rounds and join us for brunch. Doug didn't stay long to chat, because the line of people waiting to be seated was growing, and he needed to help out the overwhelmed hostess.

Claire and Maude picked oatmeal to eat.

A minute after its arrival, Maude spiked her spoon on the table. "No want this. Too lumpy."

I stirred it for her, trying to break up the lumps. "That should be better. Try it again, honey."

Claire motioned for the bowl of sugar packets, and Wolfie's daughter, Carly, handed it to her. Instead of natural sugar, she ripped open and dumped several packets of an artificial sweetener—a white mountain grew in the center of the bowl. She reached for more packets.

Maude didn't like the way I had stirred her oatmeal; it was now too smooth and dried out. She wanted more milk.

I reached for the pitcher of milk. Maude shouted. "Daddy, I do it. I pour."

"Okay, honey, not too much," I said. Claire was making a bigger mess of the sugar. "Carly, could you take the sugar away from her? Thanks." Claire was too quick for Carly and grabbed the balance of the sugar packets. She ripped them all open and drained the contents on the floor. Alden laughed.

Wolfie sighed and tried to clean the floor with a wet napkin. I was getting frustrated. "Claire, that wasn't nice. You're making Uncle Wolfie clean the floor. Say you're sorry."

Claire scrambled from her chair, armed with a napkin. In her attempt to help clean up, she knocked over her bowl of oatmeal with the back of her head. The sharp sound of the dish smashing against the hardwood floor momentarily silenced the restaurant. I looked around, embarrassed. A few small kids from neighboring tables enjoyed the show that Claire was putting on for them. Once the noise was identified, background conversation resumed. A busboy rushed over with a broom and a scoop. Muttering in Spanish, he waved for Wolfie and Claire to stand clear.

Our male server returned after the floor was cleaned. "Something else for the little lady?"

"Do you want to try egg whites, Claire?" I said. She nodded.

As soon as the server left, Maude abruptly shoved her oatmeal away. "I want egg whites too."

"Is there a way to ask nicely?" I forced a sweet tone.

Maude scanned the table. Her eyes stopped at me. She shouted, "I want egg whites! Please!" Looks of disapproval shot at me from other tables. It seemed that my kids were always the most unruly in public.

I exhaled a cleansing breath, a stress management trick. "I think you have lost the privilege to ask for something else. Please finish your oatmeal. This isn't the right way to behave." When dealing with the twins, I often thought that I sounded like an airline flight attendant who had been trained to manage hostility from travelers when they could not get a second bag of peanuts or go to the restroom during takeoff. I had read several current books on child rearing; none discussed how to manage brazen hostility.

Maude slid her oatmeal off the table in slow motion. China fragments and oatmeal now coated the floor.

I tried to subdue my anger. Carly and Alden snickered. Wolfie shook his head for them to stop.

Almost immediately, Doug returned with a busboy. "Can we be careful girls?" Doug said. The busboy pushed the sticky oatmeal into his scoop with a broom.

Doug said, "Help me out, buddy. No more messes, please."

"No problem, Doug. I'm really sorry we're busting the place up today. We'll be out of here soon." Doug retreated to the kitchen.

My anger flashed. "Maude, if you're hungry, you can eat at home. Just wait for everyone to finish. No treats on the way out. I am very disappointed with you today."

"I'm sorry, Daddy. Can I get bagels and lox like Uncle Wolfie?" Maude asked. I was surprised at her deft ability to feign remorse for her actions when she wanted something else.

I paused at her choosing a nonwhite food option. Lox was pinkish, and high in protein. "I'm sorry, honey, but you've not been acting very nicely today. We can try lox tomorrow if you like. I won't be ordering more food for you today." I hoped she would be willing to try it tomorrow.

"She can have some of mine," Wolfie said. "Then you won't be breaking your word since it will not be a new order."

I understood that Wolfie was trying to help break the cycle of white food, but it still allowed Maude room to wiggle around my authority. I needed to establish limits for Maude, consequences for poor behavior. I was torn. But, basically, because I'm a wuss at heart, I decided ultimately that this was not the time to make a stand. I prioritized a balanced diet for Maude; learning discipline could start next week. "I guess that's a good compromise. Go ahead, Maude; you can have some. Say 'thank you' to Uncle Wolfie."

Wolfie placed half a bagel, topped with lox and layered with cream cheese, on a plate. He set the plate before Maude. "Thanks, Uncle Wolfie." She eventually ate most of it.

Claire's eggs took a long time to arrive. Everyone had finished brunch.

Maude asked for a bite of remaining french toast from Alden and a piece of toast with jam from Carly. She even managed to eat a little bacon from me. I thought that maybe she was starting a growth spurt. I secretly was happy that she was eating real food again. Miraculously, for no reason at all, it looked like the curse of the white food had lifted from Maude. Kids are strange critters.

After a few bites, Claire noticed that her eggs were not white. "Daddy, these eggies are yellow." I had asked for egg whites. It was annoying that regular scrambled eggs were delivered. I didn't want to spend more time waiting for a reorder. I wondered about Liz's lateness. Where was she? Late again. "I want white eggies." Claire's voice was getting louder. Tears welled in her eyes.

"Look, honey, it's getting a little late. We have to get home for naps. Just take a few more bites. Maude just ate several different kinds of food." I took a chance and squirted a big mound of ketchup onto her plate. "Try some ketchup with them. You used to love it on your hot dogs. Remember? Eat these and we can get you a treat downstairs."

In computer parlance, Claire had the equivalent of a software error. Upon seeing the ketchup, civility froze up and the system seized. Hunger and tiredness collided, and she swept her plate off the table just like her sister had. But unlike her sister, she put top spin on the plate, which sent it flying recklessly. Claire began to kick and to scream like a banshee.

The plate splintered upon impact on top of the neighboring table that seated eight. Pieces of the plate tipped over glasses of supersized orange juice and virgin marys until, finally, it tumbled into the french toast of—as I would later find out from Wolfie—a New York Post editor. Scrambled-egg shrapnel stuck to sweaters and hair. Ketchup stained clothing. As if on a predetermined cue, the son of the editor flipped his bowl of macaroni and cheese onto the floor. He giggled, while his father frowned. In the ensuing minute, two other little protesters in the screaming section followed suit with a "me too" response of tipped crockery.

Doug would later tell me in the next music class that he had not been having a particularly good Saturday morning that day. Not only had he been two people short on the waitstaff, but the restaurant's industrial-sized dishwasher had just decided to give up the ghost. Getting somebody to fix it in less than two weeks would require a miracle no less daunting than finding a cab in the rain.

He descended upon our table with a few people from the waitstaff in tow. "What is going on here?"

The activity of the restaurant ground to a halt. Attention focused on the back part of the restaurant. Conversation turned to critiquing the situation.

"I'm so sorry." I cast a hard look at both Claire and Maude. "They've never been this bad at a restaurant. Let me pay for the dishes." I turned to the table next to me. "I'd be happy to pay for your brunch—all of you—even your dry cleaning." The table eyed me with disgust. Their body language screamed, "No thank you. Now go away." The newspaper editor waved his hand in a dismissive manner.

A disembodied voice shouted above the din of the restaurant, "Those kids deserve a good smack."

Anger swelled within me. I rose to my feet. "Who said that? What kind of savage hits his kids?"

Doug rushed over to me. With voice lowered, he said, "That's it. Brunch is over. I don't want a fight to break out here. This is a family place. Forget about your bill. It's on us today." He patted me again on the shoulder. "Please find another place to eat on Saturdays."

As disappointed as I was at Liz for not showing, I was grateful she had not witnessed this latest example of my lack of control over things. My star was definitely falling in her eyes. I decided to put the kids on a restaurant ban. Maybe six months.

5

WAKEY-WAKEY, RISE AND SHINE

Tuesday morning came, and I was back on the hamster wheel. At the butt crack of dawn, Maude dropped her wet pull-up on my pillow. "Daddy, wake up. I change all by me self. See."

Maude did a mock fashion pose by the bed. She was wearing a menagerie of clashing colors and patterns, two or three layers deep. Is it legal to wear, on the Upper East Side, a polka-dot tank top over a green plaid turtleneck shirt?

My usual trick of playing possum was not an option when smelling the aroma of pee. I mustered enthusiasm, despite having been up way too late playing video games. "You're such a big girl, getting all dressed by yourself—very good, sweetheart." I removed the pull-up and tossed it into the trash near the bed. It would take about thirty-six hours before the ammonia smell would compel Liz to empty the trash. "Next time, honey, just put your pull-up in the diaper pail?"

"I want to show Daddy I can dress and do it too."

I hoped for a miracle. "Are you sleepy, Maude? Do you want to go back to sleep for a while?" I was close to offering her a spot in the bed next to me, but I thought better of it. I knew too many parents who had made that fateful mistake and wound up having an additional bunkmate, in the marital bed. Not good.

"I want play now," Maude said.

Maude was named after Liz's maternal grandmother, a short little woman with an annoying laugh. I did not particularly like the name, but it was very important for Liz as a remembrance. Her grandmother had often watched Liz and her brother after school when her parents were at work. The name reminded me of the seventies eponymous television show. As a result, the show's catchy title song had frequently become an annoying earworm for me.

I was in zombie mode. "Let's play here." I pulled a nearby plastic tub into bed. It's important to keep an emergency stash of toys on hand by the bed. Maude rummaged through the collection of fast-food-restaurant and dollar-store toys. I sunk back into the pillow, regretting staying up an extra three hours the night before, playing Pillage and Plunder with former co-workers. Monday night had always been a big game night. I decided right then to chill out a little on the whole staying up late thing. Not as much fun as it used to be. I began to think that online games might be a waste of time. It was really unfortunate that I couldn't include "laptop warrior" as a marketable skill in my job search.

Liz was already up getting ready for another day of surgeries. She was out of the bathroom. "Morning, Maudie. Is Claire Bear still sleeping?"

"Yes, Mommy." The kids shared an adjacent bedroom. Claire had been my third choice for a name, after Victoria and Diane—but I had lost a series of coin flips with Liz during a naming discussion.

Liz pulled on her surgical scrubs. She was pretty; I had always thought so, since we had first met. She hadn't gained a ton of weight like I had since college, despite doing little to no exercise and having a rampant sweet tooth. She was a few inches shorter than me, although I certainly was not a giant. I often stared up into the nose hair of most men. Her dirty-blond hair was shoulder length. Her eyes were sort of blue, I think, and had some greenish highlights. I've never been the best at remembering details about people—which Liz often joked would make me a bad news reporter or witness to a crime. Anyway, for some reason, that Tuesday morning as she pulled on the poorly tailored lime-green, man-made fibers of her scrubs, I realized just how impressed I was by her talents, grace, and stamina. It was not an easy thing to be a woman in the male-dominated world of ortho-pedic surgery. I was lucky to have her in my life, even if it meant living in a shoe box as an NYC grad student.

Our living room and dining nook measured twenty sneakers by fifteen sneakers. The two bedrooms were equally sized and measured out at twelve by twelve sneakers. The galley kitchen did not allow for the dishwasher and oven to be opened at the same time; two people made the space inop-erable. The apartment vents continually hissed out questionable-smelling air, as if a moldy burlap sack impeded their function. In the winter, the air was hot and dry and created continually stuffy noses and scratchy throats; while in summer, the air conditioning was nearly worthless. Opening the window gave us the buzz of city traffic, mixed with periodic ambulance sirens (three hospitals were within two blocks: Memorial Sloan Kettering Cancer Center, NewYork-Presbyterian/Weill Cornell Medical Center, and Rockefeller Institute Hospital). Have I mentioned yet how much I missed San Francisco?

One of the many challenges of our move had been trying to fit our oversized furniture into our new, diminutive space. After several failed attempts at reconfiguring the plush leather sectional couch, it, like most of our furniture, was stored in New Jersey by the moving company. The only pieces of furniture that could fit in the living room were a few book-shelves, a pullout sofa, and a tiny kitchen table set from Ikea. Liz and I stepped down from a king-sized bed to a double. The twins graduated from dual cribs to junior beds made from pressboard. Everything else, like toys, clothes, crockery, dishes, electronics, knickknacks, and the like, was creatively stored in closets and cupboards, under beds, and on wall shelves and wall racks, until almost every empty space was claimed, save for a tiny walking path through every room. The secret of New York City cramped apartment living is height for storage—or so we thought, until crates stacked to the ceiling invariably fell on each of us from time to time. The walls were institutional white, except for those in the twins' room, where we had painted a color of purple that resembled a dyed Easter egg.

As Liz finished dressing, I said, "No one makes scrubs seem as sexy as you."

"You're a weird bird."

"What does sexy mean, Daddy?" Maude said.

"It means that mommy is as beautiful on the inside as she is on the outside."

"A little Lifetime channel, but I'll take it." Liz kissed the top of my head. "I've gotta rush. It's going to be a long day. I've got several surgeries lined up, but I'll try my best to get home for dinner."

"But you've got ballet with the girls at five."

"Can't do it today; not gonna happen." Liz slung her leather satchel over her shoulder. "You're going to have to handle it."

"But it's called 'mommy and me' ballet. Not really my style, Liz."

"I'm sure your manhood will remain intact." Liz was off to work. Lately, she had become dismissive of me. I was losing my status as alpha male since being home with the kids.

"I'm drawing the line at wearing tights," I said as she left. Maude giggled.

I first met Liz sitting in the front row of a morning sociology class, Deviance and Social Control. I had overslept that day and, upon arriving, had found that all the other seats had been taken. Liz was the typical first-row type: punctual, studious, and/or nearsighted. As a freshman, she had waived into an upper-level course. The lecture was about cannibalism, and the professor asked, "Do you serve red or white wine when you eat the cabin boy?" I mumbled to Liz that I would have skipped the wine and just eaten the cabin boy. Liz smiled. "I'm a born-again vegetarian. Guess that means I'm dinner." After two years of hanging with a red meater like me, she was back to chewing on fat and sucking on the bones of the best ribs from KC's Bar-B-Q in Berkeley.

At this point, I should frame our roles in the relationship as being that of counterbalancing opposites. Play the Donny and Marie song "A Little Bit Country, a Little Bit Rock and Roll" in your head—if you don't know the words, just use Google to find them. I'm creative. She is type A. I like to avoid conflicts and arguments. She is a dragon slayer with the take-no-prisoners attitude that most surgeons have. I tend toward low-energy activities like writing code and screwing around with computers. I like ska, punk, classic rock, and jazz. Liz rarely listens to music, but when she does, it is bubblegum pop. I like science fiction and fantasy books. Conan the Barbarian rules. Liz prefers classic English literature (Jane Austen or the Bronte sisters) but has expanded her taste to include American authors, especially ones that have won the Pulitzer. Secretly, she enjoys historical romance novels, which she hides in stacks under our bed. So her tastes aren't all bad. When we go to the movies, we see mostly art-house chick flicks, since Liz does not like anything with gunplay or kung fu. Occasionally, I'll find a foreign film with some assassins, like the original *La Femme Nikita*, for both of us. My movie treat is gummy bears—and anything else that has artificial dye, tastes like bug juice, and possesses sugar. Liz gets a king-sized chocolate bar.

I once asked Liz why she had ever bothered dating me in the first place, when my qualities and tastes were so divergent from her own. Her response was "Dating you pisses off my parents, and you make me laugh." After we got married, I asked why she had chosen to be my lifetime mate. "I still want to piss off my parents, and you draw the best cartoon doodles."

Claire screamed from her room for me.

She probably wanted room service again in bed: milk in a sippy cup and dry cereal in a bag. Not a good sign for the day.

It was going to be another mundane and busy day. I had set up a playdate for the twins with two other kids from their music class. The plan was to meet before lunch at St. Catherine's Park (three blocks from the apartment). Prior to that, it was my turn to be on playroom duty for the family association in the building. I didn't relish the idea of having to supervise other people's snotty little kids for two hours. All the kids were under four. What may be construed as cute in your own child quickly seems bratty from the child of somebody else.

However, the playgroup had merit. Drop off your kids twice a week all month—Tuesdays and Thursdays—with your reciprocal supervising duties being just one Tuesday and one Thursday a month. Two hours of freedom twice a week was always a good thing. Duties included riding herd over twelve kids with another parent, providing snacks, changing pull-ups and diapers, negotiating countless toy conflicts, and making sure the kids stayed happy, or at least did not whine or cry too much.

I knew little about the origin of the family association, other than that it seemed to be a by-product of the medical bureaucracy. The official name was the Upper East Side Hospital Family Association, or HFA for short. Membership required a physician spouse working at one of the neighboring hospitals or Rockefeller University, residing in hospital-provided housing, and at least one child. Over 95 percent of the families were transplants from other cities—some from other countries—working in residency or post-residency programs, which included surgery, oncology, and biomedical research, for as long as one to five years. Most of the families had a stay-at-home parent. I was the only stay-at-home dad. Dues were fifty dollars a year. The hospitals kicked in a nominal toy-and-activity fund. On holidays like Halloween, Christmas, and Valentine's Day, the family association would hold parties for the kids. I liked HFA. It made being a stay-at-home dad a little easier, since everybody had a natural connection. Otherwise, I felt handicapped because a stay-at-home dad was viewed with suspicion—like what is wrong with you for not having a regular job.

I stumbled into the bathroom while the intervals between Claire's shouts grew shorter. I quickly did my morning toilet routine, which included a quick gargle of mouthwash. My morning breath could strip paint off the wall. Upon entering the kids' room, I smelled an aroma not that dissimilar to that of a barnyard. Claire needed a tire change rather than food. It was a code-orange cleanup—diarrhea in a pull-up. The only thing worse was a code red, which was diarrhea in a wet swim diaper. It would take about thirty baby wipes to clean her toxic spill.

When I was done, Claire kissed me good morning. "Daddy, can we play Play-Doh now?"

I needed to get a job.

6

BIG MONKEYS AND LITTLE MONKEYS

The building we lived in was the architectural equivalent of a gerbil habitat. The complex was thirty-eight stories of what looked like modular concrete boxes stacked askew. This wacky design optimized both indoor light and views of the Queensboro Bridge and the East River, but offered little interior charm, with its gray stucco walls. We were home base for most of the members of the Hospital Family Association. The building was family friendly, with three indoor and two outdoor playrooms, a rooftop lounge and exercise room, and a full front desk and custodial staff. There were more people in our building than in the tiny Northern California town I had grown up in.

By the time I came downstairs to the main playroom, it was already full of screaming kids. Worn plastic toys were strewn everywhere. The playful scent of carpet mold was in the air. Maude and Claire made a break for the wooden pirate ship that was an indoor jungle gym. Morning greetings were being exchanged between the mothers who gathered near the door. I overheard loose strands of kid stories: Joshua would not sleep in his junior bed again, Sammie was coloring purple men on the furniture, and Sofia just couldn't stop coughing—she had even thrown up on Matías's white coat when he had come home last night.

Some of the mothers had been together for years and were close friends, especially the wives of the surgeons who endured near-single-parent lives. I was an interloper and a substitute mom. My presence was confusing; it bucked the traditional roles of men and women. Having been home with the kids full-time for such a short time, I felt like a featherweight parent. The moms must have thought I was a loser—that I should get a job like other men and stop playing at being a mom. As I entered the playroom, nobody shouted out to me, "Hey, Nick, how's it going?"

I put down my backpack. Supermom and Good Heart were nearby. Supermom was her uptight self again this morning. "Looks like you and I are on duty together." Good Heart originally had been scheduled with me to watch the kids, but she had traded duties with Supermom to attend a doctor's appointment with her obstetrician. The day was not shaping up the way I had planned.

Good Heart said, "Sammie is still working out the potty thing. Can you just take her to go pee-pee every fifteen minutes?"

"No problem," I said. But it was a problem. It meant more work, more anxiety over whether a slight facial expression or an extra body wiggle meant an accident was near. However, I needed to show that I was a member of Team Mom and was willing to do the "dirty work." Most women in the group were used to doctor husbands who avoided any of the hard stuff when it came to the kids. As a guy, anything I did to help would give me double brownie points. Besides, Good Heart was always helping me out by watching the twins when I had errands to do. I owed her.

"I've got four extra pairs of underwear and more clothes in her bag." She motioned to a worn neon-purple canvas bag emblazoned with the logo of the Kansas State Wildcats. "And if she doesn't like the snack you've brought, I've got cut grapes for her in a little plastic container."

Whoops! Was it my turn to bring a snack for all the kids? "Got it covered," I said as I did a mock half salute. "Get out of here before Sammie decides to not let you leave."

Supermom politely smiled at me. She guessed that I had forgotten to bring food. She loved lording over the rest of us mere mortals. And she loved being president of the family association. She had not been elected or chosen, but, rather, she had been unopposed when she had assumed the mantle of duties, coordinating all the activities. As annoying as she was, no one could have done it better. Supermom was omniscient when it came to knowing about activities available to kids in Manhattan. If the Metropolitan Museum of Art was having an art appreciation class for three- and four-year-olds every other Wednesday during the fall, Supermom knew about it. She was aware of every child-related activity in Central Park, from the children's zoo to the carousel to the subtle merits of assorted playground equipment throughout the park. She had the schedule of every library's open story-time hour memorized: East Ninety-Fourth Street Library branch, Wednesdays at 3:00 p.m.; East Seventy-Sixth, Tuesdays at 2:00 p.m. Supermom organized weekly outings throughout the year for the kids: American Museum of Natural History, Scholastic Bookstore, Staten Island Ferry, Roosevelt Island, Coney Island, and the Bronx Zoo.

"How many do we have today?" I asked.

"Eleven—including your girls."

"How do you want to do this—zone defense or two groups?" I said.

"I think groups are better. I'll do activities with Claire, Maude, Ariel, Steven, Eva, and Sofia." Supermom had an easy group. My kids were always behaved for other people. They only gave me a hard time. Sofia, Nifty-Fifty Wife's daughter, was low maintenance. Steven and Eva were the rare kids that did what they were told and were quiet like the kids portrayed in soap operas. I never got Steven and Eva in my group, nor did I ever have to speak to them. After three months, I still did not even know their parents by name. They were the phantom clan of the family association; they showed up at all the activities, but no one really got to know them. Supermom was good at picking her group. I was left with the overactive and high maintenance kids: Sammie, Joshua, Aaron, Mitch Jr., and Hillary.

Supermom preferred organized play along the lines of an uptight pre-school, rather than free play. The only benefit of her groupings was that I didn't have my kids in my group. I noticed early on that kids paired with their own parents in group settings tended to be super bratty and high maintenance. Kids tend to have better manners when out of the company of their parents. Supermom was my least favorite partner for the play-group. With the other parents, I just chatted while the kids ran amok.

"I forgot to bring down a snack for the kids. Do you think going upstairs now or later is better?" I said. It was better to admit my failure of memory early.

"We don't have time for that now, but I brought something healthier than your usual selection of Cheetos, Fritos, or Doritos." She held up a bag of sliced carrots and broccoli florets. "And, if everybody behaves, organic oatmeal-raisin cookies."

"Are you serious? What kind of kid eats vegetables at ten in the morning?" "Mine do."

■ ■ ■

"Can we play 'zombie monster'?" Joshua was four and he was getting really tired of playing duck, duck, goose. His five-year-old brother, Aaron, had been flicking him in the ear. Joshua was one of Lion Tamer's five kids, and the youngest of four boys. His little sister, Ariel, was in Supermom's group and was a year younger. Lion Tamer and her family were transplants from Israel. Her husband was doing a hard-core urology fellowship that included being on call every other night for six months. Being on call meant that he worked all night at the hospital with maybe a catnap here and there. After a month of this schedule, he developed night sweats; after three months, he had lost twenty pounds; and by the end of the rotation, he had developed a severe case of acne that bled when he shaved (his fellowship did not permit beards). Lion Tamer's twin boys were eight, and they usually appeared in the playroom after school, to harass the smaller kids.

"I'm the zombie king. Now run," I said. I was slow to get up from the floor since my legs had gotten stiff from sitting crisscross applesauce on the floor. I was out of shape and tired, a match for my role as undead sloth. The kids scattered to avoid being tagged and becoming zombies themselves. Banshee screams and bedlam ensued. Finally, the kids were having fun.

Across the room, Supermom had her kids doing stretches that looked akin to Pilates. She was not pleased when running kids broke her circle of serenity. "What's going on here?"

"A zombie is after us. Everybody run." Joshua scrambled beneath the pirate ship.

Supermom frowned. "Nick, somebody could get hurt. Let's try something else."

I felt like a real dork. Supermom could really harsh my mellow sometimes. I pulled the kids together and tried to do a group sing-along to kill time until the playgroup was over. I barely knew the words to most of the songs. For the words I didn't know, I garbled and hummed sounds that seemed to fit in. What adult male knows the words to either "Wheels on the Bus" or "Head, Shoulders, Knees and Toes," let alone their choreographed hand motions?

Good Heart deserved a big shout-out for the private tutorial she had given me a few weeks earlier, when she had noticed me floundering during our music class. Every mom knew the words to every kid song. It seemed as if they had somehow been genetically downloaded into their brains at birth. Sometimes, before I sing with the twins during bath time, I consult their picture books to remind myself of the lyrics.

Song time didn't last nearly long enough, so we switched gears yet again. With such a young age group, I had to be doing something different every ten minutes. Supermom suggested that we do reading time. The kids elbowed and clawed each other and whined about which book they wanted to get from the playroom shelves. This infighting took ten minutes. Aaron pushed his little brother Joshua down and smacked him over the head with a book. Not too hard. I was unsure if I should give Aaron a time-out for hitting his brother. My big brother had smacked me all the time as a kid—that's just par for the course. Since Aaron used a softback book, I gave him a verbal warning with no penalty time. As for my big brother, I had always repaid him by doing stuff like spitting into his soda when he was not looking. Knowing Joshua, I figured he'd come up with his own comeback pranks in a year or two.

I am not very good at reading to kids. It's actually not such an easy feat to read aloud to kids with the words either upside down or at a weird angle as you hold the book away from you for the kids to view. In general, I am a lazy reader, which means I skip words or mispronounce character names, because I'm busy daydreaming, or thinking about how bored I am, reading a book about fairies, princesses, or talking cows. The twins always caught my errors and pointed out any deviations from the prior twenty readings. Repetition is a security blanket for kids.

Hillary was the first to pick a book, and she thrust it at my face. It was a flap book. Flap books are the second worst book to read to a group. The worst are books that play sound effects to go along with the text. The whole time you're reading, the children are squabbling every second over who gets to push the button for the crashing cymbals. With flap books, the big problem is trying to stop the kids from tearing the flap right out of the book. It helps to have tape handy.

After finishing the flap book and keeping the book damage to a minimum, we started to read the jewel of a book that Mitch Jr. had brought from his collection upstairs. It was entitled *There is No Tomorrow*. A gift, no doubt, from his father, Mitch Sr., Liz's weaselly surgical colleague. It was a movie tie-in book, which meant that it had lots of pictures and a herky-jerky narrative that was awkward to read. The other difficulty was that I had to paraphrase on the fly all the inappropriate themes that it included, such as the premature death of a parent, widespread use of guns, a maniacal villain that held children captive in dark confined places, and the attempted killing of an entire city by giant robots spraying chemical weapons. In my abridged version, everything was a big misunderstanding. The villain apologized for not using his nice words and promised to repair the city with the help of the giant robots. The dead parent was explained as just being on vacation.

"How come we don't see the daddy once he comes back?" Mitch Jr. said.

"Good point, Mitch Jr. I think the artist forgot to draw him. Maybe you can take this book home and draw a picture of a daddy with your markers right inside the book. Then show your mom."

I smelled the tart scent of poop. I scanned my charges' faces. No one seemed to look like he or she had a load in his or her pants. "Sammie, did you make magic in your pants?"

Sammie shook her head—all quiet on the western front.

I chalked the smell up to a passing fart and not something more. I hated to change diapers, especially the diapers of other people's kids. Until the twins were born, I had never changed a diaper in my life. During playgroup, I tried all sorts of tricks to avoid having to change diapers. I would avoid the kid in question by always being on the other side of the room, knowing that eventually the mom on duty with me would pick up the scent and take care of it. A woman would never let a child go too long without a change. Guys are always willing to wait until reinforcements arrive. With Supermom, I could not take a pass on potty duty, since certain kids were assigned to me.

Story time for Supermom was going much better. The kids sat in a neat circle around her and listened carefully. Claire and Maude didn't interrupt with tangential questions. From a distance, the twins looked like model children. Did I bring out the worst in my kids? Would my kids be happier once I got a job? I had been able to have more fun with them, when I was not around as much. I wondered what was wrong with me.

Mitch Jr. stuck his tongue out at me and rolled his eyes.

Supermom had to be a robot or, at the very least, a former mental patient. Did anybody else agree with me? Everybody else seemed to accept her natural ability with kids. She was always telling everyone how much that she loved being home with the kids. She always had good days. Her kids were never a burden. These could only be the statements of a phony or a whacko. Good and bad days exist side by side. At playgroup, she made everything seem effortless. She only spoke to the kids in a gentle way and yet somehow was able to get them to behave and respect her. She rarely got the monkey business from the kids, and when she did, she was able to do a "horse whisperer" thing and chill them out. Can a perfect parent exist? Was she a natural? I looked at Mitch Jr. How could the perfect mom have a kid as mean as Mitch Jr.? He knew I knew that he was a little shit. But he instinctually knew also that everybody thought I was lame, and that he was considered a perfect little prince. Maybe I was the crazy one.

But I didn't think so. Something, though, was out of whack.

■ ■ ■

"Snack time—let's wash our hands and potty," I said. There was one hour left to playgroup.

Supermom brought out a platter of sliced carrots and broccoli florets and placed it on the long table in the corner of the playroom. She acted as if she were placing a Thanksgiving turkey in the center of the table. Maybe she had read one too many healthy living magazines, because I think she was totally clueless as to how sucky her snack was. I laid out the animal-decorated paper plates. Instead of juice, I filled little plastic cups full of water. Obviously, the food selection did not go over very well. At first, the kids nibbled on the carrots but grew bored. The broccoli had an even worse response.

Most of the kids just pushed the green and orange objects around their plates like checkers. Even though my girls had lifted their ban on non-white food, neither took one bite of the organic fare. Joshua chose to crush his broccoli and sprinkle it on the floor. Mitch Jr. threw his behind the pirate ship when Supermom was not looking. When he saw that I caught him doing it, he offered a look that said, "What are you going to do about it?" Remembering the swing incident from Friday, even Mitch Jr. knew that I was loathe to not piss off Supermom again by accusing her child of foul play. It did not pay to embarrass Supermom.

Supermom did not let on that her snack choice fizzled. Nobody really ate. I predicted that the kids would get progressively cranky in the second hour of the playgroup. The kids needed artificial sugar to keep it together.

Art time with the kids was a nightmare. Beyond supervising the use of crayons, I am useless as an art teacher. Of course, Supermom chose to do an art project that included the dual nightmares of glitter and glue, which is the bane of any lazy parent. Both groups together did the art project at the big table of the playroom. Supermom played the role of art teacher.

This left me the role of cleanup flunky. The project that day was a picture frame of Popsicle sticks sprinkled with glitter. To Supermom's credit, she was a good teacher. She demonstrated how to do it and then worked with her group to implement it.

Mitch Jr., as expected, got bored with the art project rather quickly. He did the overkill thing with the glitter, creating mounds of glitter over pools of glue. Discreetly, I put together a simple and moderately ugly version of a frame so that Mitch Jr. could have something to show his mother later. As for the rest of my crew, none of the projects even remotely resembled the work of art that Supermom had demonstrated. Some weeks later, while in the playroom, Joshua's chair got overturned; I discovered then that Joshua had been gluing Popsicle sticks to the bottom of his chair.

While cleaning up the wreckage of glue and glitter, major tragedy struck for Claire: Doo-cho-baa was kidnapped by Joshua. Claire had left it on the back of a scooter she had abandoned. Joshua discovered it and hid it somewhere in the playroom. Now he was taunting her.

Claire went straight to red alert. "Daddy, Joshie took Doo-cho-baa." From then on, static noise might just as well have been coming out of her mouth, because I had no idea what she was saying—her words were garbled in tears. Claire just stood by the scooter, not moving. Maude started chasing after Joshua, yelling. I hated having Doo-cho-baa in jeopardy. In a way, it felt like the security blanket had become part of the family.

"Joshua, buddy, where's Doo-cho-baa?" I said. The twins had a pretty good track record of intimidation that kept the other kids from playing with Claire's security blanket. Joshua must have been feeling particularly feisty that day.

Because he was bigger, Joshua was just able to keep ahead of Maude's wrath, as she threw toys at him. He danced around the room chanting, "Oh where is Doo-cho-baa? I no tell'a."

I looked to Supermom for help. "Did you see where he put it?"

"I was busy cleaning up our art project," she said. A minute later she added, "I've tried to avoid security objects with my kids. They diminish a child's self-image and turn them into victims."

A little harsh, Supermom; I guess not having one turns you into a bully like your asshole husband and snot-ball son.

I told Joshua to go sit on the time-out chair. He dutifully complied. Most kids cracked at the thought of going to the time-out chair, spilling their guts in confessions and apologies. Joshua, though, was a hard case. Lion Tamer was constantly giving him time-outs, and he never relented. I kind of admired his toughness. He took his punishment like a hardened convict.

After a few minutes of fruitless searching and trying to sooth Claire, I noticed that Mitch Jr. had dropped off the radar. Everyone else was in plain view and active. After a quick inventory of the room, I saw that Mitch Jr. was over in the construction nook, where the building blocks were kept. It was an intentionally quiet space, away from the action, to avoid destructive interlopers when kids wanted to play with blocks. It was not a usual spot of play for the hyperactive Mitch Jr.

When I found Doo-cho-baa, it was like discovering a crime scene. Its form was twisted and torn among a tumble of blocks. Instead of blood, glitter and glue covered Doo-cho-baa. I didn't think I could wash it without literally turning it into threads. Claire was going to be in bad shape at bedtime. Mitch Jr. had fled by the time I had reached the building nook. I didn't think there had been a conspiracy between the two boys. Joshua had pulled a prank and dumped Doo-cho-baa. It was Mitch Jr. who had carried out the crime, smearing glue and glitter on the fallen Doo-cho-baa. In an odd kind of way, it felt like I was witness to a murder.

My first impulse ran to anger and a need to vent at Supermom about her son. A pound of flesh seemed in order. But unlike in the park, I was able to bring myself out of kung-fu mode and chose silence for now. Things had to change. I was not a happy camper with the status quo. I was not in control of the flow of my life. I had no idea how to fix things.

As Claire sobbed, I placed Doo-cho-baa in a plastic bag to bring home. "I'm so sorry. Tonight, I will spend some time seeing what I can do to clean it—but it doesn't look very good. I love you, sweetie. This was not fair." I held her.

With wet brown eyes and slowly rolling tears, she nodded and stopped crying. I was surprised that just a hug worked, because I was about to offer either a chocolate bar or an ice cream to stop the waterworks. I'm such a weak parent.

Sammie peed like a racehorse. She peed right in her pants at the top of the slide on the pirate ship. The pee rolled down the plastic slide and made it nice and slippery. At the time of the peeing, she didn't tell anybody. It was a silent pee. After snack time, I had forgotten to ask her about her bladder. The countless times she had sucked on her sports bottle of Gatorade had not even registered in my brain as an early warning of the waterworks to come.

Since Sammie told no one, at least three kids slid down her liquid trap and had their backsides covered in urine. Whether you're over five years of age or not, the feeling of accidental piss sliming your body is a trigger for screaming and getting freaked out. The victims were Hillary, Maude, and Ariel. Sammie stood by and looked ashamed.

Supermom and I grabbed changes of clothes from the backpacks of the children. "Sammie, why didn't you tell me that you had to pee?"

"I thought I wearing my pull-up."

As Supermom and I fumbled to get all the kids dressed again, parents started coming into the playroom to collect their kids. I was in the middle of changing Sammie as Good Heart walked in.

"Did you remember to take her to the potty every fifteen minutes?" Good Heart said.

"Nick was off his game again today," Supermom said, shaking her head.

"Of course, I did. Things just got a little crazy the last half hour or so." Sammie was too young to rat me out on my little lie. Supermom just shook her head at me.

"Thanks for trying." She took over changing Sammie's clothes.

The playroom was a mess. Instead of cleanup being just the responsibility of the monitoring parents, everybody pitched in and straightened the clutter with lightning speed. The efficiency and rapidity of the cleanup would have made the Cat in the Hat proud. Most people would have left

Supermom and me high and dry, to clean the whole place up by ourselves. It was our turn after all. The stay-at-home parents cared about each other. They were a team, and I was the mascot who had left his costume head at home.

7

DOING STUPID THINGS

I'd never cut hair before. It's a lot harder than it appears. What made me think I could? A lot of parents, especially from the Midwest, give their kids a home-style bowl cut. Growing up, I had received such a style of cut from my mom at the start of every summer. (My mother had grown up in the Midwest, before moving to California, where she had met my father.) Mom was pretty handy with the pruning shears in the garden. It turns out haircutting is not similar to pruning a rose bush. Not even close. Precision counts. Proper haircut training was required. Recalling an old picture from childhood, I now know that Mom really should have taken me to a professional. I looked heinous with uneven bangs, buckteeth, and a fuchsia Adidas tee shirt—synthetic fiber was king back then.

With Claire and Maude, bath time every night had become a drama of screaming and crying, as I tried to get the knots out of their long, wet, golden tresses.

"It hurts," Claire said, wailing.

"I do it myself." Maude moaned.

Sometimes, I just pretended to comb it, not touching a single hair, and they still screamed.

And of course they often said, "Mommy does it better." The only problem with that argument was that they said the opposite when Mommy actually did it.

Liz adored the girls' hair. The creation of elaborate braids and ponytails was one way for Liz to subdue her guilt about not being as available to her kids as she wanted to be. She purchased special shampoos to moisturize and expensive conditioners. She even bought detangler lotion to soften their curls, so that hair combing was less painful. Fathers have absolutely no expectations placed on them to have their children's hair neatly combed. I should have just elected to keep my amateur status. What made me think that I could cut hair? I thought I was being helpful. Less hair meant less tangles and fewer knots. Long hair meant more maintenance.

I had spread out towels on the tile floor of the bathroom to avoid a cleanup mess. Now, most of their hair was on the towels, and the girls were freaking out. I'd just wanted to thin it out a little. After a few initial cuts, I had become emboldened with my perceived skill. Eventually, as I tried to fix small mistakes, I created bigger mistakes, which forced me to make more correcting cuts. Dozens of corrective cuts later, I had reduced the mass of their three years of hair growth considerably. I knew I had messed up in a big way. Their hair looked horrible. It was a humpty-dumpty moment.

The decision to cut their hair myself must have been born of fatigue-created madness. After playgroup and mommy-and-me ballet, I was spent. Being forced to dance like a mermaid had taken a toll on my manhood. No doubt, the mothers in the class were telling their friends about the fat bald guy with razor stubble that had gone to class to prance and to twirl, with brown stains on his pants. (Claire had an accidental diarrhea squirt in her tights as she was sitting on my lap.)

When we got back from ballet, Liz was still not around. Dinner was rushed, and the kids put me through the hoops with odd dinner preparations. That they had gotten me to use chocolate milk in their macaroni and cheese is a testament to how whipped I had become. So it is no surprise that I went batty at bath time, when the kids decided to have a water fight.

Like hyenas on the plains of Africa, the twins sensed I was weak prey. They went amok.

"Let's get out of the tub. No more monkey business, girls."

"No. I don't want to get out," Maude said. "Mommy lets us play. Daddy mean. I hate you."

In case of emergency, break the glass, pull the alarm, and yell like a banshee: "Both of you! Out! Now!"

The twins were stunned. I was able to wrap them easily in towels. "I want no more trouble today. We're going to comb hair, brush teeth, and go straight to bed. No stories tonight."

Maude said, "We want stories."

"I said no." It was rare for me to be firm.

When I reached the first knot in her hair, Claire screamed.

Later, over the next couple of days, as word spread around the building that I was the bonehead responsible for the butchery of the curly locks of the twins, our apartment neighbors above and below us recalled hearing their screams through the ventilation ducts. At the time, our neighbors had paid little mind to it, since they were used to the twins screaming a lot, much like people in the suburbs who live next door to a high-strung, barking dog.

Everyone had a good laugh, knowing that I was in the doghouse with Liz. At the end of the fellowship program, as we moved out of the city, Good Heart told me that my nickname behind my back was "Nick Sweeney Todd, the demon barber of York Avenue." She never admitted who had given me that moniker. My guess was that it had been Supermom, because she was the only one of the group who was a fan of the theatre.

It was not easy getting the girls to bed that night. They had cried over their hair as it had fallen in wet tangles about the bathroom. By bedtime, they were close to inconsolable. Claire was bleary eyed as the shock of Doo-cho-baa's ruination settled in, and she realized that she could not sleep with it until I was able to remove the glitter and glue. It would take a week of slow cleaning with paint thinner and a toothbrush before she could hold its smelly ragged form again. Finally, the offer of taking the girls to the toy store the next day to buy something made them calm enough to close their eyes and let the fatigue of the day wash away.

The kids had been asleep for an hour when Liz got home. I had two choices: I could tell her later, hope she did not see the kids in the morning, and take the kids to a hair salon to fix the damage I had wrought. Or I could take responsibility.

"How much do you love me?" I said.

Liz was picking through the refrigerator, foraging for dinner. "What did you and the girls eat?"

Verbal diarrhea ensued. "Today, I didn't get dover sole. I made macaroni and cheese for the girls with chocolate milk—don't ask. For me, I made pasta, and I put the leftovers on the bottom shelf. Also, I cut the kids hair in a fit of crazy. I really made a real mess of it. Tomorrow, I will take them down to Kid Hair Hut."

No answer.

I continued. "It was one of those days. And I was having so much trouble with the knots in their hair that I figured it would be better if I thinned it out a little and made it shorter. They had to get a haircut at some point."

Liz, without making eye contact, walked into our bedroom, with a Tupperware bowl of cold pasta. She smelled of dried sweat, and a hint of surgical antiseptic. "Good night."

"Honey, are you pissed at me? I'm sorry. It's just hair."

If you have to ask someone whether they are pissed or not, they usually are. I followed her into the bedroom. Big mistake. In the five years that we had been married, I had not yet realized that I should allow Liz time to cool off. Whenever I followed her after the cold-shoulder treatment, I regretted it. I somehow had it in my head that we had to resolve everything before we went to sleep. Don't they say things like that on all the daytime talk shows? If I were in Vegas, my odds would be terrible for having any level of success at a productive discussion with her during such moments. First, Liz had just come off twelve hours in the OR. Second, she had not eaten. Third, I was tired and not on my game, and certainly not capable of being either charming or witty. So why did I go into the bedroom and corner an animal while it was feeding? I must have taken another stupid pill again.

"Let's talk about it. I screwed up."

Liz ignored me. She left the room to see the damage.

She came back and sat in the center of the bed. I thought she was going to cry, and Liz rarely cries. "I love their blond curls. I wanted to let their hair grow out. Did you ever wonder why it's never been cut?"

"You're usually not here at night or in the morning, when I have to comb out their hair. They scream and fuss. It's a nightmare—tonight in particular. I'm flying solo here."

Long pause. "Flying solo? You're lucky I'm too tired to comment on that one. You've been watching the girls a short time, and all you do is complain about how hard it is, and how much trouble the girls are."

"I don't complain that much, do I? That's not fair."

"Let's face it—you're not happy at home with the kids. Hurry up already, and go find a job, and then we'll get a nanny, and you can stop being so whiney. I'm not happy with our situation either. You're not really pulling your half of the load. I can't afford to be doing mommy-and-me classes and all the other things that you think you're too macho to do. I'm running on fumes right now. You've got to do a better job for your family. The girls are out of control right now. Look at what happened at Mandarin Deli on Friday. The kids were better off when my mother was taking care of them and you were working."

"The kids being 'out of control' is not all my fault. You're never around, and they miss you. You were around a lot more with the kids when you were in medical school."

"That's a really cheap shot. I've no time to give. Don't you get it? I'm scheduled up all day. Did you ever wonder why most people don't go to medical school and become surgeons? Because it's hard. When you're a student, it's different: you have more flexibility. In school, you can sacrifice sleep, study late at night, and organize your time to be with the kids. *You* would never think to change *your* work habits or routines. *You* do little to accommodate others. I know you really loved working at happycarpooler.com, so I compensated, so you could have your dream. I expected very little of you in terms of helping out with the kids. Now, it's your turn to help me, and my career."

"I should've packed my bags, 'cause your sending me on a guilt trip right now."

I should not have said that, even if my fragile male ego was bruised.

There was another long pause. Painful seconds of waiting. I assumed she was taking great effort to edit her response to my over-the-top sarcasm. She had better control of her anger than I did. "You can be pretty selfish sometimes."

"And you don't know how hard it's been for me in New York. I'm dying here."

"We made the decision to come here together. Now that things are rough on you, everything seems wrong. It doesn't always have to be about you. Did you ever think you could have fun being home with the girls, instead of treating it like a job?"

"Look, I'm tired, and you're tired. I'm pissed; you're pissed. Things are out of whack. I'll make double time to get a job, and then we can get back to normal. We'll get a great nanny, and all our problems will be solved. We're fighting way too much lately over bullshit."

"This is not bullshit; this is our life."

She was right.

I decided to soften my edge and take a little blame, to get out of the hole I was digging fast. "I guess I'm feeling a little depressed right now, and I don't know what's going on with me. I gotta figure things out."

"Figure it out in a hurry, because nothing's working here." She went into the bathroom and closed the door.

8

STATIC CLING

I have now learned not to use bleach when doing laundry. It should only be used by someone who is either a professional launder, or is a naturally careful person. I'd rather have yellow stains around the collar, a little discoloration to my whitey tighties, than to suffer the humiliation of bleach gone amok. In San Francisco, I did not have to grapple with laundry; it had been done for a mild sum by the folks at the Laundry Neat Laundromat. Just drop twenty pounds of clothing in a bag outside your door, and a day later, it would be returned clean and folded, better than Mom could have done. With our present limited income, and with New York prices, I was forced weekly to the airless laundry room in the basement of our apartment complex. The one time I had used bleach unsupervised was about a week after my unsuccessful stint as a hair stylist.

I fumbled into the laundry room with kids in tow, pushing a wire-frame grocery cart full of dirty clothes—bottles of detergent and bleach teetering on the top. Claire hung on the cart, trying to catch a ride, while Maude clumsily bounced a big rubber ball against the walls and floor. The twins disliked being involved with domestic chores.

"You're breaking the cart; please get off," I said.

"I tired." Claire did not move from her perch. She was my low-energy twin.

"It's a full house today," Good Heart said from across the room. "Good luck finding machines." I had come at the wrong time again. It was the midday rush hour for the washing and drying of clothes.

Nifty-Fifty Wife was also present in the basement bunker. She was pulling some wet darks out of the washer and pushing them into one of the many large industrial dryers. From the sound alone of two dozen machines whirling and thumping, I knew it was going to be a long afternoon. No way was I going to be able to do four loads of wash at one time and be done in an hour. The walls were sweating from the humidity.

Claire and Maude ran over to Sofia, who was playing on the floor with a couple of half-naked Barbie dolls. "Where's Sammie?" I said.

"She's napping upstairs," Good Heart said.

"Is that safe?" Good Heart's apartment was eighteen floors up. Liz told me never to go to the laundry room and leave the kids unattended. She worried about the risk of a fire and being separated from the kids.

No answer—add another unwanted, awkward comment to my list of gaffes.

Way in the back, I found an open washer, but my laundry card didn't work. "Do either of you have any quarters? The card swipe is toast."

They shook their heads but agreed to watch the kids for a few minutes.

I returned from the corner newsstand with quarters and the unwanted purchase of *Popular Mechanics* and Tic Tacs. (I hate having to buy something just to get change, but that is exactly what I had done.) Maude was prancing and jumping about the room on top of the machines.

"Not safe," I said, "please get down."

"Catch me, Daddy." Maude jumped across the machines as if she were playing hopscotch.

Good Heart said, "Sorry, she just climbed up while my back was turned."

Claire tried to join her sister atop the machines, but I scooped her up just before she mounted a machine. Sofia wanted to break for it as well, but Nifty-Fifty Wife had her checked. Maude wiggled and danced away from me while I tried to get her, still holding Claire.

It was then that Supermom entered the scene. The day was yet in further decline. Just an hour earlier, I had been scrubbing toilets, while trying to stop the girls from floating their toys in the porcelain bowl. "Management will complain to me if they see dents on the tops of the machines."

"I know. I know." I lunged again for Maude and grabbed her. She had been distracted by the entrance of Supermom.

Supermom revved up into third gear and turned directly to Maude. In a singsong sickly sweet voice she said, "Mommy would not be happy if you had to go to the emergency room to get stitches."

I was in her cross hairs. In the past week alone, Supermom had reported me to the building manager for storing my stroller outside my door in the hall, had "accidently" given me the wrong meeting time for the association's field trip to Central Park, and had blocked me on a couple of playdates I had tried to set up. At this point, I longed to get back to her having just apathy for my existence.

I decided to cow down, after the week I was having in the land of humiliation with Liz and the building moms. "Sorry."

Supermom appeared not to hear me. She went to a table near Nifty-Fifty Wife and began to separate her dirty clothes. Mitch Jr. had followed her into the laundry room, and when he finally saw my cart, he jumped into it. Did he think it was an imagined jail cell or shark cage? Who knows what went through Mitch Jr.'s brain? The wire frame squeaked in protest under his weight. My girls at first avoided Mitch Jr. and continued to play with Sofia.

I said nothing, recalling how my tongue had gotten me into hot water in the park earlier when I had chastised Mitch Jr.

When he began to push my cart into the machines like it was Sunday-afternoon crash derby, I said nothing. Supermom did not even appear to notice her son's exploits as she chatted to Nifty-Fifty Wife and Good Heart. Was she hoping that I would blow up at Mitch Jr. again? Could she really not notice?

I continued separating my clothes: white, dark, almost dark, almost white, delicates, towels/linens, bras in laundry bags, and superstained little-kid clothes that required gobs of stain remover. My life had gone from bits and bytes to grease and grime. I filled the washer I had already found with darks, and I went to find another for the whites.

Mitch Jr. pushed the cart into me as I passed him. It was an injury akin to a grocery cart hitting the ankles. I almost cried out in pain but caught myself. Conan the Barbarian did not recognize pain.

Nifty-Fifty Wife had finished with a washer, and I quickly dumped my whites into it.

Behind me, Good Heart said, "Nick, do you have any quarters left?" The card reader on her washer was not working either. I made a mental note to talk to Clarence, the building super. He could fix anything. I gave her some of my precious quarters and turned my attention back to my whites. When I was I done loading, I poured bleach into the machine's reservoir and began to measure a cup of detergent.

"Oh, dear." Supermom looked at me. I stopped midpour.

"What's the matter?" I said.

"I was getting ready to use that machine, and you jumped ahead of me."

"I didn't know you were going to use this one."

"What do you think I'm doing down in the laundry room?" She pointed to three piles of separated dirty laundry.

"I'm sorry," I said. "Let me take these out."

"Don't bother now." Supermom sighed.

"I insist." I was embarrassed. I guess I should have asked if anybody was hoping to use it.

After I removed my whites, I offered the machine to her. She nodded and began loading her clothes.

Always one to break the tension, Good Heart said, "Do you need me to bring anything to the wine-and-cheese party tonight?"

"No. Please, just bring you," Nifty-Fifty Wife said.

"Big party tonight? What's the occasion?" I said.

"It's a party for stamping," Nifty-Fifty Wife replied.

"What's a stamping party?" I said.

"A bunch of us in the building make scrapbooks by mixing pictures with rubber stamps," Good Heart said. "Everybody brings their stamp kits to the party."

"You may come if you want," Nifty-Fifty Wife said.

I quickly said yes. I was feeling left out of things, and my instinctual thought was that it might help me connect better with the moms in the building. But my second thought was, why would I want to waste time doing arts and crafts with the moms in the building? What a stupid hobby.

I caught Supermom rolling her eyes to Nifty-Fifty Wife.

While waiting for our machines to finish, we engaged in idle chitchat. Supermom was either curt or dismissive to me, whenever the conversation happened to weave us together. Others in the building came and went, in the process of doing their laundry. Slowly, wash rush hour was digested. Surprisingly, the kids, including Mitch Jr., played well together.

One of the bigger dryers stopped. I opened the door; inside were assorted bed sheets and linens. The adage "one man's trash is another man's treasure" can be applied to laundry as well. No matter how clean someone else's laundry is, it just feels "cootie filled" to the touch. I wondered if there was an underwritten law about how much time you should wait before taking out items from a public machine and using said machine yourself. I began to take the linens out and pile them atop the dryer.

"What are you doing?" Supermom said. "They're still drying."

"These are your sheets? They're hot to the touch—done."

"The outside of the sheets are always hot. You have to separate the dry ones from the damp ones." She reached into the center of the compressed pile inside and pulled out damp sheets.

"I'm sorry again," I said. "I'm not doing anything right today."

"Not just today," Supermom said.

After saying sorry again, I retreated. Minutes later, another dryer opened, and I used it to fry Liz's undergarments. I paid for that lack of attentiveness later in the week, when she tried to put them on.

Suddenly, Supermom made a long hissing sound, like a cobra. She glared at me.

"What happened?" Good Heart said.

Supermom glowered straight at me as she asked through gritted teeth, "Nick, did you put bleach into the washer I just used?" One by one, she held up assorted garments with random bleach stains. Her last exhibit for the court of public humiliation was her prized, crimson Harvard sweat shirt.

"I'm so sorry. I don't remember. I may have had my whites in there." My heart raced, while my skin got clammy. I felt terrible. No matter what I thought of Supermom, I certainly did not mean to destroy her things. "Please let me replace your clothes if I can. I made an honest mistake."

"I don't want your money." She shook her head. "I can't be here right now." She hastily scooped up Mitch Jr. and left all her laundry behind.

After a few awkward minutes of silence, Good Heart and Nifty-Fifty Wife proceeded to finish up Supermom's laundry. They folded it all neatly, separating the damaged clothes into a separate pile.

"I didn't mean to do it," I said. "What can I do to make it better?"

Good Heart said, "I don't know. Let her calm down a little."

"Should I stop by her apartment to apologize again, maybe on my knees?"

"I wouldn't. Maybe at the stamping party tonight you can say something."

"What can I say to her that will get her to stop hating me?"

Good Heart smiled. "Tell her that you found a full-time job again."

I decided not to go to the wine-and-cheese party that night. I could not bear the thought of being somewhere where everyone would be laughing at me behind my back. I was a total failure. The next morning, I slipped a note under Supermom's door, once again expressing how truly sorry I was for destroying her clothes. I labored over the sentences, trying to write something that would bridge the gap between us. Later that day, I found my note unopened under my door, with the words "return to sender" written in thick red ink on the envelope.

9

LOST IN SPACE

Rain plus Saturday morning equaled watching TV. My all-time favorite guilty pleasure was on—*Conan the Barbarian* with Arnold Schwarzenegger—and despite my best effort to stay velcroed to the couch, I could not finish it. A rare thing happened that day: Liz did not have to go into the hospital. And, of course, rather than just taking it easy around the cave, Liz wanted to fill the day with multiple activities. She wanted to do something fun with the kids, to dispel her ever-present guilt that she was not spending enough time with the girls. The main mission for the day would be to go to the Museum of Natural History and suffer the crowds, boring exhibits, and swarms of overexcited kids.

Liz flopped on the couch, coffee cup in hand. She was minutes away from her caffeine spike of energy. "I need you to pack lunch for us and the kids—something healthy."

Conan had just lost his true love, Valeria, to an arrow from the evil wizard, Thulsa Doom. After a long pause on my part, I said, "Can't you just take the kids yourself? I'm bushed."

"Are you kidding me? I'm tired from the week too. Don't you want to be with us? The girls can't stay trapped in the house all day."

"It's a mess outside; what's the hurry to rush out? Wouldn't it make sense to take it easy today?"

"I wish I could take it easy, but this is the one Saturday I have off all month, and I want to make it count."

"I bet the girls would love quality time with just you."

"Nice try. I thought you were going to man up and start pulling your weight around here?" Conan's eyes glowered at Thulsa Doom. The barbarian would get his vengeance.

"That's not fair," I said.

Liz clicked the TV off and walked to the girls' room. "I'm going to get the girls dressed and fed, and then we'll go." Her caffeine was clearly on board, and I was going to have to run my paces today. I bet Valeria never made Conan go to any museums.

■ ■ ■

We slogged through the rain, careful to avoid getting trounced by the side splashes of passing cabs. Our stroller was covered by a plastic tarp, which kept the girls dry, but Liz and I did not fare as well. By the time we had crossed the city, we were soaked. We bickered over the mundane, like which side of the street had more covered storefront awnings or whether I had been careful enough in avoiding bumps and cracks in the sidewalk to make the ride smooth for the girls. It felt as if going on a family outing were a gauntlet to prove something that I did not yet understand. Her general criticism of my efforts was wearing on me. Some of her negativity I had earned, but some was born of something else: perhaps fatigue, stress, or her agitation with me. Things between us were not as liquid as they used to be.

The bad weather drove people with kids to the Museum of Natural History. It was one of the few big indoor spaces in the city. The lobby was full of a commotion, as people fretted over numerous ticket packages and waited on long coat-check lines. Couples spat over the cost of seeing *Penguins 3D* on IMAX and whether it truly was worth the effort to check raincoats. Those of us with strollers had a big decision at the coat check, especially those of us with the double chassis for multiple kids. Did your kid(s) have the stamina for hours of hiking around, or would you use the tiny overcrowded elevators, strategically hidden throughout the museum, to move between floors? My kids were not good hikers.

"I don't want to wait in this line. Let's just load all our coats on top of the stroller," I said.

"It's too much weight for the stroller. My parents will be upset if you break their gift for the girls," Liz said.

"They're just rain coats," I said. "I'll carry the backpack."

"You can't carry the lunches all morning. They're way too heavy. You'll break your back."

"It's not too heavy. It's really mostly light snack food. We'll grab something fun for lunch."

"I thought I asked you to pack a good lunch for us," Liz said. "What are the girls going to eat? What about me?"

I hated packing lunches. It always seemed like a lot of work. I preferred to live off the land—just grab something wherever. "They'll have chicken fingers for the girls. You and I will have options."

"We'll find grease, carbs, and gray-lettuce salads. Thanks," Liz said. "We can't afford to spend forty dollars for lunch at a museum cafeteria."

"Don't worry about the money," I said. "It'll be fun, our big treat for the day. I'm sure they'll have ice cream."

The girls cheered at the mention of ice cream. Liz shook her head. "That's what we need, Nick, more ice cream for you."

That was the first time Liz had ever made a comment about my burgeoning obesity. It startled me like a thunderclap. I was emotionally disoriented. "I'm sorry about the lunches."

"That's the least of our problems."

As we wandered about the second floor, surveying the dioramas of ancient people throughout the world, I tried to make small talk with Liz but had little success beyond a few occasional neutral comments from her. The girls ran ahead from display to display, showing little interest other than to shout and tumble, as if they were on the playground. They had liked the exhibits with animals, especially the ones where one animal was pouncing on another, ready to eat it. For them, the animal displays of the first floor had been much more exciting. I doubted they would last much longer, given their growing level of hyperactivity. There was no way they would sit through the astronomy show we had planned that afternoon.

Eventually, I foolishly ended my strategy of small talking Liz out of her funk. "You hurt my feelings with the ice cream remark. You've never said anything about my weight before."

"And you hurt my feelings by not making lunches, and by not taking seriously things that I worry about, like our money situation." A good defense is a strong offense.

"We don't always have to do things your way. Maybe I didn't want to go to the museum or eat some boring old lunch that we made at home. I would've preferred to stay at home and just watch TV," I said.

"And have me watch the kids on my day off while you're a couch potato? I bet if I didn't say anything, you would've played that stupid PC game Pirates of Plunder all day."

"It's an online game called Pillage and Plunder."

"The fact that you corrected me on the name of that moronic game shows that you are still not getting it."

"Getting what?" I said.

"I need a partner. I need somebody who is not always thinking about what feels good for them at that moment. Most of life is the boring, hard work between big events."

"That's a pretty pessimistic attitude, Miss Sunshine."

"Always got a one-liner? It was cute in college; now, not so much."

"If I had made the lunches, walked on the right side of the street to get here, and not been so glib, would you still be so angry? Why are you so mad at me?"

"I'm not mad. I'm just disappointed."

The kids got crankier and crankier before lunch. Museums were not their thing—maybe in a couple of years. We tried to make it as exciting as possible, but our ability to make exhibits on climate change as exciting as a Barbie movie proved woefully inadequate—much like I was beginning to feel around Liz. As Liz had predicted, lunch at the museum's cafeteria was a fiasco. We argued with Maude to have the protein of her gnarly chicken tenders rather than to slurp her coveted box of berry Juicy Juice. Claire avoided all the bought food and kept asking for Cheetos for lunch. While not an entirely bad request from an adult, even my limited child-rearing skills understood that this was not good for a growing three-year-old. I negotiated one Cheetos curl for every bite of ketchup-drenched tender. Perhaps the girls' previous ban on nonwhite food had been a mixed blessing in disguise.

Liz clucked as she pushed her plastic fork through the brownish and cheesy remains of her Mexican burrito. "Maybe you can work out a deal for one ice cream bite per limp fry she eats."

We ditched the remains of our half-eaten lunches and decided to do a quick loop of the astronomy exhibits before we headed home for the girls' nap time—big mistake. The girls only wanted to play tag in the vast space of the glass atrium, which housed a scale model of the solar system. I still think Pluto should be a planet; it seems unfair to have a bunch of astronomers vote you out of the planetary club, just because you're the runt of the litter.

Liz's beeper chirped. "I've gotta get this."

"I thought you had the day off."

"I do, but I promised someone I would take their beeper for a couple of hours, because they're at a funeral." She went to find a quiet space to make a call.

"I'll meet you by the restroom. Maude has to potty." Her massive intake of berry Juicy Juice had run its course through her digestive tract. She tugged at my arm.

I took the girls to the men's restroom, but Claire hesitated to go inside. "I can't just leave you here. Just come and keep us company, even if you don't have to go."

"No, Daddy. I big girl now. I stand right here," Claire said.

"I don't think that's a good idea," I said. Maude was now screaming, making sure that the rest of the museum knew that she had to pee.

"Please, Daddy. Mommy is coming right back," Claire said.

Maude struggled to open the door to the men's room. When it was just wide enough, she slipped in. I panicked—two kids, two directions. "Claire, stay here. Don't move. Wait for Mommy."

Even though I was mere steps behind Maude, I failed to catch up to her, and she closed herself in one of the stalls. "Do you need help—number one or two?"

"Number one and two."

That would take more time than a quick in and out of the men's room—I silently cursed. "Let me know when you need help wiping."

At a urinal, a younger father was holding his infant in one hand and doing his business with the other. Is that legal and/or sanitary? "Nice dexterity," I said, as I did my business at an adjacent urinal.

He sneered and left without a word.

I finished up with Maude, and we left the men's room, after arguing as to whether she should wash her hands. The whole side trip might have taken less than five minutes, but that was just enough time for Claire to have gone missing. She was not outside the men's room.

My stomach dropped. I struggled to control racing thoughts of bad outcomes. Kids wander off all the time, I said to myself. I told myself that she had just gone around the corner into the planetary atrium again. I sprinted, and I didn't immediately see her among the dozens of people milling under the model of the giant sun hanging from the ceiling.

My phone rang. Instinctively, without checking the caller ID, I answered. It was my in-laws: Mimi and Henry Lynch. At some point, I should assign them a distinct caller ID song, maybe the theme song to *All in the Family*, since they all think I'm a good-for-nothing son-in-law.

"Where's Liz?" Mimi said. "I can't reach her on her phone."

"She's on the phone." I continued scanning for Claire.

"Is everything okay? Where are you?" Mimi said. She was the paranoid type—a junkie for feeling anxious.

"We're at the Museum of Natural History," I said. "Listen, I got to go. I'll tell Liz to call you back."

Maude was now getting upset that Claire was missing.

"What's the hurry?" Mimi said. "Why is Liz on the phone?"

"She's on with the hospital."

Maude started crying.

"I thought she had the day off?" Mimi said.

"She does, but she said that she would take somebody's beeper because they had to go to a funeral."

"Who died?" Mimi said.

"Mimi, please don't take this the wrong way, but I've gotta go now." Maude started screaming for Claire.

"Is that one of the kids screaming? Is everything all right?"

"Sort of—Claire is a little lost."

"What have you done?" Mimi said.

In what seemed like less time than it takes to blink an eye, Henry Lynch was on the phone. "Where are you? Did you call the police?"

"Not yet?"

"What are you waiting for? How could you be so irresponsible?" Henry said.

"I just found out, and then Mimi called looking for Liz."

"Why did you answer the phone? Why are you chatting on the phone with us? You never take anything seriously."

"I don't have time for this, Henry. I'm hanging up." I pushed the phone back into my pocket.

Liz was behind me. "Why did you hang up on my father?"

"I didn't—well, maybe I did, but he'll understand, I think. Claire is missing," I said. I filled her in on all the details.

Before I had finished my sentence, Liz had informed a nearby guard that Claire was missing. Announcements went out to watch building exits, and museum staff appeared to help us. We had to give a detailed description, which included the fact that she would be holding the ever-grimy Doo-cho-baa. I split from Liz and Maude to search. I went with the theory that Claire had wandered off to look at something that had caught her attention earlier.

After a few minutes, it came to me: she had taken the stairway to heaven. Earlier, we had denied her wish to walk a spiraling ramp between floors, citing our lack of time. She had not forgotten. The Heilbrunn Cosmic Pathway was intended to be a multimedia guide to billions of years of cosmic history in the Milky Way. To a three-year-old, it seemed like a giant jungle gym, just waiting to be conquered—forget about the boring science stuff.

I ran up the ramp, and, there at the top, I found her. Claire didn't appear all that upset, despite seeming confused over which way to go. "I knew you would come, Daddy. This is so pretty."

I scooped her up and called Liz to tell her I had found her. Claire hugged me, nuzzling her head on my shoulder. Nap time was close at hand. I probably should have yelled at her or something for running away, but it felt so good to have her hug me that I decided to just leave it be.

Later that afternoon, as Liz and I closed the door to the girls' room for nap time, she motioned to the couch. We had barely spoken since the museum.

"Do you want to talk?" I said.

She shook her head. "That's where you're sleeping tonight."

"Can we talk about it? I'm really sorry about the day. I get it now."

She held up a hand. "Earlier you asked me whether I was mad at you, and I said I was just disappointed. I've changed my mind: now I am mad at you."

She went into our room and closed the door.

10

KNIGHT IN DISTRESS

Somewhere between Third Avenue and Sixty-Fourth Street, our new double stroller finally broke. The weight of hanging bags from Grace's Market had been too much for the right wheel bracket. I shouldn't have bought that extra gallon of milk. Now, the stroller was unusable, since the wheel would no longer stay inside its flimsy-ass plastic bracket. My in-laws had spent several hundred dollars on the stroller, as a moving gift to New York for the twins. Such decadence was unusual for them.

Liz had done research on high-end strollers, looking for the sweet spot of specs required for the transport of her spawn around the Upper East Side. Strollers in New York City have similar requirements as cars in the suburbs. Basic child comforts include soft padding, reclining seats, and the ability to add rain and snow shields. Of course, you must have slots for snacks, drinks, and toys. Other considerations include adequate storage, to not only haul all of the above, but also to be able to simultaneously hold three to four grocery bags, either in the storage bin underneath or from hooks on the handle bars. A stroller, even one for twins, had to be able to fold up quickly and to not be too wide for the narrow aisles in tiny, Manhattan retail stores. Finally, you had to purchase a brand that best conveyed both your economic status and your superior sense of style. Liz wanted only the best. I frankly wanted to get the cheapest. I think strollers are like umbrellas: no matter how much you pay for them, they get pretty beat up in little time.

When the stroller finally died, Claire was sleeping. Maude appeared not to notice that we abruptly stopped, when one of the wheels fell off. She just stared ahead, sipping juice from her cup. We were still pretty far from the apartment. A cab or a bus seemed like my best option, even while having to juggle kids, groceries, and a diaper bag.

"Need any help?" A woman coming out of a nearby apartment building had been slowed by the site of our calamity.

"My wheel fell off. I suppose there's no AAA for strollers," I said.

She laughed. "I don't think I've ever seen a wheel fall off like that." She had a very white and perfect smile. I don't have good teeth. Mine are slightly yellow. I'm jealous of people with good teeth.

"That's been my luck lately. I'm like the cartoon Ziggy, where everything goes wrong."

"Who's Ziggy?"

I feel like a dork whenever I make a pop culture reference that falls flat. "Never mind," I said. "We'll just take a cab back home. Thanks for asking to help."

"Today, your luck has changed, Ziggy. I have a double stroller. You can have it."

"Are you messing with me?"

"I have a double stroller from when my kids were younger," she said.

"You don't even know me. Who gives away an expensive double stroller to a stranger?"

"Charity is big on the Upper East Side, and you seem to be a knight in distress."

My benefactor was a very attractive woman, with a model-thin body. She was dressed for the gym in tight exercise clothes. Her brown hair was pulled back in a ponytail. She was the type of woman that could easily draw your attention from a crowd, even if you just passed her on the sidewalk. I suddenly felt self-conscious about my looks, in the presence of such a beautiful person. I was Quasimodo to her Esmeralda. Like most guys, I had not been comfortable talking to the hot cheerleader in high school, and I had been a lot thinner then. Now, I was a chunky monkey, and my self-esteem was in free fall. I should have stayed away from the free pizza a little more at work or eaten less junk food while writing code.

"That's very nice of you. Let me give you my name and number, and I can pick it up sometime. I'm Nick. My daughters are Claire and Maude."

"My name is Kelly. You can take the stroller now. I'm not in a big rush today. Just come up with me now." She went back into her building and sent out the doorman to help me collect my bags and junk. The doorman told me to leave the stroller on the curb. Garbage collection was tomorrow. I felt a little guilty leaving my in-law's gift on the curb so soon after getting it. Maybe a homeless person would grab it and turn it into something useful again.

We entered a stone prewar building. With the girls in tow, we took the small elevator up to Kelly's apartment. She told me that the apartment co-op had just finished a major renovation on the lobby and hallways a few months ago. It had been a two-year project that had been nothing but a big hassle in terms of noise, dirt, and debris. She had almost been driven to move out but had decided to stay since she was going through a divorce and wanted to keep the apartment in the settlement. At the advice of her attorney, she stayed while her husband still lived there. Not a fun time for her. It surprised me how she was able to share so many personal details with a stranger, in the span of a short elevator ride. She was a chatter monkey. I even found out that she was a vegetarian and that green was her favorite color. I wonder what percent of vegetarians chose green as their favorite color.

"Here you go." From a closet just inside her apartment, Kelly pulled out a double stroller that was nearly identical to mine. Behind her, past the living room, I could hear the sound of someone in the kitchen clearing and washing dishes. I smelled real flowers, not the chemical smell of the morning-dew scented Stick Ups I had in my apartment.

Even though I was in a posh building, it felt weird coming up to a stranger's apartment right after meeting her. I had seen too many horror movies. I wanted to go. "This is such a nice stroller, and you are being too generous. Let me give you some money for it." I fumbled for my wallet. I wasn't sure how much cash I had.

"No money. This is my good deed for the week."

Maude spotted a large, ornate Victorian dollhouse in the living room. "Can we stay and play?"

"No, Maude. We have to get going, and Kelly probably wants to start her day. We shouldn't intrude. I don't think you would like it if strangers came over to our home and started playing with your toys," I said.

Kelly said, "If it's okay with your daddy, you can take a quick peek at it."

I shrugged, and the twins darted through the living room of contemporary furniture to play with the dollhouse. Had we wandered into a photo shoot for *Architectural Digest*, I would not have been surprised.

The footfalls of the girls across the hardwood floor awakened the biggest black dog I had ever seen. He rose from his sun-drenched spot beneath the dollhouse, barking loudly as he hurtled toward them. He was a Great Dane, an elephant compared to the girls. I sprinted to intercept the dog. Claire and Maude screamed and tried to flee but collided into each other instead. As they fell to the floor, Doo-cho-baa tumbled from Claire's grasp.

I stood between the girls and the dog, urging him to stay away. My heart was in high gear—big dogs scared me. I waved my hands erratically, hoping that I wouldn't be spending the rest of the day in an emergency room getting stitches from a dog bite. The dog held his ground in front of me, with Claire's beloved blanket in his tooth-filled maw.

"Daddy, save Doo-cho-baa," Claire said, whimpering.

My first thought was that the dog could keep the ratty blanket, as long as he didn't eat me and the girls, but I chose to rescue Doo-cho-baa because Claire needed me to. I held out my arm and made eye contact with the dog like the trainers do on Animal Planet. "Give it back." I was firm, trying to assert dominance over the canine beast.

Kelly joined the action. "Licorice, drop it. Bad dog."

Licorice whimpered and took a step back. Without thinking, I reached for the blanket and pulled it in a quick attempt to snatch it free. The dog held his ground; a smaller dog would've been yanked forward across the hardwood. I was surprised that the ragged blanket didn't rip. Who keeps a

Great Dane in their New York apartment? I could easily imagine it roaming free in the wild, terrorizing some village somewhere, maybe absconding with a baby.

The game was on. Licorice arched his back and used his leg muscles to jerk me off balance. Stubbornly, I kept hold of Doo-cho-baa, and Licorice dragged me through the living room. My spinning legs and body tipped a coffee table, knocking picture frames to the floor. I heard the sound of glass shattering. At the end of the ride, once I willingly let go of Doo-cho-baa, I smacked into a ceramic Mexican pot containing an ornamental fig tree. Dirt spilled to the floor as the container plant fell on top of me. I slowly rose from the floor, humiliated.

"Carmella, come quick, and help me with Licorice." Kelly shouted.

"Coming, Miss Kelly," a voice said from the kitchen. "Is that hound up to trouble again?"

Kelly and the short, stocky Carmella came at Licorice from different angles, forcing him into a corner near the window. When Licorice lowered his head at Kelly, Carmella grabbed him by the collar. Both of them struggled to bring the dog to a bedroom in the rear of the apartment. Once the creature was contained, Kelly and Carmella appeared again. Behind them, Licorice threw himself against the bedroom door.

"I'm sorry I destroyed the place," I said. Claire and Maude were hugging each other against the wall. I righted the coffee table and picked up the picture frames that were unbroken.

Carmella nudged me aside, throwing a dismissive look. "Don't bother. I clean now." She sighed as she picked up the broken glass.

Kelly retrieved Doo-cho-baa and knelt before Claire. "I'm sorry Licorice scared you. He was just playing with you, but sometimes he's a little rough." She handed Doo-cho-baa to Claire. "My girls adore him. They ride him like a pony sometimes."

Claire and Maude seemed to relax. Eventually, they went to play with the dollhouse as originally planned. Kids are resilient. I was still shaken.

"Not a big 'dog person,' I gather." Kelly looked at me and smiled. "You certainly know how to party. You really freaked out there."

I blushed, repeating my apology again.

"I'm the one who should apologize. I should have warned you about the dog."

"I'll pay for the damaged frames and the chipped pot," I said.

"Please, no need. Besides, chipping the pot gives me an excuse to get rid of it. My ex-husband gave it to me in better times." Kelly was oddly too good a sport. I don't think the moms back at my building would have been as gracious if I had ransacked their homes in the same way. I guess people with money live in a different reality.

Licorice continued to hurl himself against the door. "How does your condo board allow such an energetic, large dog in the building?" I said.

"My ex-husband is very arrogant, and pushy. He twisted arms to make it happen. He likes to make demands people can't refuse. I wanted a lap dog."

I was getting nosy. "Why do you keep it if it is his dog?"

She smiled again. "Because it pisses him off. He loves that dog so."

Kelly ushered me to sit with her on a leather sectional near the girls. It was nice being in a clean home that didn't have a film of institutional grime. I was embarrassed about how Liz and I lived. We were living like students again. I wanted to start making money again.

"I wish my daughters were not in school, and could play with them," Kelly said. "My husband, or rather ex-husband, bought the dollhouse in England while on a business trip. It was right before he moved out, so he went overboard on gifts for the kids. For me, he brought back a box of Scottish tea biscuits. Do you think he was trying to tell me something?"

I liked Kelly's sarcasm. I didn't know quite how to respond, so I went with humor. Most people would have gone with the awkward silence. "I bet he's sleeping on a park bench right now, while you get to keep the apartment."

She smiled. "Not quite. You can't keep a good lawyer down for long, no matter how hard you try."

"I heard that," I said. At a comedy club, Liz and I had once sat through a show in which a comedian from Oklahoma had said that "I heard that" was a one-size-fits-all response, even if you're not entirely sure what the other person is talking about.

"Do you want something to drink? Water? Or do you want a cup of tea to go with my Scottish tea biscuits?" Kelly was being really hospitable, especially in light of the fact that I had just met her—and had broken stuff in her home within minutes of entering it. Niceties from the opposite sex had become unusual lately, especially from the stay-at-home moms I was dealing with on a daily basis.

I declined at first, but she insisted it was no trouble. Shortly, Carmella brought us tea. I wished I had a cleaning lady helping me around the house. I hated scrubbing toilets and cleaning Liz's hair out of the drains—not very manly things to be doing.

"Thanks, Carmella," Kelly said. After Carmella left the room, she whispered, "I got her along with the apartment." Carmella was a live-in maid.

"Not a bad deal. If I got a divorce I would only get a collection of dust bunnies."

Licorice switched from colliding against the bedroom door to just rampant howling. How could Kelly's ex-husband have managed to muzzle the neighbors to this racket? Nobody who could afford a condo in that building would sit quietly and not complain to management to eject the hound from hell. Maybe she had not been joking, when she had said that he had twisted some arms to make it happen. And made demands that people could not refuse. My mind leapt to quick conclusions. Was the ex-husband a lawyer for the Mafia? Was he having the building watched? What would this guy think of me visiting with his ex-wife while his kids were at school? I pushed these thoughts away. I wanted to enjoy sitting in a clean apartment, drinking tea, and having biscuits. I also made a mental note to have my testosterone level checked next time I saw my doctor.

It was a welcome change to talk to another stay-at-home parent who wasn't as reserved as the batch of people I had to deal with back at the family association. With them, I had to be guarded, careful not to say something that would offend or be politically incorrect. In a way, the stay-at-home moms were like work colleagues, with all the formal stiffness that comes along with it, since all of our spouses worked together at the hospitals. There was a certain self-righteousness that I found to be stifling.

It should be all right to say that sometimes being around kids is a pain in the ass. Could the moms chill out a little? Something or someone was holding them back from being normal human beings. I put my money on Supermom being the villain. She was doing a "cult leader" thing to the family association. It was fun to frame everything in the context of a good-versus-evil plot line. It relieved my boredom.

Kelly was in her thirties, and her bio was brief. She grew up in what she called the crotch of the Black Hills of South Dakota. She got a degree in women's studies at a tiny liberal arts college in New Hampshire. Later, she did some modeling and then got a job at a fashion magazine in New York. She lived the single-life scene, until she met her now ex-husband on a booze cruise for some charity involving what I think was an endangered species. I missed a lot of the details, since she spoke fast. At some point, she had kids, and she did the stay-at-home thing with their two daughters.

"What are you going to do now? Go back to work?" I said.

"I don't know. It's fun not being bossed around anymore by my ex. What about you? Are you home with your kids full-time?"

"Not by choice, since I'm not good with kids. The dot-com company I was working at went bust, and we came here from San Francisco for my wife's training. She's an orthopedic fellow at the Hospital for Special Surgery. I'm trying to get another job writing code, but nobody's hiring. But I have an interview next week, and we'll see what happens," I said.

In a rare moment of calm, Maude and Claire continued to play well together at the dollhouse. Licorice had finally stopped barking after Carmella had repeatedly poked the door with a broom handle.

"Do you like being home with the kids?" Kelly said.

"In a way, I do, but I never realized how much work it was for no pay and no recognition. The kids seem less happy with me than they were with my mother-in-law. And I live in a building with a really weird group of stay-at-home moms."

"I think it's great that you're home with the kids. It's treasured time the kids will always have."

"Everybody says that. Don't know if I really believe it."

"It sure beats having to be in the working world. You get to set your own schedule and play anytime you want." She raised her hand for a fist bump. We touched knuckles. Her skin was a lot softer than mine.

I checked my watch. "I've got groceries in your lobby that need to get into the fridge, and I should let you go. Weren't you on your way to the gym or something?"

"Yes, but I don't have to be there for another hour, to meet Dom, my trainer."

"Which gym do you go to?" I said.

"The Workout Pit, which is about two avenues over, closer to York."

"That's right near us. My mother-in-law just got me an annual membership at the Workout Pit, including forty sessions with a trainer. I'm planning on starting up there next week. I love that they have daycare for the kids during workout time." I patted my belly. "Do you think she's trying to tell me something? Liz is always getting on me about my weight." I had a theory that Liz and her mother, Mimi, were concerned about my health and wanted me to get in shape. It was odd that her parents had given me such a nice present for my birthday, since they didn't really like me very much. No doubt, Liz had begged her mother for the money. She was not pleased with my growing Buddha physique.

"It is what it is," Kelly said.

"People use that phrase, and I really don't know exactly what it means."

"To me it means acceptance. When you're ready, you'll lose the weight." Was this hot chick really this cool?

"You have certainly been very kind to us this morning. Come on, girls; let's go. Maybe we'll see you at the gym," I said.

"I'm there every morning."

I shouted good-bye to Licorice, who responded by jumping into the door again.

Kelly rolled her eyes and whispered a good-bye to the girls.

The girls and I collected our groceries from the doorman and walked home using our unexpected gift. I was careful not to overload the stroller. This time, I chose to carry the gallon of milk, pushing the kids with one hand.

"Daddy, she was nice," Maude said. "I like dollhouse. Can we get one?"

"Maybe for your birthdays we'll get one," I said. "Let's add it to your wish list." There would have been about two thousand items on their joint wish list if I had ever bothered to keep up with their gift requests. Fortunately, for my bank account, they forgot about the vast majority of things they requested.

"Kelly was pretty," Claire said, "just like Sleeping Beauty."

I smiled and nodded, but Claire didn't see me because of the stroller's canopy. "I guess fairy-tale princesses really do live in New York City."

11

DOUGH BOY

The Workout Pit is a cavern located two stories beneath an apartment building. It has a minimalist industrial décor. Club music plays throughout the gym, forcing people to talk very loudly over each other. Street art and graffiti replace the slogans and corporate images usually found in a national-chain gym. I did not fit the profile of the typical gym rat found at the Workout Pit, which was thin, muscular, tan, well groomed, antsy, and dressed in trendy workout clothes. As you can imagine, my green "Kiss me, I'm Irish" tee shirt and gray sweatpants did not distinguish me as a workout deity.

As soon as we stepped out of the elevator, Claire and Maude, as if on cue, started complaining about the noise and their hunger. When the receptionist greeted me with wide eyes and an overly generous smile, I knew that I was not going to be playing on home field at the Workout Pit.

I placed a sandwich bag of crackers into the stroller. "Where is the kid drop-off?"

"Are you a member?" At some level, she wanted my answer to be no.

"Yes, this is my first time; I'm supposed to meet with Dom the trainer for a walk-through session."

She put on a big smile for the girls. "Aren't you the sweetest little things? Come with me, and I'll take you to the playroom."

Maude and Claire were not buying what she was selling—until I said, "We'll get ice cream later."

A few minutes after the girls left for the gym playroom, Dom came to the reception desk. He was a thug with an odd charm. I would later find out that his stats were the following: six feet tall, two hundred forty pounds, with something like 3 percent body fat, if that is even possible. Dom had a big square head, with a crew cut, a thick neck, and limbs chiseled like an action figure. He was from "how yo doin'" Queens, and had a firm handshake grip that made me feel like a little girl by comparison. Dom was a little scary, and I had a passing thought that he could crush my head on a whim, if I pissed him off.

"You wanna stop being a fat boy and train with Dom?"

"I wanna be a lean, mean fighting machine, sir," I said.

Dom kind of smiled, I think. "How'd you hear about me?"

"A friend of mine named Kelly recommended you."

"She's a good kid. Now, if you want to train with Dom, you gotta be serious about it. It ain't gonna be easy. 'Cause if you sluff off, it makes me look bad as a trainer." He poked his meaty finger at a couple of people in the gym. "They are with me. The people that train with me look the best. The other members know who Dom's guys and gals are."

I felt like I was joining the US Navy SEALs, instead of a sweaty gym. This was the first time that I had ever heard of someone being interviewed by a trainer. Did this mean I was in for a world of hurt? I wondered if there were a trainer for lazy posers. Thanks to my mother-in-law, I had a one-year membership and forty training sessions to burn through. I wish she had bought me a gift certificate from a game-electronics store, or a bakery.

But I needed this. I was fat and squishy. There was something motivational about Dom. It was like being in middle school again and wanting the football players to be your friend. "Let me be your big makeover story."

"I like that," Dom said.

We did a walk-through of the gym. He pointed out key weight-lifting machines, which for the most part looked like torture devices. When we arrived at the free-weight area, Dom smiled. "When you're ready, this is where the big boys play. This is where you'll become a lean, mean fightin' machine, fat boy."

The free-weight area was located at the farthest point from the entrance of the gym. A good design decision if you didn't want to hear the screams of pain from those whom Dom trained. The area was surrounded by a chain link fence, which seemed a waste, since I couldn't imagine anyone wanting to steal free weights. Inside were kindred spirits to Dom: bulky men with socially inappropriate-sized muscles.

The free-weight jocks did callouts to Dom. "Hey Mr. Dom, I feel the burn today. Bench me two hundred, I did."

Dom ignored them. "My training is also about the diet. I'll give you a list of foods that are okay to eat. I want you to keep a log of what you eat and show me when you come in. Your diet should be low in fat and high in fiber, with lots of protein. Total calorie count is important. Make portions the size of your fist."

My head was spinning. Did I really want to train with this lunatic? "How often do we need to meet? Once a week?"

"You're on the three times a week plan for three months. And you're going to do your cardio workout three other days. Pick either Saturday or Sunday to let your body rest."

Six days a week. Who has the time for that? Dom told me that the gym opened at 5:00 a.m. and closed at midnight. Sundays, the house of pain was only open until 8:00 p.m. He suggested that I do my cardio first thing in the morning, at five—slim chance that would happen. I realized that my schedule was suddenly getting full, just because I didn't want to be fat and lazy anymore.

"What's your favorite food?"

"Pizza."

"No pizza while you're working out with me."

I laughed as if he were joking. He wasn't.

"Let's get started," Dom said. "How many sit-ups and pull-ups can you do?"

I cannot remember the details of the pain of the next thirty minutes. During my time with Dom, the kids had fun in the gym playroom.

Wanda, the gym's babysitter, was a student at a fashion-and-design school. She had brought in watercolor paints and was doing art projects with the kids. I had worried that the kids would not want to go to the gym because it would be no fun, but instead the daycare option was a winner. Wanda was an instant hit with Maude and Claire. Maude especially liked her because Wanda let her paint whatever she wanted, which was often pictures of dragons spewing fire. Most people guide girls into painting flowers, fairies, and rainbows. As a bonus, she would later teach the kids a little Spanish and do occasional babysitting for us.

As I was gathering up the twins into the stroller, Kelly came into the childcare center. "Fancy meeting you here," I said.

"A little birdie just told me that you're training with Dom." Kelly had just done her cardio routine, and she looked radiant. I looked like I had been mugged and left for dead after my brief workout.

"I might live to regret training with Dom. He wants me here six days a week."

"Dom can be lots of fun. He just likes to play tough guy."

"I suspect he has a little more patience with you than with a dough boy like me."

Kelly's daughter ran into her arms from the other side of the playroom. "This is Zoe."

I asked Maude and Claire if they had met and played at all with Zoe. No response.

"I'm embarrassed by their lack of social grace sometimes. A small downside of twins is they're a little antisocial to other kids."

"With little kids, I don't take things personally."

"That's a better attitude. I take everything Claire and Maude do personally."

"You're too hard on yourself," she said. She pulled a drink of water from her glass sports bottle.

"Thanks again for the stroller. You saved my life. My wife doesn't even know that the other one broke. She would have given me the business for having broken the one her parents gave us. Luckily, she hasn't yet noticed that yours is slightly different from ours."

"It will be our secret."

On the way home from the gym, the kids wanted pizza for lunch. Normally, I would consider that to be literally and figuratively a slice of heaven, but now I was supposed to be on a diet, and pizza was supposed to be off the list. I pushed the stroller into my favorite pizza restaurant nearest the apartment. It was called John's Pizza. I loved that place. It offered brick-oven pizza and had a garden patio in the back. The restaurant was a little crowded for lunch. After reviewing the menu, and finding little that inspired me other than pizza, I realized that the only healthy option was salad. I wasn't quite ready to be the fat guy who only eats salad and cottage cheese. At that moment, I chose to make the rationalization that you can't start a diet in the middle of the day. Diets start at midnight.

"Don't even think about it, Pizza Boy." Dom was behind me in line.

"What are you doing here?" I said. Is this guy going to stalk me?

"I'm on a lunch break, and I saw you from across the street coming in here. No pizza for you today."

"I was going to get a salad. The kids wanted pizza."

"I know the owners here really well. I'm going to do you a favor and tell them not to serve you any more pizza."

Dom seemed a little nutty. But maybe I needed a little "tough love" to get into shape. Getting into shape might help things with Liz and give me more energy to not be a lazy bum. I needed to pull it all together and be more of a partner to her. She was still pissed about the girls' hair.

12

WHEN THE CAT IS AWAY

The vibe around the building got a lot better in late August, when Supermom went on vacation. She trumpeted the news that she and the kids were going to her parents' ranch in Jackson Hole. Later, I would find out that it was not quite the hunting lodge she hoped we all would imagine, but rather, a small log cabin on a couple of acres, with one horse, a few miles from town. Supermom was a shameless self-promoter. Mitch Sr. remained in New York to work at the hospital. His status was still that of an indentured servant as a fellow, along with Liz, in orthopedics. Neither Supermom nor Mitch Sr. seemed all that upset about being apart. Some couples do better with breaks.

For those two weeks, Good Heart and I spent a lot of time together. We arranged to meet for playdates midmorning, before it got too hot. It was important to get the girls out of the building at least once a day, to avoid cabin fever, especially in such small apartments. New York City tends to empty out in late summer. People with any bit of money go to the Hamptons; only worker bees remain in the concrete hive. Avoiding the heat becomes top priority. I missed San Francisco and its cool summers. I was not used to having damp, clingy tee shirts and boxer shorts.

Good Heart and I mostly went to the playground, and when we needed a break, we went to Le Pain Quotidien, a French bakery, located nearby.

The gimmick of the place was a large oak common table that patrons sat around for morning breakfast. The kids loved the place, since they could gobble chocolate-filled croissants and smear entire pots of jam on their bread. During the past few weeks, as my kids had slowly weaned off a diet of only white food, for reasons I still didn't understand, my standards for a healthy meal had become low. Good Heart and I had gone so often to Le Pain Quotidien together that the manager said to me one day as I waited for Good Heart to arrive, "Tell your wife that we have the sourdough bread in today she likes so much."

"She's not my wife," I said.

The manager seemed a little confused. "I'm sorry, sir. The twins look so much like her."

Good Heart was amused when I reported that story. "What a scandal. We can't meet like this anymore."

Bakeries are a hard place to maintain a diet. Since I had started working out with Dom, I was on a diet of small protein portions and tons of greens and grains. My only option was to order hamster food like greens and water. I was hungry, all the time, but early results were starting to show on my body, after just a few weeks.

The joys of pregnancy were allowing Good Heart to push a sesame bagel packed with cream cheese into her mouth. "It's very impressive what you're doing with your diet and exercise." Some of the cream cheese remained on her teeth as she spoke.

"I'm like a Buddhist monk now. I'm working out six days a week. I'm not a happy camper, but I've got to take off this weight"

"After thirty, your metabolism just slows down," Good Heart said.

"And your body just does not recover the way it used to. I feel like somebody hit me with a bat. I'm sore all over. My trainer is a sadist."

"Tell him to take it easy," Good Heart said.

"A guy can't do that. It would be a sign of weakness."

"Maybe the workouts are too much. You need to tell him."

"I'm just going to have to tough it out," I said.

"You have such a guy attitude. What does Liz think about the new you?"

"She likes that I've lost a few pounds already, but she thinks the time with the trainer is taking away from my quality time with the kids, since I put them in babysitting during the sessions."

"I agree. Those babysitting services in the gym are just horrible. The kids are ignored, and those rooms are a germ farm." Good Heart was overly kidcentric. One time, Good Heart admitted that she had once peed herself because she had not wanted to wake up her daughter, Sammie, who had fallen asleep on her.

"The world is a dirty place, but somebody has to live in it."

"Maybe so, but you can at least try to avoid the dirt you know about." Good Heart touched Claire's hair. "It's finally starting to grow in."

"Thank God. I've been in the proverbial doghouse with Liz over it."

Good Heart and I hadn't really talked about the tragedy of my act of cutting the golden locks of my kids. It was one of those gossip items that was only discussed behind my back. I noticed the lingering glances and occasional headshakes from the other stay-at-home parents in the group.

"What were you thinking?"

"Apparently not much," I said.

After the big blowout fight with Liz, I had decided to help more around the house. I picked up after the kids and kept the bathrooms and kitchen clear from health-code violations. I even managed to stock the crazy types of yogurt that Liz eats. Wolfie was teaching me to cook things besides pasta and boiled chicken. Sometimes, he snuck in leftovers from his restaurant that Liz liked into our refrigerator. Nobody can be grumpy after eating Wolfie's roasted chicken and potatoes.

My cell phone did its text chirp. *Nick—can you take Zoe home with you after your workout with Dom? I've got an appointment that I can't miss. Thanks.* After only a few weeks, Kelly had become my new best friend.

"Does Liz send you text messages during the day? I'm jealous," Good Heart said.

I quickly typed *yes* to Kelly's message. "My friend Kelly wanted me to pick her daughter up after my workout tomorrow morning. All the girls can play together over at my apartment. But in answer to your question, I only get one or two texts from Liz a week."

Kelly, on the other hand, was a text-message fiend. She sent at least a dozen a day, mostly seeking my opinion on a variety of things, including what she should get at the food market for dinner. From a guy's standpoint, it was a little too much communication, but it was worth it, since Kelly was fun to be around, easy to hang out with, and willing to spend time with my personal baggage. And she laughed at my jokes. Friends like Good Heart from the family association required a certain level of guarded care, since we all lived together in the same building. With Kelly, I could also gossip about everyone else, since the circles did not overlap.

"Daniel is always telling me he's too busy at work to talk. Maybe text messaging would be an easier way to contact him," Good Heart said.

Good Heart was not having an easy time with her pregnancy. The air conditioning in her apartment was not cutting the heat of August. She was due mid-October, and she had a high level of fatigue, mostly due to the fact that she had trouble getting a comfortable night's sleep. Her hubby, Daniel, was little help around the house. He claimed to be working all the time, either in the clinics or in the research lab. Daniel was the self-absorbed type. He seemed to be a practitioner of busy work, in order to seem important.

"Have I met Kelly?"

"I brought her by the playroom last week. I think you were there. She's got shoulder-length brown hair—works out a lot. She brought her little girl Zoe."

"I remember now. She was very pretty. Didn't talk to me much. Where did you meet her?"

I told her about being rescued by Kelly and the gift of a double stroller. "She's just survived a tough divorce. A lot of her friends were through her ex-husband, and she's feeling a little alienated now."

"Nick to the rescue."

"She's a lot of fun. We've been hanging out a lot lately. Great sense of humor. Her older daughter, Tasha, is good with my girls, too. Sammie would love Zoe. Maybe I'll set up a playdate for all of us."

"That's okay," Good Heart said. "She seems like the type who takes care of herself fine."

I wasn't sure what that meant. Maybe Good Heart had already met her quota on friends? Heaven forbid she had a life outside the family association. Either that or she was turning a cold shoulder to an attractive woman. Nobody likes competition.

■ ■ ■

After breakfast, Good Heart had to run an errand to Bed, Bath, and Beyond for junior sheets and baby bedding. The girls and I decided to join her. She had just received a gift certificate from one of her aunts or uncles—too many relatives to remember. Every story from home included the name of a different relative. I think the gift certificate had come from the second-youngest brother of her father who was only a half brother by marriage. Good Heart was one of ten kids, her parents had many siblings, and nearly all the family resided in or near Wichita, Kansas. Once a year, the family met for a weekend of barbeques, beer drinking, and baby greeting of the new members. I imagined that if I ever went to Wichita to visit Good Heart, we would bump into a relative every few minutes going around town.

Bed, Bath, and Beyond in Manhattan is a great place to let your kids run around indoors, away from the heat. Manhattan has very few free indoor play spaces for kids. Maude and Claire loved to go down to the bedding section and run amuck among beds and linen displays. Every once in a while, I might catch a dirty look from one of the employees, as the kids dove and jumped from bed to bed. But I would feign ignorance and apologize, and then the kids would continue with their ruckus once said employee was out of site. The only problem with my strategy was that I could not go with an upstanding parent, like Good Heart, who was not as permissive as I. Good Heart clucked and yelled at Sammie to stop being corrupted by my brood. Kelly had had no such problem when we had gone together and let the kids have a pillow fight in aisle seven.

As we left the bedding area and headed toward the checkout, I put assorted crap—impulse items like a banana slicer, a lime-scented candle, and a DVD screen saver of a fish tank for my TV—into my cart. (I can never resist the allure of the deep-discount aisles. I feel that I'm one-up-ping the store.) Maude and Claire desperately wanted reindeer plush toys left over from Christmas, which I also threw into the cart. They were 80 percent off. Credit cards make buying junk easy.

Good Heart and I draped the bags on our strollers and pushed our kids home in the heat. Good Heart needed to get back to the apartment, because she had set up a playdate between Sammie and Sofia.

As we entered the lobby of the apartment building, Nifty-Fifty Wife was in the lounge area with her daughter and was clearly upset.

"What's wrong?" Good Heart said.

Nifty-Fifty Wife's English was not exactly perfect when she got excited. "There will be a mouse in my kitchen and the building no help until next week, when the exterminator return. No can be in that apartment alone."

Good Heart said, "You poor thing. Go get some traps at the grocery store, and Matías can take care of it when he gets home. Just come stay with me this afternoon."

"They need to be no there, before Matías get home. He think I keep dirty home, if there are many mice."

I reflexively chuckled at the situation, which made Nifty-Fifty Wife more uncomfortable. I regretted my laughter and tried to make her feel better. "In any city, rodents are everywhere. It's normal, particularly in an apartment building. Having mice doesn't mean you keep a dirty house."

"At home, Matías is of a very proud family. Please no let him know you know of mice. I ashame. Matías is a doctor—no mean to catch mice. I can no ask him to do this," Nifty-Fifty Wife said.

The thought of catching and killing a mouse did not seem like a good way to spend the rest of the day, but I wanted to help. Nor did I like the idea of her pig husband yelling at her over a stupid mouse. Nifty-Fifty Wife could not bring in an outside exterminator, since she had no access to money. Matías gave her just enough cash for groceries every week. Good Heart and I could not pay for one, since we were broke, and our spouses did not make very much either. "I'll be the great mouse hunter. Don't worry; it will be gone before Matías gets home," I said.

The smile of gratitude from Nifty-Fifty Wife made me feel good. It was the first time since arriving in New York that I felt part of the stay-at-home fraternity. Good Heart offered to take care of all the kids at her place, so that Nifty-Fifty Wife and I could go focus on the task at hand. I worried a little that Claire would start fighting over toys with Sammie if I weren't there to referee. It was embarrassing when Claire would take a bite of someone's arm. Her tell was a crazed eye roll before she bore her fangs. My hope was that she would outgrow it by college. As I left her, I gave Clair a half-stern, half-begging look which I think she understood to mean "be good."

Nifty-Fifty Wife and I asked around for mousetraps, and Lion Tamer gave us some that she had. Lion Tamer was always prepared. I bet if we needed a blowtorch, she would have had one of those as well in her pantry.

■ ■ ■

I know very little about trapping mice, other than what my friend Froggie had told me. Froggie was an undergrad buddy, who—last I had heard—was stomping around Africa playing with monkeys as part of a research study. He told me that all you need to know is that mice love peanut butter and that they don't like coming out into the open. They hang out in tiny crawl spaces. The reason that I know this is that Froggie, a devout animal-loving freak, once felt the need to rescue a mouse hidden in the walls of our dorm and release it into the wild, before the university exterminators killed it. Needless to say, I didn't get much studying done that night of my junior year in college, as we went from room to room, trying to get the mouse to crawl into a cardboard tube.

Unlike Froggie, I had no desire to take the mouse alive. I slathered the traps with chunky peanut butter and laid them around the galley kitchen, in all the tight spaces I could find. The traps were the spring-loaded wooden kind that are scary to set, since they frequently released and snapped your fingers without warning. I daintily placed them, using kitchen tongs. Nifty-Fifty Wife waited from the living room. She repeatedly thanked me in both Spanish and English.

We turned off a low-playing radio and pulled down the shades. I motioned for her to come to the couch and sit down. "Let's try to be super quiet. I want the mouse to think its nighttime and safe to come out."

She nodded, as if this was the wisest thing she had ever heard. Some women are very good at giving subliminal ego rubs to men. "Do you think it will come out?"

"I don't know. This ain't my day job." Or was it?

She laughed. "You are funny. Men in my country are very serious—very macho. They would not tell a woman that they are not the best in something."

"Being from San Francisco means I'm in touch with my insecure inner child."

"What child you insecuring with? I no understand."

"It means saying what you feel is not so bad."

Nifty-Fifty Wife smelled nice. Using perfume was uncommon among the other stay-at-home moms; I could not remember the last time that Liz had worn perfume. Nifty-Fifty Wife had dark eyes and a large nose, which would not have seemed as exotically attractive on anybody else. She was a naturally beautiful, full-figured woman—definitely out of my league, were I to be single. She always took care to be well dressed, with all her makeup in place, before she ventured into public.

Her husband had clearly married "up" in the looks department. He was not quite a gnome, but if it weren't for his family scratch and the fact that he was a doctor, he could not have done nearly as well. I had talked to Matías a few times, and he was not the life of the party/talk show–host type. He treated anyone that was not a doctor as if he or she were of a lower caste. In the food chain of doctors, he was not well placed, since he was relegated to being trapped all day in a dark room, looking at X-ray films as a neuroradiologist. I would later find out, after they had moved back to South America at the completion of Matías's program, that their marriage had been arranged. Finding this out made me sad, because I came to know Nifty-Fifty Wife well. I thought she could have done better.

While we waited for the mouse to set off one of the traps in the kitchen and hopefully break its neck, we talked about how we felt about moving to New York City. She missed her life back home, and despite having made friends like Good Heart and Supermom, she felt isolated in New York. She admitted that she was a little disappointed by Americans. Our pop culture made it seem as if we were all happy, but her experience revealed the opposite. She told me something bizarre that I paraphrased as, "American life is like a giant buffet. Its people take a lot of tastes for their plate, throw away a bunch, and, in the end, become fat and bloated. And they wind up regretting the meal."

I told her about some of my initial bad experiences being home full-time with the girls and how things were starting to get better. "But a lot of times, I feel like I'm missing out on things. And when I tell people, especially other men, what I'm doing instead of working, I see disappointment flash in their eyes before they say something like, 'Hey, that's a great thing you're doing for your kids.'"

Nifty-Fifty Wife seemed touched by my candor. "I get bored at home. I want that my papa had allowed me to go to college. Sometimes I wish I could follow people into all these office buildings around here and spend the day doing what they are doing."

"Maybe when Sofia is a little older, you can go to school and get a degree in something you like," I said.

"That is a pretty thought, but Matías have need for more kids. A big family be very wonderful too."

There was an awkward pause between us, until she asked if Liz was being supportive while I was looking for a new job.

I didn't know how to answer. "Yes. No. A little impatient, like we're in pause mode or something. We don't seem to be going anywhere. These medical programs here can really suck for the families. It's like a treadmill." I regretted being so honest. I was not sure if Nifty-Fifty Wife could totally keep my confidence.

She smiled. "It is hard when you don't have people to talk to. Being with someone in a big career is like always being in second place." Nifty-Fifty Wife fixed her eyes at me.

The conversation was getting a little too deep for me. I realized the oddity of my current situation. I was sitting in a dim room, alone with a very attractive woman from somewhere in South America, and we were both complaining about not being happy with our spouses. Warning bell. Thank heaven I was unattractively plump, or else I might have been in trouble. I wondered if she was hoping for a hug or a kiss right now. I shrugged off my thoughts as male drivel; we were just two people idly talking as friends, wasting time while waiting to trap a mouse.

Eventually, a crisp snap told me that one of the traps had gone off. We grimaced at each other as we heard a high-pitched squeal from the kitchen. "This is the ugly part," I said.

I went to the kitchen and found the wounded mouse behind the refrigerator. Its tail was pinned in the trap, and it was furiously moving its legs in the tight space. I pulled the refrigerator to the side, planning to push the mouse into a bag with a broom. Nifty-Fifty Wife was in the other room, moaning words in Spanish.

As soon as I moved the refrigerator and a wider pathway opened, the mouse shot forward, dragging the trap behind it. I gave chase into the nearby tiny master bedroom located just off the front door. It went under the bed, while I scrambled across it, making a mess of the sheets, pillows, and bedspread that had previously been arranged like a Martha Stewart catalog picture. The mouse eventually ran out of real estate, and I pinned it in the corner of the room with my broom. I pushed it into a plastic trash bag and knotted it closed. "I'm the big-man game hunter," I shouted.

Nifty-Fifty Wife was now in the bedroom, and she replied with equal enthusiasm. "You're the best, Nick! Muchas gracias."

A key pushed into the lock of the front door; someone was coming in. Matías had come home in the middle of the day. He spoke in Spanish to Nifty-Fifty Wife.

Quickly, I opened one of the bedroom windows only a few inches, given its child-safety-lock protection, and pushed the bag with the mouse out. Fourteen stories below was an alley. I will never tell anyone, including my friend Froggie, about my mouse safari that afternoon. It's not an animal-friendly tale, not something you want to share with dinner guests, as you sip cabernet sauvignon and eat goat cheese on water crackers.

"What are you doing home?" Nifty-Fifty Wife said from the bedroom. She spoke in English for my benefit and as a way, I guess, to warn him that she was not alone.

"Who's here? Who was shouting just now?" He walked into the bedroom. His English was much better than that of Nifty-Fifty Wife.

"It was Nick a shouting," Nifty-Fifty Wife said.

"Hey, Matías, how's it going?" I said.

"Nice to see you. What brings you over? Are Sofia and your girls here?" Matías was stocky, and his ill-fitting doctor's coat was buttoned over his full, round belly. If the roles were reversed, I would not have played it as cool as he was at that moment.

Nifty-Fifty Wife kissed him on the cheek. From the look on his face as he waited for my answer, I couldn't tell if he thought her kiss was a cover-up for guilty action, or if he was simply surprised because he normally didn't get that kind of reception upon coming home. Because of what Nifty-Fifty Wife said would be his reaction to the reality of a mouse hunt in his house, I was empty for an excuse, until I saw a desktop computer in the bedroom.

"She said the computer was freezing up on her, and she wanted me to take a look," I said. Matías and I really didn't know each other that well. I didn't know whether he remembered I was a software programmer.

"But it's not on now?" he said. This was indeed true.

"I have to restart it now that I fixed the reboot file of the operating system." I find that the more technical and detail-laden a lie, the better its reception.

He nodded. "You're very emotional about fixing a computer. I heard you shouting something about hunting."

"I'm just a computer geek." I reached over to turn on the computer.

"Thanks for your help," he said. He was one to always keep his manners.

"What do you need for lunch? Sofia is playing upstairs with Sammie. Nick go to gym, so you and I will have quiet. How much fun that you are home," Nifty-Fifty Wife said.

Matías and Nifty-Fifty Wife went to the kitchen. As they left the bedroom to supposedly let me finish fixing the computer, I heard him say something to her in Spanish in a harsh whisper. Later, Nifty-Fifty Wife told me he had been upset and said, "I thought I told you not to touch my computer."

One day, I hope she feeds him a grilled-mouse sandwich for lunch.

13

NATHAN'S HOT DOGS, CONEY ISLAND, AND SKINNY VEGETARIANS

A few days before Labor Day, Kelly sent me a text message.

I'm bored. Let's go to the beach with the kids.

I called her back and told her I had a playdate with Nifty-Fifty Wife to go to the Central Park Zoo. It would be rude to cancel on such short notice.

"So bring her and her daughter along. I can invite some of my girlfriends whom I haven't seen in a while. We'll have a beach party. And you can show off your new workout body," Kelly said.

"Appreciate the moral support, but I'm still about forty pounds shy from taking my shirt off at the beach."

When Nifty-Fifty Wife agreed to come to Coney Island, I was surprised. Normally she disliked spur-of-the-moment invitations. "How are we to get to Coney Island? Do your friend Kelly have a big car?"

"Not anymore, since her ex-husband sold her car out of spite. Kelly will show us how to get there by subway," I said.

"Does the subway go to the beach?"

At the last minute, I decided to call Good Heart and see if she wanted to come. "No way," she said, "too pregnant for the beach."

I offered to take her daughter as a courtesy, giving her a chance to rest for the day. Surprisingly, the ever-stoic Good Heart agreed to let me take Sammie. In addition, she accepted my secondary offer of letting her spend the day in my apartment, where the air conditioning was a little better than the one in her sweatbox apartment.

The beach expedition gathered near the entrance to the subway at the Hunter College station on Lexington Avenue. There were thirteen of us: me, the twins and Sammie, Kelly and her two girls (Tasha and Zoe), Nifty-Fifty Wife and Sofia, and Kelly's two girlfriends and their daughters, who were two or three years older than the rest of the kids. With the exception of Kelly's friends, who wore tiny sling bags, the rest of us were laden with heavy bags and strollers. Kelly's friends did not speak to me at the subway stop, or all day for that matter, and only spoke minimally to Nifty-Fifty Wife. Later, Kelly told me that they were pissed about having to slum it at Coney Island and had only gone because they felt sorry for her current social and financial predicament. I didn't bother to learn their names, and they never took off their sunglasses, even in the subway.

Maude and Claire were excited about a day at the beach. With sand toys in hand, they led the kids in a tiny parade down the steps toward the dank smell of the subway below. Our expedition wore tee shirts and cover-ups over swimwear, which made for a sharp contrast with suited business commuters and the students of Hunter College. I called forward to the twins to slow down, as I helped Nifty-Fifty Wife collapse and carry her stroller through the turnstile leading to the tracks. She seemed overwhelmed by the noise of the trains and press of the crowd.

"Sofia and I should go back. I am too slow, and you working too hard," Nifty-Fifty Wife said.

"Don't be silly," I said. "We look out for each other."

Nifty-Fifty Wife smiled.

Kelly was the natural leader of the group. Her enthusiasm for the trip buoyed everyone's spirits, including her "too cool for school" friends. She navigated our route among subway lines and transfer points with relative ease to Coney Island in Brooklyn. "Not bad for a girl from South Dakota," she said.

I hadn't seen Kelly for a couple of days, so I went and sat next to her during the longest leg of the subway ride, in order to catch up. Her really skinny friends seemed content to ignore us, while Nifty-Fifty Wife spent most of the trip being occupied with Sofia's demands for food, water, and constant entertainment. Claire, Maude, and Sammie managed to entertain themselves by trying to mock-surf in the aisle of the subway car. Occasionally, they would knock into the other riders, who were becoming annoyed with their antics, but at least the kids were not bothering me.

"I'm humiliated that my friends are seeing me like this. I should be going to the Hamptons, instead of going to a loser beach like Coney Island."

She noticed my hurt look and touched my knee. "Don't take offense. This is fun too," Kelly said. "But it's hard having to admit a loss of social standing when your husband leaves you. Our place in the Hamptons was quite nice. I just have to adjust to the new norm, that's all."

I felt bad for her. "How are you going to pay your bills? Is Kirk going to do some sort of alimony?"

"We'll be okay. Not good or great. I won't ever have to use coupons for groceries. My monthly child support should cover the basics, plus a little extra, because Kirk does love the children, and he would never want them to suffer. The apartment will be mine in full."

"Are you going to get custody?"

"If Kirk could, he would take them from me. But let's say we are at détente regarding many things."

"I'm sorry you're going through this. You deserve better," I said.

"You're sweet, Nick. But let's talk about something else. How did that interview of yours go? You were really excited about it the last time I talked to you."

"Great, except the comic book start-up has no money. My friend Morris is having trouble. He feels terrible, but he's barely making it himself. If he gets money, then he can pay me. But that's probably not going to happen any time soon."

"What job were you going for?" Kelly said.

"I would've worked on what they call the back-engine software, which is something like designing a warehouse and showroom for a retail store.

It's a website for people who want to buy and sell comic books. Trade rare stuff, buy collectibles, and read comic book news."

"I have no idea what you're talking about, but I'm sorry you didn't get it," Kelly said.

"I'm less upset about not having a job now. I'm starting to like being home with the girls, even though it still feels weird. It's not something that feels natural, but I'm starting to think I'd miss it," I said.

"Liz must be happy that the girls are in good hands while she is putting in long hours."

"I guess. We don't really talk much anymore. With so little time together, it's mostly us exchanging information about the kids—transactional talk. Things between us have been a little tricky since we moved here. It's taken a while for us to figure out who does what anymore. Basically, Liz works, and I pick up the slack everywhere else. Whatever free time she has goes to the kids."

"Sounds a little lonely," Kelly said.

"It can be, but sometimes it's not. But that is part of the slog of being married to someone going through medical training."

"I think Kirk's long hours had a lot to do with why we split. Corporate law is cancer on relationships. I was not getting the emotional support that I needed, and I took out that anger on him when we were together."

I wondered whether Kelly's use of the word "corporate" was a euphemism for what I suspected was Kirk's real job: lawyer for the mob. I had no real evidence, and Kelly never gave any more details about how he made his buckets of money, nor how Licorice managed to keep his current address despite his proclivity to being high-strung and loud. What guy in his right mind would neglect Kelly? I wanted to meet this wise guy.

I said, "When we got married, one of Liz's aunts, who is also married to a doctor, said that a large percentage of couples don't make it through medical training. It puts too much stress on things."

"That aunt seems like a real toad."

"Her warts have warts."

Kelly laughed. I liked seeing her smile. Her easy sense of humor reminded me a lot of how Liz used to be, when we were in college. In some ways, I regretted Liz's choice to attend medical school. Each year of training seemed to make her more serious, less carefree.

From the Coney Island station platform, I saw the giant Ferris wheel and roller coaster that I had always seen in photographs and movies. I was a little disappointed with the reality of Coney Island, much like I was with most tourist attractions that I had known from the media. Four things composed my first impression of Coney Island: the sticky heat, the smell of fried things, the grime and graffiti, and the fact that most people, including myself, look horrible in a swimsuit. We were definitely not at the Hamptons.

Along the boardwalk, we pushed through crowds of people. I was amazed at how many people were there on a Wednesday morning. One could only imagine what it was like on the weekends. If I wanted a picture of a mermaid tattooed on my arm, this was the place to do it. If I wanted to eat cooked meats that I could not identify by either sight or smell, I had the opportunity to indulge myself either from a food truck or a restaurant stand. If Claire or Maude wanted to buy useless trinkets or play with broken glass on the beach, their daddy could make their dream come true. This was my first and hopefully last time at Coney Island.

After about five minutes, I thought about cutting my losses and leaving. I sensed that everyone in our expedition felt the same way. But I didn't want to disappoint Kelly, and I enjoyed watching Kelly's skinny friends try to keep stone faced as the flower of Brooklyn chivalry whistled and catcalled after them. On either side of us, the contents of tiny stores spilled onto the sidewalk, in thrown-together retail displays that sought to hawk junk. Saltwater taffies, anyone? Carnival-game barkers shouted to the kids to throw balls, squirt water, and toss rings for a chance to win toys and stuffed animals, which I would have to schlep home on the subway, to one day find forgotten, in a wet cardboard box, in the back of a future garage, a dozen years from now. One place, which almost tempted me to play, was a place where, for ten dollars, I could shoot paint balls at a live person as he ran for cover from crate to crate in a pit below street level. Try to find that in Sag Harbor.

Claire spotted a homeless person begging from an alleyway. He was lying on a box. "Daddy, give him money. He hungry."

"We don't have enough money to give to everybody, honey, just because they ask," I said.

"Why not?" Claire said.

"If I give him money, then he might buy something that is not food and is not good for him," I said.

"Like what?" Claire said.

"Never mind," I said. "He needs special help like a doctor or social worker to help him. We are not professionals."

"Mommy a doctor. Can she help?" Claire said.

"Mommy is not here. But that man needs more help than we can give him. The government should help him," I said.

"Who's Gobber Man?" Claire said.

Nifty-Fifty Wife jumped in. "No money for him. He needs to get a job. He is a very, very lazy man."

"That's not always true. A lot of these guys are out-of-luck veterans, or have mental problems," I said.

Nifty-Fifty Wife rolled her eyes.

"No money, Daddy. He lazy. Let's go to beach," Claire said.

Was this what they call a teachable moment? I didn't like that Nifty-Fifty Wife was programming my kid to be so callous to the misery of others. The problem of homelessness was not an easy thing to describe to a three-year-old. In fact, it is not an easy thing to describe to anybody.

I fished out a couple of dollars from the pocket of my cover-up. Maude had been listening to us. "Claire and Maude, we can't do this all the time, but I want you to know that helping people is very, very important."

I tossed the money into the homeless guy's collection box.

"I think he will follow us and want for more money," Nifty-Fifty Wife said.

I stormed the beach with the stroller, when the twins got tired of walking from the train station. The sand on the beach was lumpy and dirty, a far cry from what I was used to in California. It was difficult pushing against the sand with tiny plastic wheels. Eventually, we found a spot in a less crowded area near the waterline, with a view of the gray water, a nearby brick housing project, and the giant wooden rollercoaster that was the hallmark of Coney Island. A website said that some considered it to be the best wooden roller coaster in the world. It looked pretty junky to me. I didn't particularly like roller coasters anyway, because they made me motion sick.

We set down our stuff and spread out our blankets. Before I forgot, I drenched the kids with sun block. Being married to a doctor, especially one with friends who were oncologists, made me extra paranoid about the risk of skin cancer. If I brought the kids back with even one red spot on their pretty pink-and-white skin, I feared Liz would throw me out of the house for good.

All the kids made a break for the water, while I went off to rent beach umbrellas. The sun was pushing out an angry heat. The adults were happy to stay put. For the rest of the day, I became the de facto worker bee. None of my companions seemed able or willing to run back and forth to the boardwalk for food, drink, or whatever we needed. It was Nick's day to be valet. In life, some people have the uncanny ability to get others to do things for them. Tom Sawyer had had that ability. I wondered how I could learn it.

Nifty-Fifty Wife and Kelly were suitably appreciative when I brought back an umbrella for them. The skinny nameless friends just tilted their heads upward at the umbrella as I worked hard to push it into the sand and gave me what I think were grimaces of thanks. Kelly pushed money at me for the umbrella rentals. I refused.

"What is this?" she said. "You're not taking us all out on a date. You're a stud, but not that big a stud." Without further insistence, I took the money—things were tight. I couldn't afford to be a big-time spender anymore.

The twins seemed to be having fun dumping sand with Sofia, Sammie, Tasha, and Zoe and making what seemed to be sand mud pies, instead of castles. The girls of the skinny friends of Kelly kept their own company. They were working on their tans and did not engage on any level with the little kids.

As for the adults, we took advantage of the temporary calm and either read a cheesy paperback or napped. From time to time, I caught the curious looks of other guys on the beach, wondering how I had managed to get a harem of pretty woman. I played cool, wanting them to think I was some Wall Street investment banker or something. I was desperate for any sort of ego rub.

I started to doze after a while, but, eventually, my cell phone belted out its "Livin' La Vida Loca" ring tone, denoting that it was Wolfie on the line. "Hey, big guy, where are you? I stopped by your apartment, and you weren't there."

"I'm at the beach, watching the medical waste float by."

"Is Liz off today?"

"No. I'm with my friend Kelly and some of her friends, along with someone from the building, and we brought a pack of kids."

"Guess who is the Sultan of Swing with his gaggle of babes? What's the deal with all this time spent with this Kelly chick lately? Should Liz be getting worried?" Wolfie said.

Kelly and the rest of the group could easily hear me speaking on the phone. "You're quite the funnyman, today. Why did you stop by?"

"I dropped off some meals for you and your lovely family. I made some turkey meatloaf that Liz loves. Just whip up some mashed potatoes and peas, and you'll be in comfort-food heaven."

"Thanks, dude. I made that shrimp-and-pasta dish you showed me, and Liz and the girls loved it," I said.

"I will make you a housewife yet, my friend. The way to Liz's heart is through her stomach. I gotta go. Don't forget to rub some more sun block on that fat belly of yours. Later," Wolfie said.

Kelly was listening. "You're quite the renaissance man, with your gourmet cooking. Liz is very lucky."

"That was my friend Wolfie. He's teaching me how to cook things more appealing than beans and hot dogs. Wolfie is both the owner and chef of L'Usine de Nourriture. In French, it means 'the food factory.'"

"I've been there with Kirk a few times. It was more his place than mine," Kelly said. "I didn't like that you sit around and watch the cooks actually cook. I prefer a table away from the smell of the kitchen."

Thanks for the unsolicited food review, Kelly. Wolfie's place rocks. Aloud, though, I said something different: "Speaking of food, who's hungry? I'm getting a Nathan's hot dog, onion rings, and a root beer. Today is not a day for diets. Let me take some orders."

"One hot dog—no cheese. Do they have nitrates inside them? And a Diet Coke," Nifty-Fifty Wife said.

"You're the best." Kelly paused. "Do you think that you can pick up a green salad with low-fat dressing on the side? If not, maybe a fruit salad? To drink, I just want water."

In an effort to be friendly, despite their obvious disdain for me, I asked the skinny friends for their order. "What can I get you?"

No answer, but they did turn their heads in my direction.

Kelly said, "My friends are vegetarians. So I think they'll have what I'm having."

"What if I can't find salad?" I said.

"Just do the best you can, and get whatever, so long as it's not deep fried, smothered in oil, grilled, or pickled. Thanks so much, Nick." Kelly handed me money for the group's food.

The lines at Nathan's Famous were long. The people working the counters were slow. From my vantage point, ten people deep in line, it amazed me how each transaction of ordering food and accepting money entailed a detailed discussion. It wasn't that the menu changed daily. The employees at the counter acted as if every order were bewildering to them. Periodically, a manager would come out with keys to override the register, whenever someone had particularly bungled a transaction. The Nathan's Famous manager had a mustache, which added further evidence to my secret theory that all male fast-food managers were required to grow out their facial hair. I hated waiting in line for fast food. It added more insult to the whole process of having to eat fast food when it wasn't even fast.

Finding junk food was easy. Finding salad or fresh fruit in a timely manner was difficult. Nobody on the boardwalk within a reasonable walking distance had healthy food, and, even if they offered it, it was sold out in the lunch-hour crush. I returned defeated, bringing only a few slices of different kinds of pizza.

Kelly was a good sport about it. "Thanks for working hard. My friends and I can split the cheeseless pizza." Until then, I had not known that cheeseless pizza existed.

"But I only got one slice of cheeseless pizza. How is that going to be enough?"

"That's more than enough." Kelly cut up the pizza three ways. "That's all we eat for lunch anyway."

"That amount of food wouldn't last me hour," I said. "As it is, I'm having a hard time on my current diet. This is my big cheat meal for the week, since Dom isn't here."

"Thank God, Dom isn't here." Kelly slipped one of my onion rings into her mouth. One of her skinny friends shot her a look. "Okay, I'm done with the onion rings now."

Once lunch was over, I buried the twins in the sand. Maude and Claire giggled at each other as they sat face-to-face, buried up to their necks in the sand. Sofia, Sammie, Zoe, and Tasha and the other girls, whose names I still don't know to this day, wanted to be buried as well. As soon as I started to dig holes for all of them, the skinny moms seemed as if they were going to actually speak and tell me not to do it, but then settled back into their magazines. Apparently, they realized they did not want to interact with their kids and do the digging themselves. I was both court jester and babysitter at our little beach party. Not even Nifty-Fifty Wife paused in her relaxation to help.

I spent the next hour burying the kids, not once, not twice, but five times each. A break was needed. "Who wants ice cream?"

All the kids shouted.

Through their liaison, Kelly, the skinny moms declined ice cream for both themselves and their kids. Their daughters protested but were silenced by the quiet shake of their mother's heads.

"How about you, Kelly?"

"I shouldn't, since it looks like I'm going back into the singles market again." She pushed on her workout-flat stomach. "Zoe loves ice cream. Tasha does not. Just make sure that its vanilla, not some flavor that can stain anything."

I took Maude, Claire, Sammie, Sofia, and Zoe to get ice cream. We ate our cones on the boardwalk, so as not to upset the daughters of the uptight, skinny vegetarian women. Sammie's scoop of strawberry slid from the cone and fell to the boardwalk in the middle of eating it. She cried, "I lost my ice cream. No more ice cream for me."

Claire said, "No worry, Sammie. My daddy will get you another one."

"I can't get another cone if I drop it. My daddy says so."

"In our family, our ice cream has an insurance policy," I said.

"What's 'in sure rant'?" Sammie said.

"Insurance is a promise that a cute kid gets another scoop if it falls," I said.

"I like 'in sure rant,'" Sammie said.

When we returned to our spot on the beach, a trio of men in their forties was in the process of constructing a large sand sculpture on the beach next to us. It would eventually become a big-breasted mermaid, lying coyly on the beach. The men, through Nifty-Fifty Wife, were trying to make flirtatious conversation with the group, since no one but she spoke Spanish. Their company was not wanted, nor their offer of free beer, except by Kelly, who accepted two light beers with a sweet giggle. The biggest of the muscled and obese trio of sand artists laughed as I approached with the returning kids. He pointed me out to his friends and spoke. All three laughed. He had a metal front tooth and a tattoo of a penguin on his arm. I felt like I was in middle school again. Fortunately, I wasn't a ninety-eight-pound weakling anymore. I was a two-hundred-and-twenty-pound weakling.

Nifty-Fifty Wife translated. "They think it funny that we women sit around and you take care of kids. They say you should wear a sundress rather than be wearing swimming trunks."

The skinny friends laughed—the first sign of emotion all day.

"Who wants beer-belly men with no jobs? Who wants somebody who plays in the sand with his two guy friends?" Kelly said. "Tell them that Nick is a macho guy who is not afraid to show his soft side. Nick goes to the gym a lot and they should be mucho scared."

Thanks, Kelly. The light beer had apparently gone to Kelly's head. I sensed a beating coming on.

Nifty-Fifty Wife spoke in Spanish to the man with the penguin tattoo. He nodded and offered me a beer. "Lo siento." I'm sorry.

I showed off a little high school Spanish. "No problema aqui. Mi playa es su playa." No problem here. My beach is your beach.

Nifty-Fifty Wife said, "He wants to know if he and his friends can build a giant sand castle for the kids to play in."

"Daddy, is the man with the bad tooth a pirate?" Maude said.

An hour later, with the help of our new beach buddies, a large sand city had grown around us. It had streets and houses, rivers and bridges. In the center was an ornate castle high atop a sand pile. Several towers rose above its walls; each tower had elaborate runes etched in the sand. We named the city Camelot, and I took a digital picture so someday Maude and Claire would know of their first time at Coney Island with Daddy. Claire thought it was the most magical thing she had ever seen. She thought it would last forever on the beach. I did not have the heart to tell her otherwise.

Late afternoon came, and all the kids waved good-bye to the trio of sand artists, as they put the finishing touches on their R-rated mermaid sand sculpture. A pile of beer cans, signifying their length of time on the project, encircled their beach chairs. We marched back to the Coney Island subway station very tired, with the smell of ocean, sun, and sun block on our skin.

On the subway ride home, I thought about the strange encounter on the beach with the metal-toothed guy. I asked Nifty-Fifty Wife if she really had translated what Kelly had said.

"I told them that you were the son of a big-time and dangerous gangster, and that we were all your girlfriends, and that the kids were all yours."

Kelly snickered. She put her arm around me and pulled me close. She was mellow from the beach-bum beer. I could smell the faint trace of mango in her hair and feel the warmth of her skin from a day in the sun. "Nicky is no gangsta; he's just one of the girls."

Why did she call me Nicky? Nobody calls me Nicky.

14

SWEAT EQUITY

"Come here." Dom waved. I was about five minutes late for our workout session.

"Sorry—the kids were giving me a little bit of a hard time in coming to the gym. I had to give them candy." The line for candy at the magazine stand was made worse by the lunch-hour foot traffic on First Avenue near the Queensboro Bridge exit. At noon, the sidewalks swarmed with office bees.

"Forget that. Come in here." He pointed to the men's room.

"I'm good; I just went. My bladder is empty, so we can have as tough a workout as you want."

"I wanna see what you got."

Dom was into some real strange training techniques. Was Dom going to kick my ass for something? I really didn't want to be trapped with him in a tiled room. If I didn't go, Dom could easily pick me up and throw me into the men's room. Would anybody at the gym come to my aide if I screamed?

I walked in. Running away seemed childish. "So did you have a good weekend, Dom? Maybe see your son?" Dom was divorced.

"Take off your shirt."

Things were getting weird. I paused.

"I want to see if you're getting any results. Let's see those new muscles of yours," Dom said.

I pulled off my shirt. "I think I'm showing a little progress."

"Make a muscle, tough guy." I did. "You look a tad better, my friend. Just have to shrink that fat belly of yours. What did you eat for breakfast?"

"Ten egg whites." I pulled my shirt back on.

"What are you going to do for lunch, Pizza Boy?"

"Pizza—as much as I can stuff into my face."

Dom laughed. "You're funny. At first, I thought you were a smacked ass, but you have heart. But do you have the eye of the tiger?"

What was he talking about? "I'll keep my eye on the ball and my pedal to the metal. No pain. No gain." I could talk tough as well.

"Whatever. Enough talk. Let's lift."

We left the men's room. "Just a little feedback for the future: I wouldn't ask another client to take off his shirt to flex his muscles for you in the men's room. It's about a seven or eight on the creepy meter."

No response.

■ ■ ■

Dom seemed to be in a really good mood during my session. The workout seemed easier, which meant that he was taking pity on me or that I was actually getting into shape. He was more chatty than usual. "Since you know a lot about computers, let me ask you about somethin'."

"I'm not really good at fixing hardware. I'm a web designer."

"No, not about fixin'—I don't even own a computer. One of my other clients is starting a web company, and I was thinking about putting some money in."

I was struggling a little during my bench-press exercise on the weight machines; it was not the best time to talk. "Investing is a big money game—gotta be careful."

"I'm expecting a big annual bonus this month. I'm the top trainer in New York, with the most billable hours and revenue for the Workout Pit chain. I live here, practically."

I started to wonder if maybe there was a job with this start-up for me. "What kind of company is it?"

"They want to start a web channel for health and fitness—show video clips of workouts. Write about nutrition info and shit. This client said it would be like an online gym. Maybe sell sports vitamins and shakes. Stuff like that."

"Are they going to charge money or make it ad based?"

"Membership only—twenty bucks a month," Dom said.

I hated to burst his bubble. "Sounds a little risky—you can get a lot of that workout and other info from TV for free. There are already tons of videos and books on the subject. Remember the old Jane Fonda workout? What kind of person joins an online gym? What exactly is an online gym?"

Dom seemed to not like my input. "All the info would be in one place. Top shelf. Premium. The best. My client said that he would make me like a video character, and I would show people how to do their workouts."

I imagined Dom's big square head in cartoon form on the computer screen. "I'm not exactly an expert or anything, but I can't see people spending twenty bucks a month for something they can get for free. Besides, your great skills are better experienced in person."

Dom smiled at the last part of my statement. "I think I'm going to do it anyway. I've got a hunch it will be big."

I was going to argue that many smart investors had lost billions in the dot-com bubble from betting on a hunch, but it seemed pointless. Dom had the money fever. People with the fever think they are on the verge of being a Rockefeller. I've been there. Now I am jobless. "If you and your friend need someone to do some web designs, give me a call."

"This client of mine is really smart. He told me he would give me something funny called 'sweat equity,' if I put in free time taping the videos. Maybe you could do that with your programming stuff."

"Sweat doesn't pay for groceries. The only sweat I'm willing to get is the kind from this workout," I said. "If he wants to pay standard rate, I'm in."

"I'll pass it along," Dom said. "We're done here. Let's do squats."

"I made poopy already this morning," I said.

"With the free weights, funnyman," Dom said.

I liked to rattle Dom's cage a little. It was like teasing the football players back in high school. How far can you go before they punch you?

■ ■ ■

We went down the stairs and back to the free-weight area. It was late morning, so a lot of the usual early workout muscle heads were gone. The only person of interest was a woman of my height, in a tight spandex bodysuit, who was totally ripped. She was doing squats with a ton of weights. Her face and arms were slick with sweat, and her long blond hair was knotted in dreads. The word "more" was printed in big red letters across her breasts. I had seen her regularly around the gym but had never spoken to her. She was a member of the exotic cool-people tribe that dwells in Manhattan; they never seemed to hold regular jobs.

"Marilyn, you need a spotter if you're going to push up that much weight," Dom said.

"My partner is a no-show today. You be my spotter," Marilyn said.

He turned to me. "Do you mind? She's also a client. You guys can switch off lifts."

"No problem." Yes, I did mind, but I didn't want to seem like an uncool guy to Dom. I was concerned that I wouldn't get Dom's full attention during my session. He was easily distracted by pretty women. I did not want to become a third wheel during my own workout time.

Since this was my first time doing squats, Dom demonstrated. "You take the bar and put it behind your neck, on your shoulders. Keeping your abs and core tight, bend your knees and slowly go down to a squat position, and then explode up to a standing position. Remember to breathe out, coming back up."

I did it a few times with low weights, to get the form right. Not too bad. Marilyn alternated lifts between my sets. Dom was more enthusiastic with his praise to her, since she was doing much more weight than I was. When Marilyn was out of earshot on a water break, he said, "When she comes back, show her what you're made of. I think you can squat as much as she does."

"Are you kidding?" I said. "She's a brute, and I'm okay with her doing more weight than me."

Dom put his hands on my shoulders and did a soft squeeze. "You can do this. It's time to break to the next level. You're ready, my friend."

"No, I'm not. I'm a chickenshit at heart," I said.

Marilyn came back.

"I'm going to be with you the whole time. If something happens, I'm here. Just trust me." Dom slammed an extra fifty pounds on the bar.

Dom lifted the bar onto my shoulders. It was heavy, but I could take it, he said. He shadowed me from behind in almost a spoon position. "I'm with you, no matter what."

I inhaled and bent my knees. The weight pushed me down easily to a squat. My muscles offered very little resistance. Getting up was a problem. I pushed up. Nothing happened. Dom helped me with a little yank up on the bar. I started to rise, exhaling.

"Is that the same weight I just did?" Marilyn said.

Dom turned his head away from me. "I wanted to prove to him that he could beat a girl."

Marilyn hooted and playfully slapped Dom. "This means war. Slam on the iron."

Dom got distracted, and he let me take the full weight for a split second, midlift. I felt something twist in my lower back. Not good. "Help." It was somewhere between a whisper and a yelp.

Dom responded immediately. He took the weight off of me effortlessly. "What happened, buddy? Lose your concentration?"

"Not exactly. That was a little too heavy." I rubbed my back. A stab of pain accented my every move. It must have shown on my face.

"We're done today. Just go home and take it easy. Put some ice on it or somethin'."

"Sorry, dude," Marilyn said. "Dom can be rough sometimes." She playfully hugged him.

"Hope you feel better, pal," Dom said. He walked me down to the playroom.

I was initially pretty angry, and I wanted to vent at him, but I thought better of it. I was still stuck with twenty more sessions with him. Accidents are bound to happen. Dom hadn't intentionally tried to hurt me. Getting the kids home, pushing their stroller down First Avenue, proved a painful trial. Midway home, the girls elected to walk, since they knew I was in pain. Maude rubbed my back (as well as a three-year-old can) that night. I was out of commission. It would take about two weeks to get back to the gym. One consolation was that I had more time to watch TV.

15

EMPEROR OF ICE CREAM

"Let's play hooky," Kelly whispered in my ear.

"What?" I said.

Kelly and I were both dropping our kids off at the Workout Pit's playroom before exercising. Wanda, the kid wrangler, greeted our kids with tickles and hugs, as she peppered them with pet names in Spanish.

"Let's slip out the back door."

Anything was better than exercising. After the time off due to my injury, I was reluctant to climb back on the sweaty workout horse. "What do you want to do?" I said.

"Get ice cream, of course." She winked as she pulled at a short towel around her neck.

The Workout Pit had a back service elevator that no one knew about except for the parents who used strollers. It was a much easier way to bring kids than the main entrance, which was at the bottom of a spiral staircase, two floors beneath street level. It was rumored that a few parents used the gym childcare as a babysitting service more often than they actually worked out. I felt a little guilty abusing both the free service and Wanda. However, it was hard to deny Kelly. She was currently the only woman in my life who was not harboring some level of annoyance with me.

We emerged from the elevator into the sunlit rear lobby of the office building above the gym. It was lunchtime. Our workout clothes marked us as out of place among suited lawyers scurrying back and forth from the lair of their offices above. I have never worn a suit to work and never will. My only suit, worn to weddings and funerals, barely fit, even after several rounds of alterations. Liz was on me to get a new suit for a wedding we had coming up.

One of the suits waved at Kelly from across the lobby, as he swept past the security guard by the elevators. "You always know somebody," I said.

"He's another corporate lawyer that works with my ex-husband upstairs," she said. "He'll probably go and tell him that I'm running around with somebody."

I didn't think mob lawyers worked in posh office buildings.

I waved at myself. "Nobody's going to believe that you are up to any hijinks with me."

Kelly snapped her towel at by butt. "Maybe I'm a chubby lover."

I rubbed my butt.

■ ■ ■

Getting a table at Serendipity 3 proved easier than I had thought. It was a famous haunt for sugar addicts and ice-cream junkies. Andy Warhol had been a devotee, even settling his bills with scribbled drawings when he had been a vagabond artist. Kelly squeezed her way through the narrow entrance hallway filled with people waiting for tables. After a few giggles and hugs to someone who appeared to be the manager, we were seated right away. Beautiful people really do have a better life.

"This dessert is going to kill us," I said. We split a platter of ice cream drizzled in hot chocolate sauce. "Between our not working out and this creation, we are down about two thousand calories for the day." Thanks to Dom, I was becoming more aware of what I put in my mouth. He told me that I should consider my body a temple. I know better—I'm lucky if my body could be considered as a drive-through church on the Sunset Strip.

"Live a little," Kelly said.

"A couple weeks ago, you and the vegan twins were fighting over one piece of cheeseless pizza," I said.

"I got into a fight with a guy last night, and I just want to have a little fun today."

Oddly, I felt a little jealous that she was hanging around with another guy. "Are you seeing somebody?"

"Not my usual type."

"What is your type?"

"I thought I told you I was a chubby lover." She giggled.

"What did you fight about?"

"We've only just met, and he's a little too controlling and possessive already. He's not a very good listener."

"Have you told him to back off a little—told him that so soon after the divorce you need to reclaim your life again on your own terms?"

She smiled. "You're better than my girlfriends at this. Have you been watching soap operas?"

"When the girls are napping, I have a show I watch."

"I wish my Kirk had watched your show."

"Wouldn't that have been bad for business?"

Kelly narrowed her face and then smiled. "How would watching a TV show be bad for his business?"

I tried to dance around the topic of her former husband being a mouth-piece for the mob. "If he were more in touch with his feelings, then his clients would sense his weakness. And weakness is not good among good fellows."

She laughed again. "I'm not sure if the practice of mergers and acquisi-tions involves 'good fellows.' From what I've seen, it involves arrogant, old white guys who could give a rat's ass whether their lawyers have feelings."

"If you don't want to talk about that part of his life, I understand. Next topic."

After dipping her hand into her glass, Kelly flicked water at me. "Are you having a brain freeze? What are you talking about?"

I lowered my voice. "Aren't you like Michelle Pfeiffer in that movie?" I forgot the name of it.

Kelly seemed amused. "The one where she's a hawk by day and a princess by night?"

"Not *Ladyhawke*. The one where the main bad guy wants her for himself. I can't think of his name." I hate when my mind goes blank on movie titles, and actor names. It makes me seem like an idiot.

"Which Jack Nicholson movie, the one where he chases her as the devil or as a werewolf?"

The Witches of Eastwick was a great movie; the movie *Wolf*, I could've lived without. I shook my head no, still struggling for the name.

Kelly interrupted. "You're talking about *The Fabulous Baker Boys*. I loved when Michelle Pfeiffer slinked across that piano in her matching red cocktail dress and heels, fluffing her hair and singing 'Makin' Whoopee.'" Kelly pretended to sing into her spoon as if it were a mike.

"There's no bad guy chasing her in that. It's the mob movie with Matthew Modine as the FBI agent who falls in love with her." Then it came to me: "*Married to the Mob*."

"I didn't see that one," Kelly said. "But are you saying that I'm as pretty as Michelle Pfeiffer?"

"Nice try fishin' for a compliment," I said. "Kirk is a mob lawyer, and you were married to him. That's all I'm trying to say."

"That deserves a double water flick." She again splashed water at me. "Why on earth would you think that? Kirk is a real wanker, but he's too chickenshit to be involved with that crowd."

I stammered. "You said that he was a nasty guy who twisted arms around the building to keep that giant horse dog in the building. And he makes demands that people can't refuse."

She leaned across the table and wrapped her arms around me in a quick hug. "Only you could jump to such a wild conclusion. That explains all your references to Tony Soprano. 'What would Tony do about this and that?' Were you trying to get me to admit that I was a mob wife?"

I started to say no, but then I decided to join her in laughter. I'm prone to gullibility.

It was easy to talk with Kelly. We talked about everything from the silly to the serious. I got more out of my conversations with her than I often did with the sophomoric Wolfie. Liz and I certainly didn't emotionally share with each other anymore. We spoke about who was where and what needed to be done—strictly business.

"As always, I'm in and out of the doghouse with Liz." It was my turn to share.

"Hopefully, you're staying away from scissors."

A crestfallen look from me got a sympathy smile from her. "It's hard to take a back seat and do the boring stuff, while she is out in the world doing something important."

"Your girls would be lost without you." She gave me a polite reply regarding the pathetic nature of my manliness.

"At some point, Liz is going to give me walking papers. She's always perpetually pissed about something." I paused, realizing that Kelly was still raw about her marriage breaking up. "I shouldn't make light about getting a divorce."

"Everybody has problems." She stroked my arm. "I'm sure things will get better. Besides, your disharmony will give us more reasons to slip out and get ice cream."

I instantly liked that thought—of having more time with Kelly—but then a stern voice entered my head and warned me to calm down. I didn't know why. Maybe because the hot new best friend felt more needy than real. Girls and guys can be friends. Repeat it over and over.

"Her new thing is that I don't anticipate her needs more."

"Liz wants you to pick up the slack for her. She feels guilty that she can't do it all anymore."

I knew Kelly was right, and it did help me understand Liz. But part of me was disappointed that Kelly was not taking my side.

It was time for a redirect. "So what are you going to do about the new barbarian in your life?" I said.

"Eventually"—she giggled—"we'll have fun making up." The restorative properties of ice cream seemed to ebb her earlier funk.

"What were you fighting about anyway?"

"The usual: he wants to control what I wear, what I eat. He thinks after a few dates we should be exclusive."

"Does Romeo have a name?"

"Sure, he does." She smiled. "You sound like my big brother...or a jealous suitor?"

I blushed and averted my eyes.

No doubt sensing my discomfort, she offered me a bite of vanilla ice cream drizzled with hot chocolate sauce from her spoon. "Relax, Nicky—playing with you."

She pushed the spoon toward me and then had to offer me a napkin when the chocolate dripped from the corner of my mouth.

Kelly was a little too beautiful sometimes.

16

NO POOP IN THE POOL

"Sure, you can use it. Just you gotta clean it all up when you're done."

"You're the man, Clarence," I said. Clarence was the building super, the go-to guy to get anything done in the building. I chatted with him almost every day. I liked him.

"Don't let the president lady know that I let you do this." Supermom scared everybody.

"Why?" We were just setting up a kiddie pool outside in the common area.

"She's a mean one, with all her demands. You would think that I worked for her or something. She wanted me to set up the pool last year and do all the work of blowing it up and taking it down—everyday. I've got enough to do around here."

"I heard that. Why couldn't you just set it up once and be done with it?" I said.

"The management doesn't want an unattended drowning hazard. So it's got to be taken down when you're done."

"It's just a kiddie pool."

"If I made up the rules, we'd all be paid twice as much for doing half the work," Clarence said.

"Don't worry about our fearless leader. She's not coming back for a few more days. I'll do it all." The first day of morning preschool was not going to start until next week. The city was still pretty hot, and I needed an activity, so a splash pool fit the bill.

"I don't worry about her. I just avoid her like the plague."

He told me about all the kooky things that Supermom had asked him to do, including deep cleaning the playroom, which entailed scrubbing all the plastic toys with soap and water. No way, he had told her. The toys were the property of the family association, not a part of his job description. Supermom had gone to management, but she had been shut down. They only wanted him to keep the kitchen, bathroom, and carpet clean. Supermom and Clarence were currently engaged in a cold war. Supermom had refused to organize the cleaning effort herself.

"She has to put all her requests in writing and submit them to management for approval before I do a thing." He smiled. "Management don't like her either."

"I heard that," I said. As a way to thank him, the next time I was at the grocery store, I bought Clarence a six-pack of beer and a steak. He loved red meat.

"I gots to get me a smoke now. Apartment fourteen-twelve called the building manager and complained that I didn't help her with killing a mouse. Everybody is all up in my grill. Now they want me to go up and help her this week, but I'm no exterminator. Not my job. So I'll let both the manager and fourteen-twelve stew awhile, while I takes a smoke break. Nobody tells me what to do. I ain't no exterminator. Using them chemicals is bad, real bad. I gots to go. I'm agitated now," Clarence said.

Apartment 1412 was Nifty-Fifty Wife's apartment. I wasn't surprised that Nifty-Fifty Wife hadn't called me to help. My guess was that Matías forbade her from allowing me in the apartment again. I wished I had the guts to put a mouse into the desk in his research office. Nifty-Fifty Wife told me that he was afraid of mice.

"That's a friend of mine, and her husband is an asshole to her about mice."

"I thought she was a friend of the queen bee. I can't stand all of them doctor wives," Clarence said.

"She hasn't gone completely to the dark side. There is hope for that one."

Clarence was a huge Star Wars fan. We fist-bumped. "I'll see what I can do for them, since she is a friend of yours." He patted my stomach. "Soon, you're going to be slim and trim—I might just get to be calling you 'young Jedi, Luke Skywalker,' instead of 'Jabba the Hut.'"

"May the force be with you," I said. I actually prefer Star Trek to Star Wars, but saying "live long and prosper" didn't seem appropriate.

He went down the steps from the lobby and disappeared into the basement below, still complaining to himself about the mice situation. "I ain't no exterminator."

■ ■ ■

Maude and Claire were very excited as I set up the kiddie pool. It was in bad shape. I hosed both mud and leaves off of it and patched a few holes with a repair kit that Clarence had found in the storage room. Water play is a license for kids to be acceptably crazy and experimental. It was one of the best ways to entertain little kids for a long period of time. The pool had been stored in an outside storage locker, and I would not have discovered it, except for the fact that Maude's purple-glitter ball had rolled under the gate.

"Should we start a swim club for all the kids in the building?" I said.

Maude and Claire cheered.

My energy level was getting better, given the new training regimen I was doing. Even a month earlier, I would have vetoed the pool as an activity, citing "Daddy's a little too tired for that" as an excuse. I turned on the air pump, and while it inflated, we set up chairs around it. The twins dragged over a plastic kitchen set and made a snack bar. Later, we would get lemonade and crackers. Luckily, a beach umbrella and a stand were in the shed. Providing shade meant that I did not have to apply sun block on the kids as often. Finally, I added a sprinkler for more water fun.

"Every pool club needs members," I said. "Let's go up, get our swim stuff, and invite everybody."

A quick round of calls, and practically every little kid in the building came running down to the courtyard play area.

I even invited some of the killjoys.

"I think the little kids should have swim diapers in the pool," Good Heart said. "Somebody might pee in the pool and make everyone sick."

"Good idea. I'll make a sign that says 'No Poop in the Pool,'" I said.

"We waste water by leaving the sprinkler on. Is not New York having a water problem?" Nifty-Fifty Wife said.

"This is not public water, but rather, the toxic water from the East River that I'm pumping in, much cheaper."

Nifty-Fifty Wife smiled.

All the kids were having a good time. For long stretches of time, none of the kids cried, screamed, or broke things. It was a rare opportunity for the adults to sit around and relax a little. No one mentioned Supermom. Instead of having organized activities that either required full parental involvement or cost money, we were able to just enjoy the day. I imagined somewhere that Supermom was instructing Mitch Jr. and Hillary on the proper etiquette of how to milk a cow. Which udder do you pull first, and do you say please and thank you?

Halfway through the afternoon, Lion Tamer's eight-year-old twins arrived unescorted—their mother and three siblings, Aaron, Joshua, and Ariel, would arrive a few minutes later. David and Saul announced their entrance by practicing their Tarzan yells against the echo-enhancing brick walls of the towering building, which surrounded the courtyard. Then, their attention turned to water fun. In less time than it takes to change a diaper, they started an aggressive water fight that splashed all the little kids in the vicinity with buckets of water. Good Heart tried to stop them by shouting for them to stop being so rough around the little kids. Between spasms of laughter, the twins' response came only in Hebrew. Later, I would find out that the twins routinely faked not speaking English in order to avoid responsibility for bad behavior.

Nifty-Fifty Wife and some of the other moms looked to me to do something. I had never been really good with confrontation, nor had I spent much time in a leadership position. Instead of yelling, I decided to take the calm approach like the Shaolin priest from the seventies TV show *Kung Fu*. Some of the child psychology shows on the Discovery channel suggested that I needed to show respect by not shouting down commands to children. I needed to create an environment of mutual respect. I walked over to the twins, shook my head, and softly said no. I held out my hands for their buckets.

If you have ever watched a network TV sitcom, you could guess what happened next. They threw water in my face and laughed.

From the courtyard door, Lion Tamer shouted at them in Hebrew; within one sentence, David and Saul immediately stopped and returned the buckets back to the kiddie pool. "We are sorry for the little kids," David said to Good Heart in poor English. They retreated to the far side of the courtyard with Aaron and chased each other in circles.

Lion Tamer helped her little ones into the pool. "I'm very sorry for the big ones. They are like animals sometimes." Her English was strained, but functional, considering she had only been in the country from Israel one year. "They are good boys. But you know boys. They do crazy things."

"I remember. I used to smash the porch jack-o'-lanterns of our neighbors on Halloween. Not a real hit with my parents when they found out," I said.

Lion Tamer told me that her husband, Avid, had been very good with a slingshot as a boy. He had often broken crockery on the *kibbutz* he had grown up on in Israel. "Now, he is a much-respected doctor." She was an apologist for her children's behavior.

"Not a very communal thing to do on a hippie kibbutz," I said.

"You have lived on a kibbutz?" Lion Tamer said.

Wolfie and I had a friend who used to spend the summers between college living on a kibbutz. His dad was a new-age granola type and a rabbi in Northern California. Our friend was a crazy, loudmouth, beer drinker, but in the summer, he loved working on the kibbutz. He used to talk about farm life—and communism—in the middle of the dessert. He loved Israel and talked constantly about it. Not sure what had happened to him after school. He had probably become a corporate lawyer, freaking out his old man.

"No, but someone I know told me a lot about them."

"Kibbutz are not always a lot of fun. Avid says that he never wants to go camping ever; it is too much like a kibbutz," Lion Tamer said.

"That makes two of us," I said. "How can anything that requires sleeping on the ground and not taking a shower be good?"

She smiled. I didn't really know Lion Tamer very well. She was a peripheral person in the family association. While the other mothers were polite to her, nobody seemed to embrace her as a friend. It seemed that many were uncomfortable with her direct manner, while others just didn't want to deal with the language barrier. Sometimes it took too much effort to figure out what she was saying. Finally, Supermom had not designated her as a socially acceptable option for inclusion. Supermom did not like Lion Tamer and her messy, clutter-making kids. And Lion Tamer didn't really buy into the whole power trip Supermom was on. Supermom would complain to the other mothers that Lion Tamer did not adequately respect the playroom, by not cleaning up after her kids. Unfortunately, Supermom was right about the extent of mess that was created by Lion Tamer's kids, but I still hated rules that others created.

Prior to my joining the family association, Supermom had compiled and posted a set of rules for the playroom, on a laminated, rainbow-colored board:

1. A clean and orderly playroom makes for a safe and fun environment. Please return the room to its orderly condition, as you should find it upon arriving.
2. All liquids and foods should be eaten in the designated food area, marked by yellow tape on the floor.
3. No hitting, biting, scratching, spitting, licking, or screaming. First offense: verbal warning. Second offense: time-out. Third offense: ejection from the playroom. No exceptions.

4. Pull-ups and diapers should be changed in the bathroom only—not in the playroom. Pull-ups and diapers should be thrown away in the orange biohazard container only.

5. Only families affiliated with the Hospital Family Association may use the playroom. A guest pass must be obtained for any other visitors.

One can only imagine the rules Supermom would have created for swim club.

■ ■ ■

I had sympathy for anyone from a different country trying to live among us. I was having a hard enough time myself. I had studied Spanish in high school, but there was no way I could go to Spain and be functional in a restaurant: "Señor, me gusta pescador." Lion Tamer gave off the vibe that she was happy in her skin and didn't really give a rat's ass what other people thought. She seemed content, and I imagined that it pissed off a lot of people.

We made idle chitchat, talking about how beautiful Israel was and how Lion Tamer missed home—blah, blah, blah. I became curious and asked her, "Is America better or worse than you thought?"

"America is safe. I am not afraid for my children being bombed every day here," Lion Tamer said. "Danger is always there. Here, I worry about cars when my children cross the street. At home, we worry about car bombs. I worry when my children will have to go in the army, like all Israelis."

"Do you have to go back home?"

"Avid wants to return, because he believes that it is our responsibility to do so."

"What about you?" I said.

"I would like to stay. It is safe. My boys would not have to be in army. Avid would make more money here as a doctor than in Israel, and we could send our kids to good schools."

"If he knew you wanted to stay, would that change his mind?"

"He would do it, I no doubt, but it would break his heart to leave our home. He has many more family than I do. I could not ask him," Lion Tamer said.

While we had been talking, Lion Tamer's twins had detached the sprinkler, and they were squirting the hose over the courtyard wall, onto York Avenue below. Unseen pedestrians on the sidewalk were screaming profanities. The other kids in the courtyard were laughing.

"My boys just love water," Lion Tamer said. She called out to them: "Just squirt the hose inside."

"I think the little kids are getting scared," Good Heart said, as David and Saul starting drenching everyone in their path. Little kids were running between the plastic playhouses screaming, looking for cover.

Lion Tamer was a little slow in picking up on cues. She was distracted by Ariel, who wanted a sippy cup full of juice. I came to the rescue by turning off the hose at the source. Claire and Maude were crying inside the pretty pink-plastic princess house. "Let's try to keep this a splash-free zone, guys. If you want to water fight, do it over there." I pointed to the big-kid swing sets on the other side of the play yard.

David and Saul ignored me again and started drawing water from the kiddie pools with buckets. They continued to chase after the kids, throwing water everywhere. I was getting angry. I didn't want to yell at someone else's kids. Good Heart, Nifty-Fifty Wife, and the other mothers looked at me to do something again.

"I think the little kids are getting scared. Do you think that the twins should have a water fight somewhere farther away from the kiddie pool?" I said to Lion Tamer.

Lion Tamer calmly said a few stern sentences in Hebrew, which caused the boys, in military terms, to "stand down." David said to me, "We so sorry that our fun is not your fun." The twins left the swim-club area and played soccer on the other side of the play yard.

"Can you teach me whatever you said that worked? My kids always ignore me," I said.

"I say to them that I will leave their closet door open at night so the big, scary monster inside will get them for being very bad boys."

"I've never heard that one before—interesting tactic." I wouldn't be including that in my toolbox as a nurturing parent. If I even joked with Claire and Maude about there being a monster in their closet at night, they would be sleeping with Liz and me until college.

She seemed to notice my discomfort and smiled. "Do not be so serious. They know that there is really no monster, but they also know that I am no happy with them. Boys like to please their mother."

Go figure.

17

HUMAN BARBEQUE

A week after Labor Day, Supermom was back from her faux-ranch vacation. In short order, the fun factor that had started to develop in the family association dropped dramatically. With the exception of Lion Tamer, I seemed the least enthusiastic about her return. I didn't relish working at the playgroup again with Supermom or having to go on contrived excursions to the Museum of Natural History instead of playing in the park. But my kids really liked the other kids in the building, and the only way they could see them on a reliable basis was to do what everybody else was doing. And everybody else was doing what Supermom was doing.

I really didn't understand her allure to the other parents of the family association. To me, she did not seem genuine. Supermom seemed to constantly strive to be the perfect mom: patient, fun, tireless, happy in her devotion to her children. But artificially so, it seemed to me. No one—Supermom and her kids included—ever seemed to actually have fun in her presence. Or even relax, for that matter. It was as if her archetype was the singing mom in the laundry-detergent commercials.

I just didn't get her. I refused to accept her practice of raising children as if they were bonsai plants: careful at each step of growth and development, afraid to let the plant grow the way it wants. I wished that the family association were less structured and that she were not the president. Maybe Good Heart or Nifty-Fifty Wife could do a better job as president.

There was only one problem with that idea: Supermom. There was no way that she was going to step aside and let someone else run the show. If someone else did her job better, then her raison d'etre and self-image would collapse.

The return of the queen was celebrated during the post–Labor Day barbeque, held every year at the building. It was sponsored by the family association, which provided all the food and beer. In a rare show at group events, most of the doctor-spouses came as well. These spouses were a serious lot, not wanting to stand around in the heat of the afternoon with noisy kids. If they were any example, then doctors are not very outgoing people. They seemed to be a breed of animal that kept to its own. In order to achieve the level of success in medicine that they coveted, they had to be willing to spend many hours alone, studying and working, with little time for a social life or family time. It was a self-selected group. Perhaps impressive, but not particularly friendly or engaging.

During the barbeque, the doctors seemed content to let others do the work to set up and cook. They clustered around the chips and beer and talked about patient cases, research, and the politics within the hospital administration. Liz was the rare breed that spread her time between talking to the other doctors and playing with the girls.

I volunteered to cook the meat. It's fun to grill stuff. Flip burgers. Roast hot dogs. Grill chicken with thick sauces, taking care to crisscross the sear marks for a better presentation. Thanks to Wolfie, I was learning that there is a certain Zen satisfaction to cooking and serving good food. It provides immediate positive feedback. Hunger. Food. Cook. Serve. Happy Family. Unlike pushing paper for a living or selling some dopey mass-marketed product, creating and sharing a meal made me feel that I had accomplished something real.

Wolfie and his family came to the barbeque. We weren't supposed to invite people from outside the family association, but I invited him anyway. I didn't really care if it pissed off Supermom. Besides, I told her that he was a semifamous chef and that he would help me do the cooking. This seemed to appease her somewhat. Of course, Wolfie didn't help me cook. He cooked for a living, he told me, so why should he do it during his leisure time? But he did give me helpful hints that only chefs know, like pulling the meat when flare-ups occur, to avoid burnt edges. He just sucked on a beer and kept me entertained while I cooked.

"You know my friend Colby? He told me a funny true story the other day about a stay-at-home dad," Wolfie said.

"You keep forgetting that I met him before in the park. He's a smug asshole with twins," I said.

"Funny. He says the same thing about you."

I was not surprised.

"He told me this really sad story about one of his friends who is also a stay-at-home dad like you. This guy lost his job at a newspaper and can't get work anywhere. So he decides to write the great American novel while he is home with the kids. Doesn't matter to the story, but his name is Roger. He turns out to be more of a poser than an actual novelist. He starts to waste a lot of time with stupid stuff like listening to the shock jock Howard Stern on the radio."

"I know who he is, but I don't really listen to him," I said, lying. I do listen to him, but I, like a lot of people, will not admit to it in public, in order to avoid that look of moral disappointment that people give you when they learn you are a listener.

"Me neither." Wolfie winked. "Roger became hooked and listens every waking hour. He even listens to it while he's watching his kids, by wearing an earbud in one of his ears at a low volume. He said that it kept his mind active while being with the kids. Prevented mush brain. Roger became an audio junkie; he even listened to taped reruns of Stern. He listened as a way to fall asleep at night. He even listened to it when he was talking to his wife, who, like Liz, is a doctor. Now that takes balls, right? Your wife is trying to have a serious conversation with you while you're only half listening—real smart move. Eventually, his wife starts to get fed up with his laggard life style."

"So why would I care about any of this?"

"I'm getting there. So when the kids are old enough to be in school, Roger has a little more free time on his hands. So he tells his wife that he wants to get into shape and join a gym. He was a fat chunk like you. Thinks the exercise will improve his health, which in turn will get his juices flowing and help his writing. His wife agrees to buy an expensive gym membership, since he's gotten a little depressed being home with the kids all the time and is obsessive about listening to Howard Stern. She doesn't want him to be listening to Howard Stern, but she feels the need to throw him a bone, since he's willing to take care of the kids. She hopes that the exercise will help jump-start his whole outlook on life, and give him more energy to actively go out and get a job again."

"Am I supposed to be this guy or something?"

"Just listen. So the exercise thing goes bust, because he's basically very lazy and doesn't go to the gym. Now, here's the kick in the teeth. His wife finally gets tired of him, starts having an affair with another doctor, and kicks Roger out. He tries to get custody of the kids, but he fails, since he has no job and is basically painted as a neglectful dad, because of his obsession with Howard Stern. Roger starts feeling really sorry for himself and calls into the radio show, telling Howard that he lost his wife and kids because he is a superfan. Howard calls him a loser but offers him a position as a lowly intern. Now, Roger gets Stern's breakfast every morning, and he pays the bills by working as a cashier in a convenience store."

"That is really depressing," I said.

"Now, when you're feeling sorry for yourself, remember that things could get a lot worse and Liz could bail on you," Wolfie said. "So the moral is, don't get any weird hobbies and keep exercising."

"Very uplifting message." Were Roger and I similar? I started thinking about a lot of negative things. Was it possible that Liz could get bored of me? Would she really leave me? Am I that selfish a spouse? Compared to some of the better-looking single male doctors, I was a real hump—a useless house hubby.

"How are things going between you guys?"

"Not super romantic, but we're pushing through. I haven't slept on the couch for a while. I've tried to pick up the slack for her, so that all she has to do is the doctor thing. Her schedule is such a crusher. We have no time to just be us together as a couple," I said.

"Have you guys ever tried a sitter?"

"Not yet. Liz doesn't want to leave the kids with a stranger."

"How about Claire and Maude do a sleepover with my kids sometime? Emma could watch them and give you guys a chance to get out one night. And I will throw in a free dinner at my restaurant."

I liked the idea. "Are you serious?"

"Absolutely."

Eventually Liz broke away from talking to her doctor friends and came over to watch me grill. By then, Wolfie was eating with his family at a nearby table.

I was turning out major amounts of hot dogs, burgers, and grilled chicken. I was a cooking machine. The food seemed a hit.

"If I'd known that you were such a good fry cook, I would've married you sooner," Liz said. I'd forgotten the last time she had said something funny to me.

"We're all full of surprises."

"Well if this job with the comic book start-up doesn't work out, your newfound cooking skills could be a fallback." Liz smiled.

"Ouch. I get the humor, but still that hurt my feelings."

"You're too sensitive," Liz said. "Don't be such a wuss. Did you go in for a formal meeting?"

"Went in, but no dice."

"What happened?"

"I met with Morris again at his office. He can't find anybody to invest in his start-up company."

'Why didn't you tell me that you didn't get it?"

"You've been busy lately. We just barely have time to say hello, let alone talk about the decline of my life."

"That's not true," Liz said.

"It kind of is," I said. "Anyway, Morris can't use me because he's merging with another start-up company, which will do essentially what I and a couple of programmers could do if he hired us. He can't get money to pay us, so a merger solves the problem of having to raise cash from outside investors."

"You'll find something. In the meantime, at least you get to be with the kids."

"But what are we going to do about money? Things are getting pretty tight. There's only so much that we can put on our credit cards."

"My parents can help us until I finish up my fellowship. I'll beg them again about lending us a little money. We'll be just fine, if I can get that job at the Hunter Clinic out on Long Island."

"I don't want to have to ask for money from your parents again. They already think that I'm useless. Your dad called me Meathead again on the phone."

"That's just his sense of humor."

"Accountants don't have a sense of humor," I said. "Do you really think that you're going to be at the Hunter Clinic?"

"I think so. I really want it," Liz said.

"What about California? Don't you want to go back?"

"I like it here. There are more opportunities for me. I've been on the West Coast since college. I stayed there for you."

I still missed San Francisco, and I wanted to go back, but I didn't want to ruin Liz's dream. She had worked so hard. I just smiled.

My phone beeped, letting me know that I had a text. *Just finished reading that book you gave me. I loved it. You're the only guy I know who likes books from Oprah's Book Club. Save the date: Sept. 18. Zoe is having her birthday party at the zoo.*

"Who's that from?" Liz said as I finished reading the text message.

"Kelly. Her youngest daughter, Zoe, is having a party, and she wants me to save the date."

"She texts you a lot, and I've never met her. Maybe I should," Liz said.

"Well, she's taking her divorce pretty hard, and her friends have all but bagged her—so she's reaching out to new people."

"Whatever—sounds a little clingy to me."

I sensed that Liz was not very impressed with Kelly. It was probably my fault, since almost every story I had told her about Kelly had not been particularly flattering. I thought Liz had handled well my hanging around with the women in the family association, but maybe that was because they seemed almost like coworkers. Kelly was something different. She was an unknown entity, and it didn't help that I had once accidently said she was pretty.

"Forget about her for the moment," I said. "Let's talk about me taking you out on a date sometime."

I pulled some burgers and hot dogs off the grill and served them. A crowd of people started to gather around us, asking for ketchup, mustard, and relish. Soon this was followed by "Where are the plates? I need a napkin. Are these hot dogs kosher?" Gimme, gimme, gimme.

"Not a good time now." Liz organized food to take to our girls at the picnic table nearby. Whenever she had a moment's free time, she wanted to spend it with the girls.

As she gathered supplies, I forged ahead. "Wolfie offered to watch the kids while you and I have a romantic dinner. It might do you some good, maybe help you stop being tense all the time."

"Maybe take your new best friend, Kelly, and cheer her up instead, since she has no friends but you anymore."

Sniper fire. I hadn't seen that coming.

Everyone at the barbeque was talking about Good Heart's husband's teeth. They were very white. Unnaturally white for a human—alien-space-saucer white. The contrast of his teeth with the skin tone of his face was shocking. If it had been Halloween and he had been dressed as a vampire, it would not have been a problem. Daniel had gotten his teeth whitened because it was covered for free under the hospital's benefits plan as part of his oncology fellowship.

We all had theories as to why he had chosen to go full-out white, instead of a more natural hue, but none of them made sense until Good Heart whispered to us that he was color blind. "Please don't embarrass him. They will get less white eventually, right?"

Daniel was feeling good about his teeth. He entertained questions about the whitening procedure and discussed how it would pay dividends with its appeal to patients. "Patients want their doctor to be like a movie star," Daniel said.

No one had the heart to explain that they were too white. The closest someone came was when Supermom's husband, Mitch, said, "Those are real teeth, right?"

At some point Daniel came over to the grill for another hot dog. I pulled a slightly burnt one off and put it in a bun. "Looking good with those pearly whites."

He asked me how it was going, being the only stay-at-home dad.

"It's getting better. I had a hard time initially, but after this summer, it seems I'm getting into the routine of things," I said.

"I couldn't do it—kudos to you." Daniel appeared to be a little buzzed on cheap beer.

"I still miss working, but there are some rewards to staying at home."

"Let's not go too far, my friend. I get wicked bored if I have to be with the kid more than like an hour. A little one-on-one park time is fine, but after that, I just pawn off Sammie to the wife," Daniel said.

"You're not good with kids." Did I really say that out loud to him? He was silent. "I mean, some people are better at going to work than being with kids. Your wife is the better one with kids. And you're good with the cancer stuff as an oncologist." I changed the subject. "For me, I think I'll miss being with the kids, once I'm back at work."

"Are you seriously looking? I thought you were going to stay on the bench until Liz was done with fellowship and you guys could move back to California."

"I'm serious about looking, but the companies are not serious about hiring. We might stay on the East Coast. Liz has her eye on the Hunter Clinic out on Long Island with some big-shot doctor."

Daniel was very chummy with Mitch, Supermom's husband. "I think she's going to have a little competition on that one." He waved for Mitch to come over. I guess I really had offended him.

"Mitch, did you know that Liz wants to work at the Hunter Clinic too?"

Mitch was a handsome guy. He was the type of guy you hated in high school because everything came easily to him. He was smart, athletic, and confident with the girls. Mitch chose to wear horn-rimmed glasses when seeing patients (even though he didn't require prescriptive lenses), to seem more intellectual. I know this because he had actually admitted it to Liz once during hospital rounds. Who admits that kind of thing to a coworker? Liz had told me that Mitch's father, a neurosurgeon, was golfing buddies with Dr. John Warner, the gatekeeper referral for any job at the Long Island practice.

Mitch paused his conversation with Matías to join Daniel and me. From the smell of his breath, Mitch seemed to be tied with Daniel in terms of beers downed. "Liz is a great girl. The Hunter Clinic would be lucky to have her, but I think I'm a lock on that position. Nick, you should try, in a subtle way, to steer her somewhere else. I'll get you some names of some other practices. It's your job to look out for the missus." He sliced his index finger through the air in lecture mode.

I wanted to slap Mitch, but I didn't, because Liz would get embarrassed. More importantly, Mitch was in good shape and would thrash me after I got in my first cheap shot. But I was seriously offended by Mitch's sexist comments. After all of Liz's hard work, she did not deserve to be dismissed in such a fashion. She had been at the top of her class in med school and had been recognized for her surgical talents many times. I hadn't decided how I was going to square things up with Mitch, but I was not going to let it pass for long. As for Daniel and his asinine attempt at creating more competitive tension for Liz with Mitch, I made a mental note to bury an unwrapped turkey sandwich deep in the back of his sock drawer the next time the girls had a playdate with Sammie at her apartment. It would take a week before the smell would become overpowering.

At that moment, I chose to be diplomatic. "There are lots of good doctors and lots of good practices looking for good doctors. The pond is big enough. Doctors have good job security."

"Thank God. All that training has got to amount to something," Mitch said. "I would hate to be in business. Take Nick's experience—he got the boot after his company went belly-up, and now he can't get a job. My wife, she has this supposedly great English degree from Harvard, and she can't get real work. She wants to do some bullshit work for a nonprofit."

"And we're stuck paying the bills," Daniel said.

Mitch said, "What is that all about? We're expected to hump it out for the next thirty years. Women get the easy half of the marriage deal by being home with the kids and spending the money."

Matías had followed Mitch to join the conversation in the grill area.

Mitch was more of an angry guy than I had thought. I said, "Being home with young kids is actually a lot of work. I thought it was easy until I had to do it full-time."

Daniel said, "You're smarter than I thought, and I mean that in a nice way. Keep saying stuff like that, especially when Liz is around. You have a good thing going, chilling out with the kids all day, while Liz does all the work. If I could've married a doctor instead of going to medical school, I would have. Kudos to you." If Daniel had said kudos one more time to me that afternoon, I would have put a second turkey sandwich between his mattress and box spring.

"My wife has been dropping hints lately that I'm not doing more around the house like Nick," Matías said. "You're making us guys around here look bad—stop being so helpful to the moms."

Daniel and Mitch laughed.

Matías did the fake chummy pat on my shoulder. "I'm old fashioned. And I'm not going to give the girls a bath at night or babysit them when I'm home from the hospital so that she can go out. What happened to the brotherhood of guys?"

Just to mess with Matías, I kept pointing to a spot on my cheek as if he had food on his face, so that he would keep wiping his face, hoping to clean the phantom spot. I continued the frat-boy-style banter the three of them had started. "You guys seem more like Archie Bunkers than like educated guys. What's wrong with balancing the load with the kids?"

Mitch said, "Of course, men and woman are equal. But there are two things that you're forgetting: women do a better job raising kids, and if the man has a more important career, he gets a pass on doing the household chores. I don't have a simple job like regular guys."

"I heard that, Mitch," I said. It just was not worth talking to him anymore.

In the years to follow, I later learned that Daniel, Mitch, and Matías held the minority view among other male doctors in terms of their attitude toward women, kids, and shared familial responsibility. But at that moment, I did not know that. I was disappointed in the family association and felt cheated about my time in New York. Why were the ringleaders of the family association two schmucks like Mitch and Supermom?

Daniel did the stuttering drunk laugh. "Nice chat—glad to have you back in the boys' club, Nick."

Supermom appeared over Mitch's shoulder. She had heard the tail end of what we were saying. "Where did Nick go?"

Mitch said, "Nick says he's working too hard for the family association."

Supermom did a nose wrinkle. "Today, you're working hard on the grill, but normally you don't seem to be working too hard. Did I miss something?"

Mitch said, "No, babe. I'm just messing with Nick. Everything is fine. Are you going to wrap up the picnic, because I'm ready to leave."

Supermom seemed a little flustered. "Can you hang in there a few more minutes? I just have to make a couple of quick announcements."

After calling for everybody's attention, Supermom went through a laundry list of announcements, mostly thanking people for their help with the family barbeque. At the end, she turned to the topic of the year ahead. "Now that summer is over, we have to select new officers for the upcoming year. I asked around, and the old officers still want to do it, and nobody seems interested in taking over their responsibilities, so unless anybody has any objections, we can forgo an election and name the officers now."

Everybody clapped. I raised my hand.

Supermom seemed annoyed by my distraction. "What's your question?"

"It's not really a question but rather an announcement," I said.

Supermom did a broad, fake, public smile. "What is it, then?"

"I would like to throw my hat into the ring and run for president of the family association."

A few people clapped sporadically; Liz and Wolfie were not among them.

18

BALLOT-BOX BLUES

In a few days, Daniel's teeth were a little less white, probably due to his big coffee addiction. I ran into Daniel and Matías the Saturday after the barbeque, on my way back from the copy store on Second Avenue, where I had been making election signs to hang around the apartment building. When they first saw me, they seemed a little surprised. In their long white doctor's coats, they sat at a sidewalk table in front of a sandwich deli, eating what seemed to be a leisurely lunch. Neither their wives nor their young children were anywhere to be seen. In fact, the deli was a few blocks in the opposite direction from the parks and other child-friendly areas of the neighborhood. It wasn't until I started talking to them that I realized they were at unease, having been caught taking lunch on a Saturday. Did they think I was going to rat them out to their wives? When they have to work on weekends, most doctors with young kids grabbed a quick something at the hospital cafeteria or at Mandarin Deli, so they could get back to their families.

Daniel came up with an excuse that he was waiting for some gels in the laboratory to finish running. I didn't even know what gels were, but it still seemed like a lame excuse. I didn't buy it. As part of his oncology fellowship, Daniel was doing what was called "bench research," in conjunction with clinical rotations at the Memorial Sloan Kettering Cancer

Center. Good Heart frequently complained to me about how hard he was working. "He spends so many hours at the lab—poor thing." Matías was arrogant with his reasons for a lazy lunch. "Doing busy things at the hospital—many patients."

For a moment, I thought I might see Liz come out of the deli, holding her lunch, coming to join them—part of the conspiracy to ditch family for a little adult time. But Liz was not like them; she always wanted to be with the kids. Maybe not me so much, but definitely with the kids. She went straight to work and back again. No side trips, like these lug heads. I was rocking the double stroller, trying to keep Maude asleep, while Claire was fingering Goldfish crackers in a plastic sandwich bag.

"You need to get a nanny or a babysitter on the weekends, pal," Daniel said. "You need a break." Daniel was quite the phony friend.

"Liz works most weekends, so I wouldn't want to bail on the twins. I always feel a little sad for a kid that I see hanging around with just a nanny on the weekends. The nanny's bored and talking on a cell phone, and the kid is bored and doesn't want to be dragged around the city like luggage."

Matías was smoking a cigarette, which seemed weird for a doctor. Nifty-Fifty Wife wanted him to quit, but it was a cultural thing for him. The best she could negotiate was for him not to smoke around their daughter or in the apartment. He noticed my stack of election signs. "You're pretty serious about running for president. Why would you want to take on all that busy work? Just let Mitch's wife do it all."

I wanted the kids in the family association to have more fun and fewer rules. What little kid wants to eat broccoli florets for a snack or go to the art museum instead of the park? Why should the stay-at-home parents be subject to the uptight sensibilities of Supermom? Since most of the parents were new to the city, social life revolved around the family association. I couldn't say any of this out loud, so I went with "What's wrong with a little change? Shake things up a bit."

"This election thing is becoming goofy. It's like we're voting on class president or something. The only problem is that you're not the star quarterback and Mitch's wife was literally the prom queen of her high school, so I think you're going to have an uphill battle, my friend," Daniel said.

"Who gets to vote?" Matías said.

"If you have a kid and are a registered, due-paying member of the family association, then you can vote," I said. "Can I count on your vote?"

"You're a character," Daniel said. "Why would I vote for you over somebody that is doing an okay job? But don't worry; I probably won't vote, unless my wife nags me to."

"You said the reason already," I said.

"What reason?"

"You just said she's doing an 'okay job.' Would you want somebody to do an okay job or a great job for you?"

"Look at you, Mr. Politician," Daniel said. "I'll bite. How are you going to do a great job?"

"I'm going to do kid stuff, not stuff that parents think kids should be doing. My exhibit A will be the swim club I put together for the kids this summer," I said.

"Sammie is still talking about it. She was excited to go every day," Daniel said. "Good point."

Matías said, "I think this is very silly business. Let the moms do what moms do. I go back to the hospital. You coming, Daniel?"

Daniel attempted to be more social. "It was good running into you. Good luck with the election stuff."

Much later, I "accidently" told Good Heart and Nifty-Fifty Wife that I had run into their husbands that Saturday, when they had supposedly been working hard. By then, I was ready to screw the boys' club.

■ ■ ■

I returned to the building from the copy store with my signs. Daryl and Bryan were the doormen on duty. It was very easy to convince them to let me hang my election posters around the lobby. Claire woke up Maude, and both pitched in, delighted to be responsible for the hanging of all signage below two feet. Some of the signs were upside down, and I thought that made a statement to the electorate that I was kid friendly. Later, I found out most people thought I was being lazy or sloppy when I hung up the signs—so much for trying to make a statement.

The election would take place the next day. I had spent the week since the barbeque informally talking to the moms about trying to make things more fun. It was a difficult argument, given that I didn't want to refer to Supermom as a stick-in-the-mud and a control freak. Even my novice political skills told me that was not a good idea. I was not sure whether I would get any votes. It seemed that Supermom had made a lot of friends over the years, while Mitch had been doing his surgical residency in New York City. My strategy was to build support from the newer families.

Daryl and Bryan were also going to be on duty for election day. The voting was to happen after the association brunch in the lobby, near the polling station that was set up in the corner. "Daryl, I'm going to bring down a bag of candy later today, as a giveaway to get people excited about my candidacy. Can you hide it and then put it out on the front desk, right before voting? I want to surprise my opponent with a stealth tactic."

Bryan later told me that Supermom also provided treats in the form of miniature chocolate bars, right before voting commenced—so much for stealth.

"No problem," Daryl said. "What kind of candy?"

"Tootsie rolls."

"No good—too hard to chew. Need something sweet, like a Lifesaver or a lollipop."

"Do you think that will help?"

"No doubt," Daryl said.

"Lollipops it is," I said. "Thanks."

"No problem," Daryl said. "Anything to get rid of the queen of too many requests. She is always asking me to carry her groceries up to her apartment, instead of just using the building carts."

Bryan said, "She wants me to take her car and try to find free spots on the street. It takes an hour, and she's a bad tipper."

"So why do you guys do it for her?" I said.

"Carl, the building manager, wants us to make the family association happy. His bosses come down on his head if the doctors complain that their wives are not being taken care of. Around here, doctors are the top dogs," Daryl said. "That president of yours has already complained a couple of times over Carl's head. Carl is not one to take criticism well."

"Is Carl here today?" I sensed I could make a political ally.

"Carl is always here. He lives in the building, with his wife and sick mother-in-law," Bryan said.

"Do you think I could talk to him?" I had a little free time before I picked the girls up from a playdate at Good Heart's apartment.

"Carl doesn't mind getting paged out of the apartment, if you know what I mean," Bryan said.

"I heard that," I said.

Carl K. Karl brought me to his office, deep in the basement, near the incinerator room. Yes, that was his real name. Carl rather quickly made it known that he was in support of my candidacy. "I can't stand her. Anything I can do behind the scenes to make anybody but her the president, just let me know. I don't care if a goat is president. She must know somebody higher up in the hospital admin, 'cause all I get is grief from my bosses. She complains that the playroom is dirty. The walls need to be repainted. The doormen talk too loudly to each other while on duty. A light is out on the seventeenth floor. Get the picture?"

"I was thinking that maybe you could increase the family association's budget and make me look like a hero. I have to give a campaign speech to the family association tomorrow."

Daryl once told me that Carl had been a sergeant in the army, stationed in what he called a smelly country that was way too hot. Carl had a square head, was as neat as a pin, and sported a buzz cut. He was the kind of guy who was always pissed off about something. "Great idea—go knock off a liquor store or something, and you got your budget money. There's no way I can squeeze another dollar out of the hospital this year. I can barely get money for extra lightbulbs, let alone money so the kids of the rich docs can have some more toys."

I went for it. "Carl, do you need a hug or something?"

Carl laughed. "Guess I'm wound a little tight today. I'm a little crazy, 'cause my wife and her mother have been screaming at each other all day. I'm like a hostage negotiator, and all I want to do is watch my Mets."

"How about letting us move some of the playground equipment and picnic tables around, so that we can set up a bike track for the kids in the courtyard. A lot of that stuff is not bolted down, and all we need is a little help moving it. No money required," I said.

"I could help with that," Carl said.

"How about allowing the family association to set up a meeting with you, once a month, to talk about issues in the building? In return, nobody complains directly to the hospital, and this gives you a chance to address stuff before it gets out of control."

Carl smiled again. His gold canine tooth glistened under the fluorescent light. "Do you want my job? Cause you are management potential, my friend."

"Carl, I could never do what you do. You are the soul of this building."

"Flattery will get you far with me, Nick, but not enough for me to get you that new air conditioner you've been wanting for your apartment. Everybody asks me for one. We are told to keep fixing them rather than buy new ones."

We shook hands. I thanked him for his secret endorsement.

"Be a politician, and in your speech tomorrow, just make promises that you have no intention of keeping," Carl said to me as I left his windowless, cinder-block office. The only wall decoration was a sign that read "The beatings will continue until morale improves."

■ ■ ■

Sunday was election day. This was the first election anybody remembered having for the office of president for the family association in the past five years. Usually, the position was given to whoever objected least to doing it. The charter of the family association did not detail any specifics for election of officers, only that an election may be held if more than one person wanted to do it. Other officers could be named by the president, without election. Supermom and I agreed to hold a brunch right before voting in the lobby. Each of us would set up a table of buffet food in the playroom and then give our speeches.

Supermom brought sushi for her brunch selection. She set up an elaborate display of California rolls and selections of fish (yellowtail, tuna, salmon, and mackerel), creating an array that spelled out the initials of the Hospital Family Association. Furthermore, she laid out a gross amount of futomaki, tekkamaki, and kappamaki. For the kids, she had udon noodles. Desert consisted of pineapples and green-tea ice cream.

I was a few minutes late bringing my food, since it took a long time to prepare and bring the food from *L'Usine de Nourriture* in catering tins by cab. I served as Wolfie's sous-chef, and we put together a french country breakfast, complete with waffles, fresh-baked muffins, fruit, fresh-squeezed orange juice, sausage, and bacon. I even set up an omelet station that included egg-white options, and I cooked to order. Wolfie bankrolled me for all the food, and I owed him many hours of babysitting in return. It was a pleasure to show up Supermom for once.

"I figured you were going to bring bagels and cream cheese, and maybe pizza—very impressive," Supermom said.

"Would you like an omelet? I won't tell anybody," I said.

"I'm fine for now."

Wolfie shouted to Supermom across the room: "Is this grocery-store sushi? Do you know if it is fresh and made this morning?" Sometimes, it's nice to have obnoxious friends.

Supermom only vaguely acknowledged that Wolfie had spoken as she continued to greet everyone at the door. "Thanks so much for coming."

As one might imagine, not a lot of people chose to eat raw fish in the late morning—especially when the siren call of sugar, grease, and syrup were present. The turnout for the brunch was good, even from the doctors, mostly because free food was being served. Daniel, lost in his own world, loaded up his plate with sausage and bacon, while Good Heart struggled to get food for Sammie, who was being adamant about pouring the syrup on her plate at the kids' table. Matías stuffed a few extra muffins in his white coat, while I cooked him an omelet with lots of mushrooms and spicy peppers. Mitch Sr. threw a couple of ornamental sushi on his

plate and then proceeded to help himself to my selection of breakfast fin-
ery. Supermom, frozen smile in place, watched as her supermarket sushi
was passed by like roadkill on the side of the highway. I overhead someone
say, "That fish does not smell good."

The reviews were positive for my brunch. Good Heart and Lion
Tamer recognized my hard work, and I was proud of myself for the first
time in a while.

Liz came as well. "This is a fabulous brunch. Everybody just loves it,
even the kids." It had been a while since Liz had complimented me for
something I had done.

Brunch came to an end, and then it was time for remarks from the
candidates. Supermom wanted to go first. She was wearing a summer
dress, which highlighted her vacation tan and athletic body. I scanned the
audience and knew that I had lost the male vote.

Supermom is an eloquent speaker, and she was able to convince a
large portion of the audience, through passive-aggressive language, hidden meanings, and straight flattery, that she was a wonderful person, who
has their best interests at heart. I'll paraphrase and decode what I heard:
"I'm president and have been for the last couple of years. So you owe it to
me to vote for me. I like to do things my way, and you seem to like it. Nick
is a clown and is disorganized. He can barely control his twins, and he cannot be given the responsibility and sacred trust of the family association.
Next year, we need to do more child-development activities, with more
parent involvement. We basically need to run a full-day preschool for our
children. No more lazy days in the park or unstructured playdates." Strong
applause followed her speech.

It was my turn to speak. By comparison, I did not look pretty, nor was
I tan or wearing a killer sundress. I had two-day stubble and was dressed
in baggy shorts and a tight-fitting tee shirt with waffle-batter stains. I had
worn my Dylan's Candy Bar baseball cap, gangsta style. I went with a very
simple speech.

"I think Supermom has done a very proper job with the family association. But I think it is time to change things up a bit, because change is
good sometimes. The change I offer is to let the kids have more fun being

kids. There is time enough for school and learning in kindergarten and beyond. Why the rush, since, thanks to medical breakthroughs, we are all living maybe a little too long anyway? Let's have more games, more silly stuff, and no more field trips to the places where kids can't scream. I have not read a ton of child-development books, nor do I intend to change that. Let's make the family association more like a year-round summer camp."

I continued. "I talked with the building management, and they are willing to help us reconfigure the play yard so that we can have a safe bike track for the kids. Also, I convinced the building manager to sit down with us once a month, to talk about issues, so that we can get solutions to problems instead of complaining to each other and getting nothing solved. Finally, in closing, I think we need to have more wine-and-beer parties for the adults." Alcohol gets votes.

I received a lukewarm response. Somebody in the audience yelled "dynamite breakfast," and the applause got stronger. The meeting broke up, and everyone went to the lobby to vote. Wolfie and I stayed back to clean up.

Liz left with the girls to go vote. I hoped that she would vote for me. My fear was that she would vote for Supermom, in order to save me from myself. Liz was not a strong supporter of my candidacy. It seemed like a lot of work to her, with little in terms of gratitude. I also suspected that she did not think that I could handle the responsibility and that I would mess everything up, causing more embarrassment to her among her colleagues.

In short order, the results came back. Carl K. Karl announced to a small group that still remained in the lobby that I had actually won by one vote. Supermom, no doubt confident of her victory, had gone upstairs to her apartment with her circle of supporters. She would later hear the results from a gloating Carl K. Karl in a phone call. A recount was demanded, and, days later, Carl K. Karl's boss had to verify that all the votes were authentic, by reviewing each ballot. Supermom never fully accepted that a fair election had occurred. She felt that Carl K. Karl had altered the results. Nifty-Fifty Wife later told me that Supermom spent the following week polling everyone in the family association to gauge who had not voted for her. It stills remains a mystery to Supermom why she lost by one vote instead of it being at least a tie by her calculations, but I know. Nifty-Fifty Wife had voted for me but told Supermom otherwise. The reason was simple. I had helped her kill a mouse. Nifty-Fifty Wife said, "She is somebody that I am friendly with, but she was not a friend to me like you have been."

19

MISANTHROPES ARE PEOPLE TOO

Claire's security blanket, Doo-cho-baa, was a tattered shred of dirty threads by the end of the summer. It could no longer be considered even good enough to be a cleaning rag. It was becoming a biohazard, since Claire used it to wipe up milk and juice spills. Putting it in the washing machine would prove fatal to it, since the hand cleaning with paint thinner after Mitch Jr.'s feather, glitter, and glue massacre had rendered it thread-bare. I softly suggested to Claire that it was time for Doo-cho-baa to be put to rest. The kids were going to be starting preschool in a week, and I did not think that their future teacher would relish the faint smell of rotten eggs at circle time.

I was nervous to bring up the topic, since Claire considered Doo-cho-baa a member of the family. Even Maude respected Doo-cho-baa and did not play taunting games with it. Claire was very protective of her security blanket, and I feared that any talk of getting rid of it would bring about a dark storm that would last for days, if not years. When I broached the subject, her reaction was unexpected. She seemed to have realized that at some point she would have to say good-bye.

"We can cut off a little piece of Doo-cho-baa and keep it in a special place," I said.

Claire paused. "Can we have a pooneral?"

"A what?"

"A pooneral."

"What is a *pooneral*?"

"A party when somebody wants to good-bye."

"You mean a funeral?"

"A funeral—yes."

"Of course, we can have a good-bye party for Doo-cho-baa."

Maude and Claire scrambled to their room to set up a party. They dragged their play table to the center of the room, setting it with plastic plates and utensils. Claire rummaged in her closet for plastic food, in order to prepare the table for a fantasy feast.

I found an old cigar box in my closet, filled with spare change, and I emptied its contents into a cookie tin. Claire would be able to decorate the cigar box with whatever crazy design she wanted, using crayons, markers, glitter, and glue; she would have a memento box for the small piece of Doo-cho-baa that would remain.

I began our service. "This is a party to say good-bye to Doo-cho-baa. We are going to have cake and ice cream and sing silly songs. Doo-cho-baa was the best blanket a little girl named Claire could ever want. Sadly, Doo-cho-baa got smelly, really really smelly." I held my nose.

The girls laughed.

"Doo-cho-baa lived an adventuresome life. He was dropped in mud puddles, lost at a resort in Florida, chewed on by my cousin's dog, and run over by the stroller more times than I can count, but he never stopped being special to Claire. Loyalty is a special thing. Unfortunately, Doo-cho-baa is tired and wants to rest, and so only a part of him will live in a cigar box next to Claire's bed forever and ever."

We all clapped and dug into our pretend meal. I cut the least smelly corner off, and the girls decorated the box. Several minutes passed and all was good until Claire asked, "Where is the rest of Doo-cho-baa going?"

The original plan was, after the girls went to sleep and could not be witnesses, to hurl the balance of Doo-cho-baa down the garbage chute, where it would land in a dumpster seventeen floors later. At some point, it would wind up in some landfill in New Jersey. "I hadn't thought about it. What do you think we should do with it?"

Claire was silent.

"We should throw it away because it is dirty," Maude said. Kids can be very direct.

Claire shook her head.

"I do it, Claire. No cries," Maude said.

Claire shook her head.

"Can Daddy throw it away?" Maude said.

Claire shook her head.

"Should we all throw it away together?" I said.

Claire nodded.

Before Claire had time to really comprehend what was going on, I got to my feet and ushered the twins into the hallway, where the garbage chute was located. I pulled opened the steel trapdoor to the chute and pointed for Claire to just throw Doo-cho-baa in. At that moment, I realized that this might not be the right way to get rid of a security blanket. Was I doing psychological damage to my child? Would she suffer posttraumatic stress after today, whenever she saw a blanket of the same color? Would she tell a therapist someday that all her problems stemmed from this point in time, when her Daddy made her throw away what was the most important thing in her life? Since I never read any books on the subject, I had no idea what one should do in this situation.

Claire stared into the trash chute as she held Doo-cho-baa loosely in her hand. She hesitated.

Maude got impatient. She snatched Doo-cho-baa from her sister and threw it into the blackness of the chute. "Bye. Bye. Doo-cho-baa."

If I had thought what I was doing might be bad for Claire, just imagine how Maude's action was going to return as bad karma, when the two of them would have fights in their teens. Claire would remember on some level.

Claire screamed her loudest primal scream to date.

When she was finished, I said, "Who wants to go to a birthday party at the zoo? I think they will have real ice cream and cake." I tried the diversion technique, which I now realize was not very sympathetic to Claire's feelings.

"Let's go, Daddy," Maude said.

Claire was not so easily swayed. She went back to the apartment and opened the memento box, with the little piece of Doo-cho-baa inside. She rubbed it with her fingers.

"You still have a part of him. And you can touch him anytime you want," I said.

Eventually, Claire nodded. I gave her a hug and a kiss. She squeezed me back, and I melted.

Later when the kids went to sleep, Liz and I would do a postgame analysis of the Doo-cho-baa funeral, under the covers before bedtime. We would dissect every detail to determine its significance in the development of Claire over the span of her life. Liz's conclusion was that I might have done damage to Claire's ability to form meaningful, trusting relationships. Thanks, Liz, for the support.

"I thought to stop and save Doo-cho-baa from the chute, but then I worried that I would be reinforcing her dependency on a security object," I said to Liz.

"I think you did the wrong thing. I would have saved it and made a rule about it staying in the memento box. The visual of Doo-cho-baa going down a hole might be a tough one for Claire Bear to get her head around," Liz said.

"The funny thing is that my parents would not have given it a second thought. They would have gotten rid of Doo-cho-baa in the middle of the night, while I was asleep, and would have just explained it away in the morning as merely something that had to be done. Just move on. They would have had no guilt about throwing it away. Suck it up."

"And how do you think that would have made you feel?" Liz said.

"Pretty crappy."

■ ■ ■

Kelly's daughter Zoe was having her fourth birthday party at the Central Park Zoo. Maude and Claire had been excited to go for weeks, since the zoo was one of their favorite places. Kelly had spent a lot of time planning it—or, rather, had spent a lot of time telling the professional party planner what she wanted. She was apprehensive about the party, because her type A, stress-monkey ex-husband was going to attend. Money was an issue, since hosting a top-notch party at the zoo with twenty-five kids would probably cost about twenty-five hundred dollars. Kelly's alimony budget would have been pressed. But Kelly was in a perception dilemma among her richy-rich circle of friends, since her kids were in private school and their peers would tease them about having a home party with stale supermarket cake. In the end, Kelly had gotten into a shouting match with Kirk, her ex-hubby, which had ended with him agreeing to foot the bill. Prior to their fight, Kelly had been smart to include some of the kids of his law firm partners on the guest list. Kirk had taught her well about leverage.

At noon, we arrived at the Central Park Zoo's party room, located in a three-story, turn-of-the-century brick building. Kelly seemed to be in a panic as she greeted everyone. Upon seeing me, she smiled. "At last, a friendly face." She ushered Maude and Claire to a table where other kids were gathered, decorating individual party bags that would be filled with candy treats at the end of the party. She directed her cleaning lady, Carmella, who also served as a part-time nanny, to help my girls get set up. "Things are just going miserably wrong today. Zoe stained her dress feeding food to a billy goat. The cake has not arrived from the bakery yet, and this room smells like cat pee. Kirk is going to have a fit when he shows up. I hope he does not bring a date."

"I never met him, but I don't think he'll bring a date to his daughter's fourth birthday party, so soon after the divorce."

"He's a corporate lawyer, Nick; nothing is too low."

I decided to change the topic. "Do you need any help? I don't know any of your snobby friends."

"And yet you'll still live a long and happy life without them."

"I could run to the supermarket and get a cake for you?"

"That's sweet, but we're not there yet." She waved to Skinny Vegetarian Mom One and Skinny Vegetarian Mom Two as they entered the party room behind me. "Remember Nick from Coney Island?"

They both air-kissed Kelly and acknowledged my presence by blinking once in my direction. I said to no one in particular, "I'm going to grab a turkey sandwich now." I didn't intend to stick around and be ignored by humorless veggie eaters again.

The food spread for the adults was impressive. It was a large assortment from the Second Avenue Deli, and it included every possible combination of meats, breads, and trimmings, like coleslaw and pickles, as well as their famous mustard. Kelly even had a separate table with assorted salad options for her vegetarian friends. I grabbed a plate and tried to stick to my diet by taking plain turkey on whole wheat, but I failed when I couldn't resist the magnetic pull of a few small slices of salami and roast beef. Screw Dom. He wasn't there. A fellow chunky monkey next to me loaded up enough corn beef on his sandwich to feed a family of five in India. He said, "This sure beats the usual junk you get at kiddie parties. Save room for the cake, though; I hear it's going to be awesome."

I took my plate and found an empty round table in the corner of the room. The girls seemed to be having fun as the zoo coordinators gave the kids a mini lesson on zoo animals and their young. At bedtime, the twins would still be perplexed that baby kangaroos were called joeys. I rushed to finish my sandwich, so I could help the girls in the treasure hunt that was coming up. Kelly's idea was to have the kids hunt for clues all around the zoo, to figure out the mystery of where Zoe's birthday crown was located.

I got a text message from Liz, who was working another Sunday shift at the hospital, informing me that Good Heart had delivered a baby boy the night before. I sent a message back telling her that I would pick up some flowers on the way home. *Good idea. Might be nice if sometime you got me flowers as well.*

"Look at all this food. Who serves this kind of food at a kid's party? What a waste of money." A new, heavyset guy sat down at the table with me. His plate was stacked with food.

"At the kid parties I usually go to, the parents are lucky if they get a slice of the leftover pizza," I said.

"I heard that," he said.

"I say that as well. Where did you hear it?" I said.

"That's what we say back in Oklahoma, when you agree with something," he said. "But you don't sound like you're from Oklahoma."

"I'm not. I heard it at a comedy show once, and I thought it was funny."

He sat in silence for a few moments before he spoke again. "I'm sitting here thinking that all this is a waste. This is a fourth birthday party, not a wedding, right?"

"When I was a kid, I got to have two friends over for my birthday. My mom would give us those paper hats, and we ate some cake after school. Birthdays were not a big deal," I said.

"I heard that." He smiled. "I wish I could ditch this party, but I have to be here for my kid. I'd rather be at a ball game right now. Do you follow sports?"

"Not really."

He seemed disappointed. "Which kid is yours?"

"I have the twin girls."

"How do they know the birthday girl?"

"The kids know each other from the gym. They sometimes play there together at their childcare center while I work out."

"I can't stand all that workout stuff. It is so narcissistic. Look at me. Ain't I thin and beautiful?"

I patted my belly. "I had no choice but to work out. My trainer at the Workout Pit is insane, and he really whips my ass. It's good stuff, I guess."

"What's your trainer's name?"

"Dom."

"I know him."

"Did you ever train with him?" I said.

"My wife does. Or, rather, my ex-wife does."

Lightbulb—I was at a loss for words.

Enter Kelly, stage left. "Kirk, the treasure hunt is getting ready to start, and I think it might be a good idea if we both walk with Zoe and Tasha on the treasure hunt."

"I'm not going to pretend we're a happy family again. You walk first with them, and I'll walk with them the second half."

Kelly noticed that I was at the table. She appeared to tone down her response. "This is already an awkward situation, since this is the first birthday party after you left us. Can we try to put on a good front for the girls?"

"A little late for that, don't you think?"

"You can be so difficult," Kelly said. She turned to me. "Is it me?"

"I have no intention of commenting on your ex–marital bliss, because I fear it might end in my bloodshed."

Kelly left.

"You seem to be a smart guy," Kirk said.

I put my hands up in a mock surrender. "I'm just here as a party guest, not an umpire."

Kirk smiled. Did he have dentures already?

Kirk was older than I thought. I pegged Kelly to be about thirty-five, and he looked at least fifteen years older. His lack of hair caused me to mark his age up a bit. His divorce with Kelly was his second, and I was not sure if he had other kids. Kelly had nothing but bad things to say about him: temper, workaholic, misanthrope, snored like a chainsaw, chronic halitosis, smoked smelly cigars, self-absorbed, bit his nails, lactose intolerant, and cheap. The cheap part I had to disagree with, since he had paid a lot of money for his daughter's fourth birthday party. Kelly delivered such a skewed picture of Kirk, it was hard to see him through any other lens. I tried to steer clear of him during the treasure hunt, but he seemed to like me, even though I was Kelly's friend. Clearly, Kelly had reasons for a divorce, but I had to ponder what she had seen in him to marry. The easy answer was his money, but I wasn't convinced. Kelly seemed to be a sincere and caring person, and she only spoke ill of him, not of anyone else. I bet he had cheated on her. That would explain her anger.

The treasure hunt was to begin. Everybody gathered near the door. The plan was that the zoo staff would lead all the little kids around the zoo, by having them hold onto an orange rope. The procession would go from animal exhibit to animal exhibit, looking for clues to where Zoe's birthday crown was hidden. The back story for the hunt was that a mischievous monkey named Max had taken Zoe's crown from the party room last night and had hidden it somewhere. Max left clues for the kids around the zoo. The first clue was a big rubber ball. After a round of guesses, the kids decided that they had to go to the seal tank, since seals can balance rubber balls on their noses.

I merged with the pack of other parents, and we followed the kids to the outdoor seal tank, where a feeding show was about to begin. As we all gathered around the tank, Kirk somehow found his way next to me. I was surprised that he kept his promise to stay away from his daughter, the birthday girl, just to avoid Kelly.

During the seal show, he quietly heckled the zoo keepers. "I wish I could balance a ball on my head and get paid."

A minute later, he said, "Do you think the zoo keepers use special soap to wash off the seal smell at the end of the day?"

Just after a seal swallowed a fish for a backflip trick, he added, "Are the seals in a union, and if so, do they strike for more fish?"

A couple parents chuckled at his jokes, myself included, but most of the others just clucked at him. One even added a loud shush, followed by "We're trying to watch the show."

On the far side of the seal tank, Kelly noticed the commotion, and she rolled her eyes in my direction, as if to say, "See what I have to deal with."

"Nick, would you rather be watching paint dry or sit through this show? If you've seen one seal trick, you've seen them all," Kirk said.

"I'd rather be eating ice cream," I said.

Kirk patted my back.

The clue of a knit ski cap led us to the polar bear cage next. Kirk stayed with me, I assumed, since I had laughed at his stand-up routine by the seal tank. I had tried to melt into the crowd of the other party parents, but he kept up with me. For a supposed misanthrope, he was very chatty. "Do you believe that for all this money, all Kelly could come up with was the crummy idea of walking around the zoo? It would have been cheaper to buy regular individual tickets for all the kids. None of these kids really cares about the tour. All they want to see is the animals eating stuff and licking their fur. The money should have been spent on renting a back room at a decent restaurant. That deli layout back there was one of every type of dried-up meat and cheese they could find. And what's up with the party room smelling like a stable? I know we're at the zoo and smells abound, but they could clean the carpet once in a while in there."

I needed to defend Kelly. "I think the kids are enjoying the treasure hunt. It's great fun for little kids."

"I've got three other kids besides Zoe and Tasha, and I've been going to these birthday parties for a long time now. At some point, you just get sick of all the wasted time and money and the bullshit that people feel they need to do now for their kids. I wanted to have a little home party for Zoe and a few of her real friends. Does Zoe really enjoy having an army of kids at her party?"

"Home parties are good, but the kids will remember this too," I said.

"They won't remember any of it two weeks from now. They keep the memory of being loved and happy. After two wives and five kids who think you're an ugly hump, you learn a few things."

I was taken aback. "Don't take this the wrong way, Kirk, but if you're so in touch with your feelings, why did you and Kelly get divorced?"

"I worked too much, and she cheated too much." He seemed eerily calm as he spoke.

"Kelly doesn't seem like the cheating type."

"She is," Kirk said.

I had a hard time imagining Kelly as a serial cheater. She was devoted to her kids, and I didn't think she would risk breaking up her family over infidelity. Kelly had told me that Kirk was venomous. He must have been trying to play a mind trick on me.

Somewhere around the monkey exhibit, Kirk demanded to trade places with Kelly, to walk the birthday girl around. Kelly seemed embarrassed to have to leave Zoe and walk in the rear. Kirk was acting like a curmudgeon.

"How are you doing?" I said to her, as we walked toward the penguin house, which supposedly was the location of Zoe's birthday crown.

"The party is going awfully. Everybody seems bored. I wanted this to be so special for Zoe, and Kirk is just ruining it."

"I think the party is going great. Thanks for inviting me and the girls," I said.

Kelly was silent.

We entered the penguin house by parting hanging plastic strips, which served as a barrier for the frigid air conditioning inside. The exhibit hall was pitch black and smelled faintly of penguin poop. Dozens of penguins were on display behind one-way glass panels. The simulated dim light of the Southern Hemisphere surrounded the penguins in the exhibit but left us in the dark. The sound of their honks was magnified by the overhead sound system. It was crowded inside, and our party was forced to stand in one of the corners. The exhibit was a replica of typical harsh, rocky conditions of the Antarctic. The penguins waddled to and from zoo keepers, who feed them frozen fish. Occasionally, the penguins would take a dive into the tank's arctic pool, and the crowd would clap and giggle. The party guide stood in front of the glass and gave the usual litany of gee-whiz statistics and facts, which regarded the care and feeding of these butt-ugly birds.

I zoned out and just enjoyed the cool air, which was a respite from the heat outside. In the tight crowd of people, Kelly was near me in the back of the room. Despite the pervasive odor of penguin poop, I could smell the perfume she had put on for the party. It reminded me of the scent pouches that sometimes fall out of fashion magazines. Liz smelled like antiseptic half the time. I stood behind Kelly and watched her unnoticed. I felt sorry for her. She was such a nice person; she didn't deserve all the problems she was having. Her social circle was beginning to thin, and Kirk constrained her with strict alimony controls. Kelly was alone for the first time in her life.

The crowd clapped for Zoe as she pointed out the birthday crown behind the glass. The zoo keepers inside the display climbed the faux rocks to the highest point, upon which the birthday crown was perched. They would bring it out to her. Zoe gave Kirk a big hug. "This is the best party ever, Daddy. Thank you."

"I did all this for you, my dear," Kirk said.

Kelly's eyes were teary. She noticed me near her, and she was clearly embarrassed. I wanted her to feel better, so I stroked her back reassuringly. "Zoe knows that you were the one who put the whole party together."

"I know." Kelly gave me a hug. "You're sweet for saying so."

Her hug lasted a little longer than I expected, so I reflexively hugged her back, so as not to seem uptight. Don't friends hug? She let her head linger on my shoulder for an uncomfortable period of time before pulling back. "Excuse me. I'm sorry, Nicky."

One of the penguins did a backward dive into the water, and everyone cheered. The guide invited everyone from the party to go back to the party room for ice cream and cake.

It felt way too good hugging Kelly. It lingered in my mind for the next few days.

20

HOMEMADE COSTUMES SUCK

I should never have decided to run for president of the family association. What a boneheaded move. It was more work than I thought. I anticipated that things would be on autopilot, since I could shed many of the organized activities that Supermom had developed. No more field trips to the museums. No more parent-run music classes or reading groups. Yet there was plenty to do, since everybody got into the spirit of doing things differently. Suddenly, everybody had ideas as to how things should be run. There were more people involved than ever before. Suddenly, we had activity committees popping up, with varied agendas. Before, Supermom had just told everybody what to do and when; now, I was bombarded by questions. Should we have a teacher come in and teach gymnastics? How about having an art class? Can the kids put on a musical at Christmas time? I attended too many meetings, both during the day when the kids where in preschool and when I had free time after the kids went to sleep. I had even less time for video games than before. There was so much enthusiasm that instead of being a fun leader like I had hoped, I became a crossing guard who said stop to anything that required any real monetary commitment. The family association had no real budget, and nobody wanted to raise the annual membership fees, since all the doctor families lived on a fixed income (a relative pittance).

True to form, Supermom did not fade into the background and enjoy her post-presidency. She started her own activity committee, comprised of her cronies. They called themselves the Child Development Committee (CDC), which just so happens to be the same acronym as the US Centers for Disease Control and Prevention. It was a de facto shadow presidency, and their goals were to undermine everything I did and to make my life miserable. Instead of my campaign promises of more fun for the kids and less work for the parents, we had become more bureaucratic. My attempt at empowering people had backfired in my face. When it came time to name the other officers of the family association, I finally relented to Supermom's obvious wish to be vice president. I should have actually paid attention in high school when my English teacher had taught Machiavelli's *The Prince*. I really sucked in a leadership role. By the end of October, forty-five days into my presidency, the vibe I picked up was that I was a lame duck. If it weren't for my pride, and the fear of getting laughed at and hearing "I told you so" from Liz, I would have resigned.

On the eve of Halloween, I finished the final touches on the haunted maze that I had built for the family association's party. The maze was a scarily decorated collection of kid-sized, moveable plywood walls, which I had spent most of the month building, at night when the kids were asleep. I was proud of it because it would last for a long time and be changeable into a different maze path each year. Clarence, the building super, had helped me procure all the spare plywood scraps I needed from a nearby hospital construction site. He knew a guy, whose cousin knew a guy, whose job it was to dispose of the unneeded plywood. I painted a castle-wall motif, while some of the moms who were quite artistically talented painted witches, goblins, and ghouls in various places. I was actually quite excited myself for the Halloween party the next day.

Liz did not share my enthusiasm for the maze, especially after being up most of the night on call. "Does this mean you finally have time for your family again?"

"That's not fair."

Liz closed the refrigerator. "You were getting pretty good at keeping up with the groceries, and now I'm lucky if there are enough eggs to make an omelet for dinner. What did you feed the kids?"

"We got pizza across the street."

"When did you start eating pizza again? I thought you said that your body was a temple."

"Still is—I ate a salad," I said.

"That's like the third time you've taken the kids out for dinner this week. I don't think we can afford for you to eat out all the time. How is our money looking this month?" Liz said.

"I haven't gotten a chance to balance the checkbook, but we're good."

"That's a real financial answer. Are we still charging things like crazy?"

"Yes, but we'll catch up. Soon you'll be making the big bucks, right?" I said.

That was not a good thing to say. "I don't have time to do the bills. You're supposed to pick up the slack." Liz did a cleansing breath. "I don't want to get into all of this, all over again, tonight. I need more help, Nick."

"I'm sorry, babe," I said. "You're right. I want to be here for you and the girls. The presidency thing is just a side thing. I'll delegate more, or something. Forget it. Can I run down to Chicken Lickin' Kitchen and pick up a roasted chicken and salad for you?"

"Too expensive—I'll just eat cereal," Liz said.

I changed the subject to the kids, which usually put Liz in a good mood. The twins' birthday was coming up in a couple of weeks. "What do you want to do for the girls' birthday? Do you want to have a party or something?"

"I do, but I want to keep it simple. Can we use the party room upstairs?" Liz munched on her Cheerios.

"Simple is good. We can do it upstairs and get a singer or something for entertainment," I said.

"How much is that going to be?" Liz said.

"The singer might be like a couple hundred, and everything else like three—maybe five—hundred?" I said.

"Can we afford that?" Liz said. "I'd like to be able to invite some people from work to it."

I think we barely had enough in our checking account to cover it. I didn't want to tell her that we were maxed out on our credit card. "No problem. Maybe your parents can help again." I have to admit that I was getting addicted to the little cash they had been providing us lately. My previous stance on getting no financial help had eroded, but I liked to call it "evolved." Also, the cheapskates had a soft spot for their grandkids, and I knew they would want to help out for the party.

Liz said, "I don't want to keep going to them. It's embarrassing. Can we still afford to have you looking for a programming job? Do you think it's time to get something outside of your field, to help out until next year?"

I got upset thinking about not being home with the girls. "I don't want to get a nanny for the girls. And I don't want to dump them in daycare."

"This is a new feeling," Liz said. "I didn't want to say anything, but I was wondering why you hadn't been so gangbusters about finding a job lately."

"Maybe on some level I feel like I'm abandoning the kids if I do. I don't know. If we were in San Francisco, we would be near your parents, and I wouldn't care as much."

"I'm embarrassed to admit this as a woman, but I couldn't be home with the kids. It would drive me crazy. You're much better with the kids now than when you first started taking care of them," Liz said.

"What are you talking about? You keep complaining that I'm not pulling my weight," I said. Her updated opinion of my child-rearing skills was news to me.

"You don't help me very much at all. I asked you to help me take my work clothes to the cleaners last week, and they're still in a pile by the door. I'm still wearing a white coat with stains. The place is a mess. We have no food. You don't make any time for me when I come home. You're off doing stuff for the family association. It's like there's no slice of Nick for Liz anymore."

"So how is my being home with the kids better?"

"When it comes to the kids, you've become better than I thought. Since June, you've gone from little grasshopper to Zen master. You're clearly the best father I know. Devoted. Dedicated. The kids are very happy with you, and that is really the important thing. You're a playmate dad to them. I don't know what changed in you, but it's pretty amazing."

"That's very nice of you to say."

"It's true," Liz said.

"But I'm a lousy husband, you're telling me."

"I don't want a third kid. I need more from you. This fellowship is burning me out."

Liz was right. She deserved better than having to eat cereal for dinner after having worked fifteen hours straight.

At the ceremony upon leaving residency, the head of Liz's medical program offered an interesting metaphor regarding the role of a spouse to a physician. He said that the spouse packs the physician's parachute. Would you ever jump out of a plane if you didn't trust the person who folds and packs your parachute?

"Can I open up a can of soup to go with your cereal?" I said. "You deserve something hot."

Liz half smiled. "Make sure it's the kind with the chicken chunks that taste metallic."

■ ■ ■

Trick or treat in a giant New York apartment building is nirvana for kids. It is the ultimate in high return for little effort. If you're ambitious, you can have a bag of packaged sugar and chocolate in no time. Take the elevator up to a high floor, go from apartment to apartment, and then use the stairwell to go down to the next floor. Avoid using the elevator on the way down, since it will, by then, be congested with the increased traffic from trick or treat.

Claire and Maude bounded from apartment to apartment, looking for people giving away candy. Claire shouted, "This one has a pumpkin picture. We can knock." And Maude would pound on the door with more effort than expected from someone not yet four years old.

"I thought you were the police or something," one of the surprised international residents said after opening the door and seeing my two small children. "And who are you?"

"We're Thing One and Thing Two," Maude said.

They smiled. "Who?"

"We're friends with the big cat," Claire said.

"You look like little clowns to me. I don't know this cat of yours, but here is some candy."

I had done a really crummy job on the kids' costumes. I don't think that many people were able to get the Cat in the Hat theme at first glance. Maybe I should have dressed as the big cat himself, with the red-and-white top hat, even if it would have made me look like an even bigger dork than I already did. I tried to keep the kids' costumes simple (i.e., cheap), so I bought two blue wigs at a discount store and dressed the girls in red long johns, with "1" and "2" written in black marker on the fronts. Unlike some of the moms in the family association, I could not sew or make a fabulous costume from scratch otherwise. Their costumes looked like family heirlooms compared to mine. Nor could I afford the theatrical quality costumes sold at some of the stores on the Upper East Side. I didn't understand how Halloween had suddenly become a big holiday now, with elaborate and expensive costumes. I can't tell you how many Halloweens as a kid I had dressed as a hobo, complete with a bandana wrapped around a stick. It had been a perfect five-minute costume, made from hand-me-down clothes.

Eventually, Wolfie and his kids caught up with us at our building, somewhere on the twelfth floor. He had taken a night off from the restaurant, so that he could go trick or treating with the kids. His kids were dressed in store-bought costumes as Batman and Robin. They actually looked like what they were supposed to be. Next year, once Liz started in practice and we had more disposable income, I would buy a costume at the store just like every other parent. I would no longer care about the

principle of the matter. The concept of a simple life would be happily replaced by the ability to spend money to make everyone happy.

Other people from the family association felt awkward that I had invited Wolfie to trick-or-treat with us. The building was like an Amish village when it came to outsiders. "They are not one of us." Everyone seemed
a little put out that they were giving candy to people they had never seen
before in the lobby or the elevator. Had I broken some unwritten rule, like
"Thou shall only distribute candy to kids from the building; all others are
infidels"?

But I really needed to be with a good friend. Lately, hanging around
with the other parents in the building had seemed too much like having
to go to work again. All they did was ask me if I could help them with
this or that. I had to be careful about what I said, lest I wind up offending
someone.

When someone was bold enough to ask whether Wolfie lived in the
building, I would use my own version of a Halloween trick. "This is my
kin from West Virginia." The use of the words "kin" and "West Virginia"
in a sentence was a little unsettling to the members of the professional
class. There were no follow-up questions. The response was simply, "Nice
to meet you. Take some candy for the kids."

Following trick or treat, we took the kids to the family association
Halloween party held on the top floor of our building. At the door of
the party room was Supermom. Dressed as Snow White, her outfit self-
made, she greeted everyone with a little gift bag of candy as they stepped
off the elevator. Her kids, Mitch Jr. and Hillary, were dressed as Doc and
Sneezy. Her husband would be a late show to the party and refuse to wear
the Prince Charming costume that had been made for him. Upon seeing
that Wolfie and I were not dressed in costume, Supermom went into fake-
smile mode. It was obvious that she was not amused by either our lack of
costumes or Wolfie's presence at yet another family association function.
"No costumes, fellows? It's bad for the other members to see the president
not dressed up for Halloween."

"My poison apple costume is still at the cleaners, Snow White," Wolfie
said.

From a box nearby, she pulled out a pair of bandit masks. "I have these for those who aren't wearing costumes."

We slipped on the masks and entered the party. It was easier not to argue with Supermom.

Good Heart saw us and waved a broom in the air. She was a witch. Her newborn, Ralph, was swaddled in a sling. "Pretty lame costumes, guys."

"We've already been told," I said. I still think real adults don't dress up for Halloween—unless it's an adult-only party with alcohol."

"Is Liz coming?" Good Heart said.

"She texted she'd be here soon," I said.

"I want to thank her for the baby gift."

"Do you like it? I picked it out myself—unassisted."

Good Heart seemed relieved. "I couldn't believe that Liz bought a baby-wipe warmer. That makes better sense, that it was you who bought it."

"What's wrong with having warm baby wipes?" I said.

"It's too decadent, but, more importantly, there have been reports of electric-shock exposures from them. Not a very safe thing to have near a baby," Good Heart said.

"I'm sure there were only one or two incidents. I don't think the baby manufacturers are going to sell anything that is really all that dangerous. I bought it because I knew you would not get it for yourself."

"Thanks for trying. It was thoughtful," she said.

Wolfie and I politely ditched her, and went for some punch.

"Is your girlfriend coming?" Wolfie said.

"Don't even joke about that, here." Nobody seemed to hear Wolfie. "These moms go crazy over any suggestion of infidelity."

"Sorry. I'm just so excited to meet your new best friend."

"She said she was coming, even though her older daughter is having a big dress-up fundraising party at her school."

"Has Liz ever met Kelly?"

"No. And my guess is Liz is not going to like her very much."

"Why?" Wolfie said.

"Kelly is model pretty. A lot of women give her the cold shoulder because of it."

"Liz is hardly the intimidated type. She's a surgeon."

"Would you want your lovely wife hanging around with a really good-looking pretty boy, while you're pulling long hours at work?"

"We have a standing rule that she can't talk to anybody that is a seven or higher in the looks department."

"That's a really good rule to protect fives like us."

"You're still a little Budda body, even if you've lost fifteen pounds. Model types don't go for dough boys with no job and two kids."

"It's more like twenty pounds gone now, fry cook," I said. "I don't want Liz having suspicious thoughts, especially since we have not been quite Donnie and Marie lately."

"Good thing, 'cause Donnie and Marie are brother and sister." Wolfie was looking over my shoulder. "What do you think of cats?"

Kelly had arrived. She was dressed as a black cat. There are two types of black-cat costumes. The first kind is the cute and cuddly and nonsexual (appropriate for children's parties); the other is disarmingly sexual. Most people can only pull off the first kind of cat costume. Kelly was the rare type of person who could look good in tight black spandex and painted whiskers. Liz was not going to like meeting her.

"I guess I don't have to tell you who arrived just now," I said.

"Why is she hanging around with you?"

From across the room, I could tell that Supermom was giving Kelly the business. I imagined that she was telling her that this was a function for residents only. It was rescue time.

"Glad you could make it." I now stood between Supermom and Kelly. "I invited her."

Supermom leaned forward. "People are going to get upset, since we told everybody not to invite guests. You brought two people and their kids. Membership dues paid for the party."

"I know it's bending the rules a little. I'll chip in a little extra money to cover," I said.

"That's not the point. We have to be fair to everyone," Supermom said. She was right, but I didn't want to admit it.

Kelly motioned for her daughters to leave. "We can go. Zoe just wanted to see the twins in their outfits, but it's not a big deal. I'll speak to you later."

Supermom seemed pleased by the prospect of her departure, as if, like in Snow White, she would remain the fairest beauty of all at the party. Right then, by comparison with Kelly, Supermom seemed a little frumpy. Kelly needed to stay. "I agree we have to be fair to everyone. But I invited her, not knowing that this was such a strict members-only kind of deal, and I won't be rude by turning her and her daughters away on Halloween. If anybody has a problem, let them talk to me."

"As you wish, Mr. President," Supermom said.

Zoe and Tasha, dressed as a pair of fairy princesses, darted across the room toward the twins. Away from Supermom, Kelly said, "Thanks. I could use a friend right about now. When you get a chance, I've got to tell you something." She noticed the homemade costumes on the twins. "I could have helped you with the girls' costumes. Why didn't you call me?"

"You've got a lot going on. I didn't want to bother you," I said. "Liz wanted to help the girls make them, but then her week was too busy at the hospital. So I threw something together."

Kelly touched my arm. "That's what friends are for! Call me next time you need help with womanly stuff."

I was slow to pull back my arm at her touch. "How did your party go at Tasha's school?"

"The usual crowd was there, throwing money around at the auction. Everybody strutting about in their Christian Dior Halloween costumes." She giggled and did a fashion-show spin.

"Looks like you got a little into the competition yourself."

"What do you mean?"

Now I was embarrassed. "Your outfit is definitely not G-rated."

Kelly said, "Are you flirting with me?"

I stammered. "I'm just saying that you went all out on your outfit and it shows. I'm sorry if I..."

Kelly smiled. "Relax. I'm just messing with you." She made a meow sound.

I changed the subject. "You said that there was something that you wanted to tell me?"

She seemed a little upset at being reminded. "Yes, but not here."

"Are you a Russian spy or something?"

"Yes." Kelly was prone to drama.

"Is something wrong?"

"Can we talk in the exercise room?"

It was a little weird to leave the party for a few minutes, just to have some privacy with a woman who was not my wife. It would draw attention if we left together. The women in the family association were a suspicious lot, and Liz was expected to arrive soon. I said, "I'll go to the exercise room now, and you'll follow me in a minute or two when you think no one is looking."

"What's with all the cloak-and-dagger stuff?" Kelly said.

Was that an insult? She pushed me to the exercise room near the party room.

Once there, she sat down on a bench by the window, which looked out over the East River. It was a sweeping view of the Queensboro Bridge, Roosevelt Island, and the neighborhoods of Queens. I sat next to her. "I wanted to tell you something before you heard about it at the gym."

"What's going on?"

"I've being secretly seeing Dom romantically."

"Our trainer? He's a thug." Kelly seemed embarrassed. "I mean, he doesn't seem your type. But you're both single. Love can be stupid."

"Dom also has a thing with another woman, and they have a son together. They aren't married, but they live together sometimes. He wants to leave her for me, but I don't really want a long-term relationship. I thought we were just having fun," Kelly said.

"How did he take that?" I really didn't have to ask.

"He took it into crazy country," Kelly said. "He got really angry, and it scared me."

"Did he get physical?" I hoped she wouldn't ask me to protect her from Dom. I'm a scared little chickenshit when it comes to fighting. I'd never been in a fight, unless you count the time that Wolfie and I got into a drunken late-night slap fight over an egg sandwich.

"No, he didn't get physical. I don't think he would hurt me. What do you think?"

"If you don't know for sure, then you gotta bail."

"He can't be my trainer anymore. And I don't think I can go to the gym anymore, because I think some of my friends saw us arguing in one of the Pilates studios. I'm pretty humiliated by the whole thing." Kelly sniffed. Tears would come next.

Like with Nifty-Fifty Wife during the great mouse hunt, I was having another secluded conversation with someone who was not my wife, and it was getting a little too heavy for me. I didn't want Liz to catch me consoling a distraught, attractive woman, alone. This was not good.

But seeing Kelly so upset made me feel really sorry for her, and I rubbed her bare shoulder, against my better judgment. "How did you start going together? Was he nice to you?"

"I've been so lonely for such a long time. Dom likes to flirt. I invited him to lunch after one of our workouts. The rest you can guess."

"It makes sense to quit the gym. Get away from all the negative people there. You've got to find a place where you can hang out with nice people, regular folk, instead of the snotty rich crowd," I said.

"There's something else I wanted to talk to you about. I need a change. I've been thinking about leaving the city, maybe somewhere in North Jersey. I'm so tired of it here."

I didn't want to lose Kelly in my life. She was the only stay-at-home mom that made me feel comfortable being a stay-at-home dad. Some of the other moms like Good Heart and Nifty-Fifty Wife were nice, but she was different. I liked hanging around her as much as I did Wolfie. She was the only true new friend that I had made on my own in New York. "Don't throw your life away by moving to New Jersey. It's row after row of aluminum-sided houses and strip malls."

"I don't like being in the city anymore. Kirk lived here when we met, and so I followed him. I can't move too far away, because we have joint custody of the kids."

"Moving is only going to make things worse. You can't run from your problems. You're going to be just as lonely somewhere else. New York has everything."

"Since when did you become an advertisement for New York City? I thought you were homesick for San Francisco."

"I still am, but like the song 'You Can't Always Get What You Want,' sometimes you have to compromise and make the best of it. Who knows, maybe Liz will change her mind, and we'll go back after her fellowship. She has to decide. It's her turn."

"I don't know what to do." Kelly sniffled. "I've failed at everything."

Since I didn't have any tissues on me, I offered her a gym towel that had been left on the floor, but she declined. "Things are better than you think." I smoothed my hand across her back. "Please don't cry."

"I'll be all right." She wiped her nose across the tight black nylon of her arm. I didn't think women did gross stuff like that.

"Wolfie and I are going to a horror movie tonight since it's Halloween. Why don't you come with us? It'll be fun. Cheer you up a bit. Maybe we can invite some other people from the party to come."

"What are you seeing?"

"*Drummer Boy.*"

"What's that about?" Kelly said.

"It's a movie about a bunch of teenagers in a marching band who are killed off one by one. It's a horror dramedy, and it's got the tall skinny guy from *Saturday Night Live* in it."

"I usually don't do horror movies, but I'm game. I could go for a little distraction tonight. Carmella can watch the kids."

"Let's take Manhattan." In my attempt to cheer her up, I spoke a little too loudly.

Behind us, Supermom entered the exercise room. "Excuse me. Am I interrupting something?" She paused. "Nick, a section of the maze fell and almost hurt one of the kids. Everybody is wondering where you are."

"Here I come." I didn't bother to make up a plausible excuse as to why we were in the exercise room alone. I should have.

As I suspected, no true disaster had happened. Supermom was being a snoop. The supposed section of maze that had fallen turned out to be a cardboard sign that had been knocked off by one of the kids. I wished at some point that Supermom would come to accept me, warts and all. It was a real bummer that she was always on my case.

Eventually, Liz arrived. The party room was nearly full. Like most of her doctor peers, she did not have a costume and was coerced into wearing a bandit mask by Supermom, who had returned to her post by the door.

"I see you're in the no-costume club as well," I said.

"No time to put one together. What's your excuse?" Sniper fire. Liz was in a hostile mood.

A possible humorous retort could have been "Bad day sawing off bones?" It might have worked on a less sleep-deprived day, but instead I went with a more moderate response. "I focused all my energy on the kids' costumes."

She glanced across the room at the kids' costumes. "Are you serious? Those are the lamest costumes I've ever seen. Why didn't you go with something simple like ballerinas or fairy princesses?"

"I tried to be creative and, obviously, failed miserably. The kids' love the Cat in the Hat, and they asked me if they could be Thing 1 and Thing 2."

"If you couldn't do a good job, you should have convinced them to be something else," Liz said. "And if you were going to do such a horrible job on their costumes, you should have at least gone down with the ship and dressed up as the cat."

She was right. Exhausted and crabby, but we both knew she was right. If I had admitted it then, things might have gone better. Instead, I replied, "Since when did Halloween become a testament to a person's worth as a parent?"

"I'm bored already with your excuses and rationales. Do we always have to bicker over stupid stuff? You're not getting it. I am embarrassed by those costumes. I needed you to pick up the slack, and you just didn't."

I blew it. "Sorry, they are pretty ugly costumes. Can I get you something to eat?"

"Thanks. I'll eat something fast and then hang out with the girls." She dropped into a bench by the window.

I returned with cumin-flavored tofu meatballs, which was the only food left in any useable quantity from the pot-luck spread at the buffet table. Thanks to Wolfie, Kelly managed to meet Liz in my absence. Apparently, Wolfie had seen Kelly alone in the corner, munching on a celery stick, and had decided to play cruise director by introducing her to my wife. He got it into his head that he was sparing me the awkwardness of having to introduce them. As I approached, the trio was caught up in idle party talk. I could tell from Liz's poker face that she was unimpressed by both Kelly and their conversation.

I handed Liz her plate. "I'll make you something better at home, if you don't like it." After a few seconds of silence, I added, "I'm glad you two have finally met."

"Kelly's been telling Liz how wonderful you are and what a great friend you've been to her during the divorce," Wolfie said.

"I only met her three minutes ago, and I already know her life story," Liz said.

Kelly seemed embarrassed. "I can be a total bigmouth sometimes. Right, Nicky?"

Liz said, "Nick can be a pretty special guy when he wants. He thinks the world of you too, and I assume he likes the extra *y* you've added to his name."

Kelly laughed nervously.

We entered a conversation dead zone. It was time for a subject change. "Pretty soon, we're going to be giving out prizes for costumes."

"Our kids are going to be getting the prize for the worst costume." Liz excused herself with a pat to my shoulder and handed back her plate of untouched food. She went to look for our girls.

Wolfie said, "Just shrug it off. Liz is not the type to put lipstick on a sow's ear. You blew it on the costumes, and she called you out on it."

"You mean 'lipstick on a pig,' or 'sew a purse from a sow's ear,'" I said.

"Whatever—I'm just a fry cook, remember," Wolfie said. His kids, Carly and Alden, came over and dragged him away toward the Halloween games.

I was left with Kelly, and I realized that I couldn't go to the movies later that night. "I think maybe I should stick around the apartment tonight and bag the movie."

Kelly said, "Liz doesn't realize what she's got."

21

FEEL THE BURN

Two days before the twins' birthday party, I got a call from Dom. He was overly friendly, which seemed out of place for his tough-guy persona. That day, I was suffering from a bad head cold, which somehow included diarrhea and a fever. In baseball terms, it was the triple play of diseases. My runny nose made me go through tissues faster than I eat jelly beans, and clumps of wet tissues circled the wastebasket nearby. When I was not unloading my bowels in the bathroom, I was sprawled out on the couch, feeling sorry for myself, as I tend to do when I get a flu. The twins tumbled around the apartment, basically unmonitored. I declared the day a TV holiday—no time restrictions on cartoons. It was ice cream for breakfast. Around noon, the phone interrupted my moaning and nose blowing.

"Nick, buddy, what are you doing?" These were Dom's first words. Initially, I thought he was going to invite me to a sports game or something, because his tone was so jovial. The call surprised me, because it had not occurred to me that he might consider me a buddy.

"I'm just laying here suffering from the mother of all flus. I feel horrible."

"That's too bad, pal. Keep your fluids up. Try to eat some soup." Dom was usually the least sympathetic person on the planet. At any other time that I complained about anything being sore, he would sneer at me and tell me to shake it off.

I had not had a training session with Dom in the two weeks since Halloween. Either I cancelled or he cancelled. But mostly he cancelled. Some of the reasons seemed valid, like he had to take his kid to the doctor or the mother of his child needed help moving, but others seemed lame. He told me that one of his clients had invited him to stay at their house in the Hamptons for a few days. It was unclear whether it was a man or a woman, and whether it did or didn't include physical training and/or romance. This lack of enthusiasm for keeping his appointments with me was starting to piss me off. I thought about getting another trainer, but I was nervous to do so, because he knew I was a friend of Kelly's. I didn't want him to think that I was talking about his extracurricular activities with the manager of the gym. It never pays to piss off a muscle head. I'd seen too many movies and cop shows to dis him like that.

"Maybe I'll try some chicken soup later," I said. "So what's up with you? Do you want to reschedule our sessions? In a few days, I should be back in fight shape, once snot stops dripping out of my nose every two minutes."

There was silence on the line for a few seconds before he spoke. "I'll get back to you tomorrow with some dates and times so we can make up all your missed sessions. I really gotta apologize for my lack of professionalism. I'm bigger than that."

Something was up. He continued. "I need a favor."

Did he want me to drive a getaway car or help him dig a really deep hole somewhere in the New Jersey Meadowlands?

"What's going on, Dom?"

"It's a little embarrassing, but I'm in jail right now—got put in late last night. I need your help in bailing me out."

There was no way I was taking my sweet little twin girls down to some jail to bail this guy out. And there was no way I was going ask someone in the family association to watch my kids while I went downtown alone. It would be quite a scandal for the holier-than-thou crowd to tell them I was associating with a known criminal. As mentioned before, I'm a chickenshit. Some seek trouble, while others run the opposite direction, like scared, small children.

"I wish I could help, but I've got the twins to take care of. Don't you have anybody else who could do it?"

"No. The only family I got is my mom's. She'd kill me if she knew I was back in jail again." Did he just refer to his mother as "moms"?

"How about your girlfriend, the one who is the mother of your child? Can she help?"

"That's the problem. We got into it last night, and I got a little heated."

I said nothing. I didn't want to piss him off.

He filled the silence. "I didn't hit her."

"I didn't think that you did," I said, lying.

"I just threw a beer bottle, and she called the cops, telling them she was afraid. All I told her was that I don't like her smoking in front of my kid. She got all up and crazy, telling me I got no right to tell her what to do if I don't live with her or pay the bills, and I got a little heated. I pay for stuff for the kid."

I wanted to avoid sounding judgmental, but I didn't blame his girl-friend, or ex-girlfriend, for calling the cops. Dom was not a choirboy. "Sounds like a long night."

"I don't want you to think that I was at fault or nothing. My girl has always been a little hot headed too. The bottle wasn't thrown at her—just the wall—not her."

"It's a little tough for me to get down there right now with the kids. I'm sure there's somebody who can help. Maybe another one of your clients would help? What about that person who you stayed with in the Hamptons?"

"You're my best client," Dom said. My bullshit meter was buzzing.

"I just physically can't get down there today. Wherever down there is?"

"I'm in jail in Queens, and you don't have to come. You can just Western Union the money with a phone or a computer."

"They have a Western Union in jail?"

"No. A friend of mine can pick it up at the Western Union down the street and bail me out," he said.

"So you just need the money from me because your friend doesn't have enough money to do it himself?"

"Something like that."

Exactly like that. "How much are we talking?"

"Five hundred."

That was pretty much all of our money in the checking account. The same amount that we needed for the kids' party. "I really don't have that kind of money right now."

Dom was persistent. "I thought you were one of them computer wonder kids, and your wife is a doctor, so of course you gots the money. We're friends, right? I have the money in the bank, but my friend can't get to it to help me out. I'm the Workout Pit's top trainer, and I just got paid a big bonus. As soon as I get out, I'll pay you back. Just give me your address. I can drop it off with your doorman in less than an hour. I'm in a pinch. Please help me. You don't know what this month has been like. I've gotta get out of jail."

"I know you're thinking that I'm giving you a line, but things are really tight for us right now. I haven't worked in a while, and though Liz is a doctor, she's just a fellow, and fellows don't even make minimum wage, if you add up all the hours they're pulling."

"I thought your wife was a girl, not a fellow."

"A fellow is a like a job title among doctors. So she is…"

"I'm just messing with you, Nick. I'll throw an extra hundred on top. Call it interest for one hour's time. I know this all seems weird and shit, but you know me well enough to know that I am not a bullshitter. I'm a straight shooter. You know where I work."

Dom was playing to my acute sense of guilt. I always had a hard time saying no to people. I decided to do it, because the extra hundred would allow the twins to have a nicer party. I had been keeping Liz in the dark regarding our finances, and I thought it would be a good idea to have a little cushion. Things were tighter than I had described to her. A year ago, I could spend a hundred dollars for dinner on a weeknight without having to think about it. Now, an extra hundred seemed like a lot.

"The extra hundred is very generous of you," I said. "When you get out, please drop it off with the doorman. I need the money back, so I can pay for my girls' birthday party this coming Saturday."

"You're the man. I'll call you tomorrow for your training times." Dom gave me the information to send him the money via Western Union. I chose to use the web and was able to track online when the money got picked up. It felt nice to help Dom out.

An hour later, I called down to the doorman and wanted to know if someone had dropped off anything for me. No. Nothing. Zilch. Nada. I described Dom to the doorman, and no one close to fitting the description of a body builder had entered the lobby. Two hours later, there still was no money. By early evening, I considered that maybe I was not going to get my money back, but the optimist in me offered other explanations. Had the doorman taken my money? Maybe Dom's friend who had waited at Western Union had run off with the money. Should I try to reach Dom by telephone at the police station to see if he was in jail still? Can you even call a prisoner in jail, or would I have to go down in person? What excuse would I give Liz as to why I had to go out at night, sick as a dog? Maybe Dom had been delayed, and he was going to drop off the money tomorrow. I decided to stop by the gym in the morning, when the kids were at the Thursday building playdate, even though I was still sick.

Going to the gym did get me some answers. Answers I did not like. It turned out that Dom was no longer working at the gym, since about the time he'd had a falling-out with Kelly. He had been fired for supposedly cheating on his time sheets. Further investigation among my usual gossip sources revealed that Kelly had finally complained to the manager of the gym. The manager had a strict rule about trainers having romances with the clients.

All of Dom's excuses for not having training sessions with me and a few other people had been lies, because he was covering up that he was out of a job. Was he embarrassed by his dismissal? Did he just make up excuses in order to save face to people? Did he hope to hold on to his clients, thinking that he could get a job as a trainer somewhere else? I would never find out the answers any of these questions. Dom had disappeared from the Workout Pit, leaving rumors in his wake. He had also played the same money scam on at least five other people who were willing to admit it. It turned out that he had never called me from jail. Western Union told me that he was the one who had picked up the money.

Yesterday, when Liz had eventually come home, the kids had already gone to bed. She was upset to have missed them. I had hoped to get a little sympathy for my cold, even though it's tough to get pity from a doctor over a little thing like a flu. But as soon as I heard her curt reply to my greeting, I knew even a little tender loving care was not going to happen. I was back in the doghouse, and I hadn't even told her the financial news.

Fortunately, I had pulled together enough energy to order online a food delivery from the supermarket, so the fridge was full and Liz had something decent to eat for dinner. She ate in silence the barbeque chicken, roasted potatoes, and steamed green beans that I had gotten for her. We made little eye contact. I made the effort to sit at the table with her, even though it was hard to remain upright in a stiff, wooden chair with achy muscles. The smell of her food made me nauseous.

I felt compelled to break the silence. Liz was not going to initiate a conversation. I first blew my nose and snorted down some mucus. My colds tend to be wet and messy. "Is something wrong, Liz? Did something bad happen today?"

"We can play this one of two ways. I can ask you straight up or you can tell me," Liz said.

"Tell you what?" I said. Now I was getting nervous.

"Are you going to play games or come clean?"

"Come clean about what? I have no idea what you're talking about."

"Are you having an affair with that woman Kelly?"

"No. Not at all. Never. Absolutely not." I wanted to be clear.

Liz seemed relieved.

"What made you think that something was going on? Have I done something to make you suspicious?" I rose and hugged her as she sat in her chair. Liz started to cry, and she was not the crying type. I told her, "I love you, have always loved you, and am one hundred percent devoted to you and the kids."

Liz rose from her chair and returned my hug. "I believe you."

"Thanks for believing me. I love you."

"It's a little weird, having you home with the kids, and me barely around. You spend a lot of the day surrounded by other women, and I sometimes wonder. I've been able to keep my jealousy in check, because I know that you're not the type, but when people at work started to talk about you and Kelly, it made me think that maybe I was being naïve," Liz said.

"Who's talking at work?"

"Mitch is blabbering around the surgical suites. One of the nurses who is my friend told me today. It was all I could do not to run home and bury myself under the covers. It was humiliating. If I can't trust you, then I'm lost."

Liz said that Mitch had been whispering to people that Supermom had caught us together in the exercise room during the Halloween party. Apparently, the version of the story going around was that I was kissing her after she had flirted with me in her slinky cat costume. I told Liz that Kelly was the emotional type and that she was upset about her relationship with our trainer at the Workout Pit.

I wanted to go into kung-fu mode on Mitch, but I didn't want Liz to get any more heat in her program for my behavior. Besides, I don't know kung fu—and/or any other kind of fighting for matter. Other options included putting a laxative in his coffee prior to his having to perform a long surgery or putting hair-removal gel in his shampoo. "Do you want me to go upstairs right now and talk to him? I can tell him to knock it off and to apologize publically to you."

"That's sweet, but it wouldn't help," Liz said. "I'll ride it out, knowing that it's not true."

"Why should you suffer? Kelly and I are just friends," I said.

"You two do spend a lot of time together. It's a little weird."

"Can't a man and woman just be friends? Kelly is going through a lot with her divorce. Her friends are dropping her because of it. She's finding it hard to date again."

"You tell me that you're not romantic with her, but you two seem to fill a need that the other is missing. I know that I'm not around as much as I used to be, but don't you think that you're both relying on each other too much emotionally? Where does it go?" Liz said.

"It goes nowhere. Just like Wolfie and I are buds who talk about stuff. I can be friends with her just like that."

"Can you? Can she? I don't think that you two realize that you've become accidental emotional friends."

"What's an emotional friend?"

"All the benefits of being a couple, without the sex."

"Kelly and I are not a couple, or emotional friends, or whatever. Our relationship is mostly based on the fact that our kids play together well. It's a side benefit that we can have normal adult conversation rather than the banal ones I have with the moms around here, about potty training, snack time, and what kind of stroller I need to buy. Someday soon, I'm sure our kids won't play together, and I will barely see her." I needed Liz to believe me, because she was hurting, but I sure would miss having Kelly around when our kids outgrew each other. I think Liz was on to something with the "emotional friend" angle, but I was not stupid enough to admit it to her at that moment.

"Are you sure that she feels the same way? Maybe from her end, there is more."

"I doubt it. Look at me—I'm a recovering fat slob. You're the only one who could love this tub of lard."

"You said her ex-husband was not a looker either."

Did Kelly think our relationship was becoming more than friends? She had seemed distant the last couple of weeks since the Halloween party. She was not as available for playdates as she had been. Was she upset with me? My life was turning into a soap opera.

"Maybe I'll pull back a little on things. Less playdates and stuff. I don't want anybody, especially you, to misconstrue or think anything more exists than just circumstantial friends. You and the girls are my top priority. Nothing else matters."

"Now you're saying all the right things, but I still don't feel as connected to you as we used to be before we came to New York."

■ ■ ■

The next day, during my inquiry into the debacle that was Dom, I ran into Kelly on the street, not far from the gym. She greeted me with a polite hello, but the chill was still there. I told her about what had happened with Dom.

She shook her head. "He was a real scumbag charmer."

"How you are handling the whole thing?" I said.

"Now you care?"

That comment was the first time that Kelly had ever tried to send me on a guilt trip. "What's that supposed to mean?" We had never exchanged harsh words before.

"At the Halloween party, you kind of blew me off when I was upset."

"I did?"

"At first you were hesitant to talk to me, like you didn't want to get hung up with my problems. I practically had to drag you away just to speak to you alone. You convinced me to go out and have a little fun at a stupid horror movie, but then you're like, no, I gotta stay home, because you didn't want to get involved with my problems. And I still don't get that Wolfie friend of yours. He was very creepy, introducing himself to me and bringing me over to meet your wife. That was really awkward talking to her."

"I don't know what to say. Liz had a bad day, and I thought I should be home with her. The reason I didn't want to talk alone with you is because I was afraid that the gossipmongers in the family association would talk. And it turns out they did. Liz came home yesterday freaked out that you and I were having an affair. It turns out that this thing of ours is upsetting her."

"What thing?"

"Not a thing. I mean two adults, man and woman, being just friends. I'm not saying anything."

Kelly eyes fell to the pavement for a few moments before she spoke again. "I'm sorry. I've been at odds since Halloween. I'm a little edgy. Forget my little outburst. You're right. It didn't make sense to go to the movies that night."

"I'm sorry, too. I could have been more inclusive at the party. You did come out so our girls could play together, and everybody treated you like secondhand goods."

"That's nice of you to say."

Did we just argue and make up like a couple? I think Liz nailed it on the head. We were emotional friends. This was not a good situation.

She changed the subject. "Zoe and Tasha are getting excited for the twins' birthday party. Are you guys ready?"

"Almost, except there is one small problem," I said.

"What?" Kelly laughed, thinking I was going to make a joke.

"Dom stole all the money I had to pay for the food and entertainment."

"Are you serious? I didn't think you and Liz were that tight on money. I thought you did pretty well for yourself, being a techie in California."

"Most of the money was in stock options that are now worth less than a sweaty gym towel. I can't get a job unless I want to flip burgers."

"I feel terrible for you. This whole thing with Dom is my fault. I was the one who pushed for him to get fired. I was so angry with him, and I didn't want to have to look at him every time I worked out. He's not very stable. Let me loan you the money."

"I can't let you do that. I don't want to start borrowing money from friends. Now that I know for sure Dom is gone for good, I gotta come clean with Liz. I'm gonna just tell her. We'll just have to cancel the birthday party, or make it just a big playdate with a cake in the playroom. We don't need a juggling clown-dancer for entertainment, or balloons, or streamers, or to serve lunch to everybody," I said. Liz was really going to hit the roof when I told her we were barely making ends meet. At that moment, I realized that she might leave me at some point. She was not happy or fulfilled with me. And I knew her parents had never really liked me to begin with—so no support from that front.

"You can't cancel the party. You told me Liz was inviting people from work, including that guy who can help her with that practice she wants to join. If you cancel it now, not only will the status of her marriage continue to be hospital gossip, but she'll be identified as somebody who is so out of control that she can't even afford a birthday party for her kids," Kelly said. "Let me do this for you. Pay me back when you can, or not at all. Besides, it's Kirk's money anyway."

I was tired of letting Liz down. I needed a lifeline. "Thanks Kelly."

22

JUGGLING JOANIE

"Why did Santa Claus leave his suit here?" Maude said.

Maude and I were in the storage room on the top floor of our apartment building. She had been rummaging around in some of the holiday boxes, while I was collecting extra chairs for the twins' birthday party.

"Maybe he leaves extra suits in lots of places, just in case he gets his dirty on Christmas Eve," I said.

The better part of my morning had been spent setting up tables and chairs, blowing up balloons, and stringing streamers. The twins' birthday party would be starting soon. Liz had managed to trade shifts with somebody to get the day off. She worked with Claire on decorating the tables and organizing party favors. Right before the party, Eli's Market would deliver its famous deli platter. Everything was working out well, except that I didn't have enough cash to pay for everything. I hadn't seen Kelly since she had agreed to lend me the money that Dom had stolen.

Maude didn't accept my explanation for the Santa suit. "Why do he not bring more suits in his sleigh, Daddy?" She scratched her head.

It was time for her to know the truth. "I'm going to tell you a big-person secret."

Maude seemed delighted at the thought of being included in the world of adults.

"What I'm about to tell you might upset you, but I think you can handle it."

"What?"

"There is no Santa Claus. Mommy and Daddy are the ones who give out presents on Christmas Eve."

"That's not true. You telling stories again, Daddy."

"No, I'm serious."

"Daddy, you're not Santa Claus. And Mommy not Mrs. Claus. How can you give presents to all the kids if you don't have any reindeer?" Maude said.

"I'm not Santa Claus, honey. Big people make up Santa Claus, so that Christmas is more fun for little kids."

"No, they don't."

"Think about it. If there were a real Santa Claus, how could he go to everybody's house in one night and carefully set out gifts, decorate a tree, and eat all those cookies and milk that people leave out for him?" I said.

"He moves really really fast." She tussled her hair.

"Think about how long it takes to clean up all your toys. Just imagine doing that for everybody in the world in just one night," I said.

Maude didn't seem that upset. "Can I tell Claire?"

"Yes, but you can't tell any other little kids. It's up to their Mommy and Daddy to tell them about Santa Claus. Do you promise? I told you because you're four and a big kid now."

"I promise, Daddy."

The Santa suit Maude found was spotted with stains and smelled of closet mold. I pushed its box deeper into the back of the storage room, hoping no one would find it. I didn't want to be forced into playing Santa Claus at the holiday party just because I'm the fat guy. We could hire a Santa Claus for the holiday party next month.

As Maude and I finished arranging the chairs in the party room, Kelly arrived early to the party with Zoe and Tasha. Maude was excited at the sight of her friends. She called for Claire to come over and play with them. Kelly waved hello to Liz, who returned a weak smile from across the room. Liz and I were still working through the whole Kelly issue. While factually it was clear that nothing was going on between us, Liz still had reservations about Kelly. Her presence made Liz uncomfortable, and I had to respect that. I decided to find a way to distance myself from Kelly yet still retain the relationship that my girls had with her girls.

Out of earshot from Liz, Kelly said, "Let me give you that money now. Come to the elevator or something."

I told Liz that we were going to hang some streamers and balloons by the elevator. "I hate having to be so clandestine with Liz."

She handed me seven hundred dollars in mixed bills. It was more than what Dom had stolen, but I needed it. "Don't stress about paying me back too quickly. I really don't care."

I stuffed the bills in my pocket. "Thank you."

Behind us, the elevator door opened. Supermom had bumped into our entertainer in the lobby and had offered to bring her up to the party room. "You guys are just an inseparable pair." She turned toward the elevator for an introduction: "This is Juggling Joanie."

I did not appreciate Supermom's remark. I decided to say something to her about it, along with her part in spreading the hospital gossip. She clearly was the source, since it was she who had interrupted Kelly and me in the exercise room during the Halloween party.

I greeted Juggling Joanie with a handshake. She was freakishly tall and muscular. At first, I thought she might be a man in drag, but a quick inventory of her neck revealed that she did not have an Adam's apple. She had arrived without her clown makeup on. Juggling Joanie had long stringy red hair and seemed to be several decades older than her online pictures. Her website had claimed that she could do all sorts of fun things at birthday parties: juggle, dance, sing creepy kid songs, perform magic with puppets, do clown stuff, paint faces, dance with bubbles, and make balloon sculptures. For adults, she could kick it up a few notches and deliver singing telegrams, belly dance, dress as an elf or cupid, sing songs from the Broadway musical *Cats* in costume, and perform *Riverdance* as a one-woman show. I had chosen her because she had received mostly good reviews from children's websites, although one client review had accused her of falling asleep during one of her magic shows.

I asked Kelly to help Juggling Joanie find a place to set up, and I talked to Supermom. "I really don't appreciate your snide remarks suggesting that Kelly and I are anything else but friends."

"You're the one who is assuming my meaning," Supermom said. "I would never accuse you of infidelity."

"We both know that's not true," I said.

"I don't like your tone, your accusation, or the way in which you are conducting this conversation. You're creating a hostile and threatening environment. I will not be intimidated. This is where I live and raise my children, and I will not stand for it. I will report you to the building management if this conversation continues or if your hostile manner happens again." Supermom went straight for the nuclear arsenal.

I retreated a few steps back. "Mitch would be better served by sticking to medicine than by participating in water-cooler gossip. I will not accept your attempt to belittle my wife in her place of work. If you want to have this discussion in a more formal setting, I would welcome it. If you can't work with me in the family association, you are welcome to leave. The only hostile situations around here are the ones you have created."

Supermom pushed the elevator's call button. "I no longer feel I can attend your birthday party. You have insulted me."

"Your kids are still invited. I would prefer to let this be our last words on the topic," I said. There was no way that Mitch was going to allow Liz to host all the doctors from their surgical suite without him around. John Warner was coming, and he was the key to the practice that Mitch coveted. Supermom would have to swallow her pride and come, but I'd let her figure that out on her own.

■ ■ ■

The turnout for the party was very good, but that didn't really mean anything, considering that everybody in the family association was obligated to turn up at each other's parties. Additionally, I had dared once again to invite outsiders like Wolfie and his family and Kelly and her girls. Unless your kid was expelling orange bodily fluid and/or had a high fever, everyone in New York City went to birthday parties, because the weekends in the cement city could get really long. People always welcomed any form of cheap entertainment. Due to the constraints of the training in the medical profession, most of us really didn't have a big social calendar or the financial resources to fuel one, so parties between us were pretty much the only option. Claire and Maude had talked their friends into a frenzy over Juggling Joanie and all her many talents. Even though they had never seen her in person, their imaginations had created expectations of the ultimate performer. For two weeks prior to the party, the kids had demanded to see the goofy pictures from her website over and over again.

Minutes before the show started, Liz and I pulled all the party kids together into a semicircle. A rough head count pegged the number of kids at fifty, with a similar number of adults. Claire and Maude were beaming with excitement.

As expected, Supermom and Mitch came to the party. Mitch was easy to keep track of, because he was a satellite in the orbit of John Warner. Never more than five steps away, Mitch made sure that John Warner was having a good time and that he was well fed and hydrated. Several times, Liz checked in with her colleagues to make sure that everything was going well, but her efforts were muted by the interruption of Mitch with some stupid joke that only got polite laughs. Mitch would not let Liz get a word in, even at her own party. He was truly a schmuck.

After my interaction with Supermom earlier, I was prepared to let my grudge with Mitch rest. I felt that I had fired an effective warning shot over their collective bow. I was not going to take their nonsense anymore. I was hoping my intolerance to their wagging tongues about our marriage would slow Mitch's gossip-mongering going forward. Everybody knows that bullies move on when it becomes too much trouble for them to hassle you. I assumed Mitch would not risk having the hospital administration getting involved in our disagreements if it could potentially affect his career track.

I know Supermom and Mitch would never change their annoying ways in general. They were assholes via DNA, but so long as they left Liz alone, I didn't want to keep expending effort to be at war with them.

They could rag on me all they wanted in private. It was better to leave them alone in their narcissism and allow them to take center stage as the king and queen of the family association. When they were not feeling challenged, Supermom and Mitch could be friendly and gracious, as royal couples tend to do. Unfortunately, my wish to let my anger go would not come true. Either Mitch hadn't heard about my displeasure with his gossiping about Liz, or he failed to care, because I inadvertently overheard him tell John Warner right before the Juggling Joanie show that Liz wanted to go back to San Francisco. "The East Coast is not for them," he said, while chewing on a pita chip. "Liz's heart is in San Francisco, and her first choice is to go to a practice out in Mill Valley, California, not out to Long Island."

Mitch deserved a little payback, and I needed Juggling Joanie's help. I went to the exercise room that served as the backstage for the show. Juggling Joanie, now in clown makeup and a giant green afro wig, was doing her final warm-up stretches, while listening to the low-volume sounds of shrill Buddhist chants from her boom box. The title of her music choice could have been called "Stubbing Your Toe by Moonlight."

Juggling Joanie stopped when she saw me. I said, "I'm sorry I haven't gotten a chance to tell you how excited we are to have you. My girls are thrilled to have you perform. It's a big deal to them. They're turning four."

"That's so very nice of you," Juggling Joanie said. Her voice was very raspy. When I stood next to her, she towered over me. The white makeup on her face made her large eyes seem menacing, which caused such an unsettling contrast for a birthday clown. If I were to meet her in any other situation, say a dark, empty parking lot, I might think I were going to become a New York homicide case.

"A friend of mine is in the audience, and it turns out that it's also his birthday—the big three-oh. Now, my friend is a little bit of a prankster, and his wife wants me to do a little something extra for him. Can you make sure that you include him in the magic show, maybe embarrass him a little bit? Treat him like you would a future groom at a bachelor party. Please don't do anything too crazy, or anything that would be inappropriate for the kids or take away from the twins' big day."

"No problem," Juggling Joanie said. "During the magic show, I can have either the white rabbit or the pigeon take a shit on him. It goes over really big at the adult parties. Which one do you want to shit on him?"

"I leave it up to your artistic integrity."

"You all seem like a hoot. Do you want me to do a little trick on his wife too while I'm at it?" Juggling Joanie was showing good spirit. Do native New Yorkers say, "You all seem like a hoot"?

"Yes, but surprise me," I said, before describing both Supermom and Mitch to her.

■ ■ ■

The show started with loud thumping music, as Juggling Joanie did acrobatic tumbles across the floor. A bubble machine filled the performance space, and the kids cheered. Claire and Maude looked like they were in seventh heaven. Juggling Joanie finished her entrance by doing a handstand followed by a dramatic split, directly in front of the kids, all in synch with the music.

"When I was a kid, all we did was play pin the tail on the donkey, eat ice cream, and then kick everybody out of the house," I said.

Liz laughed. "This is great."

The magic show began, and, quickly, Mitch was included in the show—what a surprise. At first, he shook his head about being included in the performance. But Juggling Joanie apparently found a way to be persuasive, by wrapping a feathery scarf around his neck and slinking her grandmotherly body around him in a manner that was uncomfortable to watch at a kid's party.

"A little birdy told me that you're having a birthday party too," Juggling Joanie said.

"Not for a few months," Mitch said.

"That's not what your wife says." With an aggressive pull, Juggling Joanie brought him to center stage and put a giant floppy clown hat on his head.

Mitch glanced at Supermom with a look that said, "Did you put this lunatic up to this?"

Supermom shrugged.

"I need you to hold this flower, Mitch," Juggling Joan said. She motioned to Supermom to come forward. At first hesitant, Supermom succumbed to the encouragement of the crowd. "Since you have flowers, you must give them to a beautiful woman."

Mitch unenthusiastically handed Supermom the flowers. "That's not how you do it," Juggling Joanie said. "You've got to smell them first. It's all about the theatrical presentation, birthday boy." She squeezed her clown horn in a short, loud burst.

Mitch rolled his eyes. His fellow surgeons were enjoying the embarrassment of their otherwise-uptight colleague. He faintly pretended to smell the obviously plastic flowers.

"Try harder. Take a deep whiff, and then give it to your lady love." Juggling Joanie let go two quick bursts of her horn.

"Can we just finish this?" Mitch said. Everybody in the audience did a mock boo.

Somebody shouted, "Come on Mitch, play along, dude. Don't make a clown sad."

Rolling his eyes, Mitch leaned his nose forward and took a dramatic sniff of the flowers. Suddenly, a funnel of water shot out of the flowers and into his face. The clown horn went off again. Mitch dropped the flowers and walked off. "Ha. Ha. I'm done here."

"Wait. Wait," Juggling Joanie said. "You've got my hat." She made a big, wide cheesy clown grin.

Mitch stopped and took the hat off. "Here."

Everybody laughed at the sight of a pigeon sitting on his head.

"What do we have here?" Juggling Joanie said. "Boys and girls, he found my pigeon. I was looking for that."

Mitch froze. He rolled his eyes up to see the pigeon. "Can you take this thing off?"

With a clownish furl of her hands, Juggling Joanie said, "His name is Laxative, and, yes, we can take him off, but we don't want to frighten him. If we frighten Laxative, he'll make a poopy on your head."

The kids erupted with laughter at the use of the word "poopy." "This is the best show ever, Mommy and Daddy," Maude said.

"Now, I'm going to need everybody to be really, really, really quiet." She put a big, long, gloved finger to her lips.

Juggling Joanie put her arm around Supermom and brought her center stage, handing her a rubber hammer. "Laxative is trained to fly back into her cage at the sound of my magic whistle. But the whistle only works if somebody hits me on the head with this hammer."

Juggling Joanie, who was considerably taller than Supermom, got down on her knees and faced her. Before she placed the whistle in her mouth, she said, "I want everybody to count to three slowly, and then she will hit me on my noggin' with the hammer."

"Won't the whistle scare the bird?" Supermom murmured.

In a lower voice that only a few of us nearby could hear, Juggling Joanie said, "Laxative is used to the whistle. Only sudden moves and screams make her poop. Hurry up and get ready to hit me. Go with the flow, honey."

The kids whispered, "One. Two. Three."

Supermom swung the rubber hammer and hit Juggling Joanie on the head. Four things happened in sequential order: One, the whistle blew. Two, Juggling Joanie's glass eye tumbled out of her head. Three, Supermom screamed really loudly at the sight of the dropping eye. Four, Laxative took a dump on Mitch's head, portions of which spilled onto his nose.

Payback was more delicious than I had expected, though it was more intense than I had really wanted. Juggling Joanie later told me that she took pride in the ability to make her glass eye fly out. What would she have done to Supermom and Mitch if I hadn't warned her not to go too crazy? The reaction to the scene was mixed. Most of the kids were happily mesmerized by the spectacle of bird poop and Mitch cleaning himself with a fuzzy purple handkerchief. This was considered a good time for them. Only a couple of the kids had been freaked out by the glass eye falling out of the eye socket. Two or three kids seemed not to have noticed anything unusual; this stuff happens in cartoons all the time for them. All the adults were stunned, not sure whether to laugh, feel pity, or vomit.

Juggling Joanie, for her part, seemed unfazed. She rubbed her glass eye on her sleeve and pushed it back into her right eye socket—show time.

A few tumbles and a dozen magic tricks later, the kids were well back in the groove, and Juggling Joanie was in her element at center stage. The adults, on the other hand, were spiritually less malleable and chose to steer clear of the freak clown with the flying glass eyeball. They chose instead to graze at the buffet table, talking to one another. Fortunately, nobody blamed me for the weirdness of the performance—mostly because they assumed that Juggling Joanie was an unpredictable, self-contained bag of crazy. Who could have known? Mitch and Supermom pretty much kept to themselves for the rest of party.

At the buffet table, I managed to have an unexpected and productive chat with John Warner. My intention was only to make a turkey sandwich, not to chat up the influential top doc in Liz's surgical group. Liz wanted to have a little bonding time with him but didn't want to hover over him during the party. She played the balance well. I, for my part, jumped into a casual discussion with him while we each made a sandwich. We talked about stupid stuff. I don't recall how we stumbled onto the topic, maybe we had started out by talking about our favorite all-time movies, but it turned out he had loved reading the *Conan the Barbarian* series as a kid, just like me. I find it pretty funny when the pop culture choices of a person contradict the initial impression I had of him or her. I had taken Dr. John Warner for an opera and classical-music type. Maybe a little viewing of *Law and Order* on the side, when he felt like being a bad boy. Instead, he turned out to be a big sci-fi, fantasy geek.

"Did you ever read the *Conan* comics?" I said.

"Absolutely—I collected all the *Conan* comics," Dr. Warner said. "I think I had the first one ever published."

"A friend of mine is starting up a website that buys and sells comics. You should check it out and see if you can pick up some that you're missing."

"They're all gone now—my first wife threw them away about ten years ago."

"That's horrible. Is that why you divorced her?"

"Unfortunately, my first wife died from breast cancer," Dr. Warner said. He must have seen the look of embarrassment on my face so he added, "But I've heard of people divorcing for lesser reasons."

"I'm sorry. I can be a blabbermouth sometimes," I said.

"Mitch is a blabbermouth. You're not," he said, whispering.

I was embarrassed, but I genuinely liked this guy, and I appreciated his gracious candor. "This friend of mine with the comic book website thought he could give me a job programming, but his financial backers wanted to use in-house guys only, so no room for me. He felt terrible. We were roommates back in the day." Was I boring Dr. Warner with too much information? "Anyway, he gave me the first *Conan* issue as a consolation prize. I'd like to give it to you. I collect the *Conan* paperback books, but the comics never really did anything for me. I'm more of a fan of the *Aquaman* comics, but he didn't have any extra of those."

"That's very nice of you. But I couldn't accept it, because the first issue, I'm sure, is worth a lot of money," Dr. Warner said.

"Comics don't mean that much to me—enjoy. You can restart your collection with it." I winked.

"Too kind—let me give you something for it, since you and Liz are no doubt struggling to get by on fellow pay. I know what it's like to be on a tight budget."

I later accepted a check from him, and I used the money to pay back Kelly. The value he placed on it was more generous than I think I would have gotten had I tried to sell it at a comic-book store. A few hundred dollars were left, so I put it in the bank as a little cushion. Sometimes the ball breaks your way.

I had been monopolizing his attention for too long. "I should let you get back to having everybody kiss up to you. It was nice to meet you."

He laughed. "It was nice to meet you too, Nick. These parties tend to be very dry indeed. All anybody wants to talk about is medicine. The next time we do something social in the surgical group, I'll make sure that Liz drags you along." He shook my hand. "It's a shame that you and Liz are going back to San Francisco at the end of the year."

I went for being candid. He liked Conan, after all. "Mitch is spreading false rumors again. Liz is desperate to join some superstar practice out on Long Island, but she isn't one to blatantly kiss your ass twenty-four seven like Mitch. The only reason she would consider something else is if I told her we needed to go back to San Francisco so I can get a job. There are no jobs for me here."

"So you'll have to go back if you want a job," Dr. Warner said.

"Not necessarily," I said. "I'm doing the stay-at-home dad thing, and I'm kinda digging it. I was crappy at it for a while, but now I have my head above water. Maybe I'll try letting Liz do the breadwinner thing, and I'll be a househusband. New York does have some benefits, even though it's not San Francisco."

"Between you, me, and my sandwich, Mitch still has some growing up to do. He's a talented surgeon, but he's not much of a personality in the OR, or outside of it. Mitch's dad is a longtime friend and golfing partner of mine, so I have to throw him some bones every once in a while. But I'm glad Liz is open to staying around—she has got real talent." Dr. Warner patted my arm and melted into the crowd.

At the end of the party, while the kids were hurriedly unwrapping their gifts, Liz and I had a quiet moment sitting together without arguing for a change. I thought about Juggling Joanie's performance and wondered why she had never juggled at the party.

23

THANKSGIVING WITH AN EMOTIONAL FRIEND

"I don't think the turkey is done yet," my mother-in-law, Mimi, said. She'd been checking on the holiday bird every ten minutes, since she had arrived from the hotel. "What time did you put it in the oven?"

"I don't exactly remember, but the thermometer I impaled it with will tell us when it's done. I'm good, Mimi—thanks for checking in," I said.

Mimi's presence in my tiny galley kitchen was as welcome as a neck cramp. I'd been working in the kitchen since early morning, trying to pull together some semblance of a traditional holiday meal. Comments from anybody, particularly somebody who announced that she would not help with the making of dinner, were not appreciated.

"It takes about twenty minutes a pound. So how many pounds again?" True to her personality, Mimi felt compelled to state again the only fact she knew about cooking a turkey. She was as competent as an army cook, and yet she considered herself the reincarnation of Julia Child. Just because she watched cooking shows and ate a lot of food, did not make her an honorary Iron Chef. Every time she opened the oven door for her inspection of the bird, she blocked my access to both the dishwasher and refrigerator, as well as bumped me with her chunky caboose, while I was trying to peel ten pounds of potatoes. The kitchen had less floor space than an elevator.

"It's about twenty pounds," I said. "I know you keep saying that you just want to be a guest, but if you feel drawn to the kitchen, you can help me peeling these potatoes, while I work on the salad?"

"I have made my last Thanksgiving meal. It took a lot of therapy for me to be able to say that. It's up to my daughter now to do the cooking. I have spent my whole life working for others." Mimi could not accept the fact that the house duties fell upon me now. Liz was supposed to do it all. My mother-in-law also appeared to ignore the fact that I had replaced her as the primary caregiver to the kids.

Mimi was one of those formerly eager-to-please people who had entered therapy because they needed permission from others to make themselves happy but came out aggressive, self-absorbed, and still unhappy. As planned, my request for help at least succeeded in driving her from the kitchen. Presumably, she went to harass her husband, Henry Lynch, who was settled in front of our old, big-box TV, sucking on a beer and eating tortilla chips. He was a somewhat decent father-in-law, albeit rather opinionated. His personality was well summarized by his career choice: accounting.

Their son, Scotty, on break from law school, was next to him, discussing the nuances of the football game they were watching. For two people who seemed to possess at least half a brain between them, they spent an inordinate amount of time talking about sports.

I was thankful Scotty left me alone for the most part, as long as I didn't say anything contradicting his world view. He was a hard-case politico type, who believed in low taxes, small government, and American imperialism. He actually said out loud that he believed poverty is an active choice and that global warming is a myth. He once told me that he was considered a wide-eyed liberal at his law school. Either his law school was a breeding ground for *nosferatu*, or he was a liar. Either way, I considered Scotty a real tool. He was in his last year at school, and he studied corporate law with a vengeance. His most memorable quote was during his wedding toast to both me and Liz, because he was able to work in that he "wanted to be greedy rich someday." Mimi and Henry were very proud of Scotty.

I was committed to making the holiday a pleasant one for everybody, for the sake of Liz and the girls. Liz had been nervous all week in anticipation of trying to provide a good meal for her family, since her mother's self-emancipation from Thanksgiving duties. Her family had traveled from the West Coast just to be with us, forgoing the usual tradition of being with their extended family in California. Liz had to work the rest of the weekend, so we couldn't fly to them. We were quite surprised when they all accepted our halfhearted offer to come to New York. Christmas was the only holiday that Mimi still was willing to host. I had promised Liz that I would pick up the slack and take care of all the details. All she had to do was entertain her folks, once she got back from morning rounds at the hospital. She hadn't been able to get the whole day off, but we were hoping Thanksgiving morning rounds would be blissfully swift.

Soon after Mimi stopped bothering me, the doorbell rang. It was Wolfie and Dr. Emma, along with their kids. I had invited them for two reasons. First, Wolfie had originally invited me for Thanksgiving dinner at his house, since we were new to the city, and I had had to decline the invite after accepting, which is always embarrassing. Liz's family had decided to fly in at the last minute. Second, I needed him as a backup, should my cooking go sour on my maiden voyage as the holiday cook. Being friends with a professional chef had benefits. I was surprised how readily he had accepted the opportunity to eat my food. Guess everyone needs a break from his or her day job every once in a while. Liz's family knew Wolfie from our college days, and they liked him a lot, since he always brought with him sensational desserts. He was not a problem to invite, unlike Kelly and her kids.

The drama with Kelly had started two days before Thanksgiving. Just before the holiday, her ex-husband had left the country on business and reneged on taking the kids for Thanksgiving as planned. Kelly had scrambled to put together a new plan for the holiday, because she didn't want to substitute for Kirk and have to take the kids to his parents in Connecticut. A trip out to her parents in South Dakota was out of the question, because their relations were apparently strained at best. She called me and invited us to her apartment for Thanksgiving, after explaining all the details.

"Can't come; we're having a bunch of people over, including Liz's family," I said. "Why don't you come as well, and join the experiment?" I realized after I invited her that Liz was not going to be happy, but what could I do? I had spoken before thinking once again. On the upside, Maude and Claire would have fun playing with other kids on Thanksgiving.

"What experiment?" Kelly said.

"I'm doing an experiment on whether anybody gets sick on the food during my first holiday meal," I said.

■ ■ ■

Wolfie did a quick inspection of my kitchen. "Not bad. I would recommend you as a cook for an elementary school anytime."

"How does the turkey look?" I said.

"It's going to be a little dry. I think it is done. I'd start getting ready to put out all the sides."

"How can it be done? The thermometer is not even close to saying its done."

"You have it shoved in the wrong spot. I would pull it now," Wolfie said.

Mimi peeked her head around the corner. "It doesn't look done at all. It's twenty minutes a pound. At least an hour more, Wolfie."

"Good to see you, Mrs. Lynch—I mean Mimi." Wolfie gave her a peck on the check. "I wish I had you working at my restaurant." He walked her back into the living room. Before he left, Wolfie mouthed the words, "Pull the bird now."

I had miscalculated the timing. Liz had not arrived, nor Kelly and her family. But all the food was ready. I called Liz. "Hey babe. What's your timing?"

"I'm rushing like crazy, and almost done. Maybe ten minutes. Just have to peek in on two more patients. How's it going on your end?" Liz said.

"Wolfie just got here. Your mom is about as helpful as a mosquito bite, and your dad and Scotty are making sure the couch does not float away by itself."

"What about your new best friend, Kelly? Is she at least helping?"

"She's not here either."

"It figures. I'm sure she's waiting until the last minute to make her dramatic entrance."

I chose to let the comment slide. It is not a good idea to defend somebody whom your wife had once thought was having an affair with you. She was being as good a sport as anybody could expect, considering that she was not a fan of Kelly and that we were primarily hosting her family. The smart move was to lay low, and for once I did.

After I hung up the phone, I started to put out the dinner on the table, making sure to keep everything warm with tinfoil with the fear of serving a cold turkey dinner. I announced a five-minute warning, which was barely acknowledged, particularly by the couch zombies.

Dr. Emma appeared in the kitchen. She was a stick-figure-thin woman; her black hair was pulled tight in a bun. Dr. Emma was a zealot runner, a member of the ultramarathoner club. Next year she planned to run the Vermont 100 Endurance Run. She was sweet, but a little too much of a health freak for me. "How are you handling the stress of your first Thanksgiving?"

"I could use a free therapy session when this day is done. Do you have any openings next week?"

"You're too crazy for my practice; I'd have to admit you straight to Bellevue Hospital."

"I need help keeping Liz's family under control today. Time with Mimi is making a straitjacket and a rubber room seem idyllic."

"If things go bad, I'll prescribe a round of sedatives." She went to supervise all the kids, who had gathered in the twins' bedroom since there was very little remaining space to play in the living room. I could hear screams and giggles as they dumped bins of Lego pieces on the ground.

It was time to carve the turkey. Mimi appeared by my side, a witness to my inexperience with poultry surgery. She impatiently pointed at areas where both dark and light meat could be mined from the carcass.

"Do you want to show me how it's done? This is my first carving."

"No. You've got to learn, if you're going to be a housewife. Henry likes the white meat, and Scotty, the dark meat, so keep them on separate plates," Mimi said. "Save a leg for Scotty, and make sure there are lots of cranberries and gravy, because this looks dry. You overcooked it."

"I thought you said just minutes ago that I needed to cook the turkey longer," I said.

"Just cut the turkey and stop being a contrarian. No wonder you're having a hard time getting a job. Do you pick fights during job interviews as well?" Mimi said.

"Interviews are not my problem. It's just that nobody's hiring programmers," I said, for the fourteenth time that day.

"Those dot-com companies are all make-believe anyway. You should have studied something more sensible in school, like accounting. Right now you could be on your way to partner at Henry's firm," Mimi said.

"I make lots of math errors, so that would be a problem," I said.

Mimi pointed to more dark meat on the carcass. "You are quite the comedian, Nick, but comedy doesn't pay the bills. You've got to go out and make some money. Poor Liz is working herself to the bone."

I could hear Wolfie laughing at some presumably lame joke that Scotty was telling. I wished he had been close at hand to referee.

"Who would take care of the kids?" I said.

"You could get a nanny or daycare."

"That might work for some people, but I want family to raise our kids," I said. "That's why it was so great when you watched the kids while we were at work."

"That was hard on me. Too much work. I just want to be a part-time grandmother now," Mimi said. "I'm too old for little kids."

"Why didn't you tell us that you weren't enjoying yourself?"

"I didn't see it as choice at the time," Mimi said.

"I'm willing to have a little less money if I know my kids are better off. Every family has different needs," I said.

"Your generation is so spoiled. You worry too much about kids; you're too childcentric," Mimi said.

"I think my generation realizes that you have to have fun on the journey. How you grow up matters."

Mimi collected the last amount of meat and placed it on the tray. She covered it with tinfoil. "That's a load of crap, Nick. Suck it up and get a job."

Once all the holiday food was set out on a hodgepodge of old and borrowed tables in the living room, I announced to everyone that we were all set to go. "Liz should be here any minute, and then we can start. A friend of mine with her kids is coming at some point, but we don't have to wait for her."

The kids poured out of bedroom, and chaos ensued as negotiations began for where each of them was to sit. I let Dr. Emma handle them.

"Who's your friend?" Scotty actually diverted his attention away from the television set.

"Her name is Kelly, and her kids are good playmates of Claire and Maude," I said.

Wolfie chimed in. "She's a fabulous gal. I think she did some modeling, right, Nick?" Whose team was Wolfie on? And did Dr. Emma hear him use the offensive term "gal"? Wolfie lost three good-cheer points.

Henry made eye contact with his wife. "Is that the one who is the emotional friend?" All the Lynches had negative points already. By the time Liz came home, I had stopped keeping score for them.

"Yes, but don't make a big deal about it, Henry. There's nothing to talk about," Mimi said.

At that moment, I had an idea for a reality TV show called *Turkey Fights*. What if an army of cameramen went out and secretly videotaped a select bunch of contentious families bickering around the Thanksgiving table, opening up old grudges and starting new fights. It would be an instant ratings monster.

I said, "Henry, welcome to the new millennium, where a man and a woman can be just friends."

"Nick, you always have your head in the clouds," Henry said. "Let's sit down and eat. It's almost halftime, and it's a good time to break."

"I thought we would wait for Liz," I said.

"I'm eating. You said she would be here soon, so she can catch up," Henry said.

The Lynch family seated themselves around the table. Wolfie and Dr. Emma gave me the "should we sit" look. I nodded with resignation. I asked Scotty to turn off the TV.

Scotty did not move.

"Just put it on mute, dear, and trade seats with me, so that you can see the TV," Mimi said.

Five minutes into the meal, Liz came home. "Nick, why did you start without me?"

"The angry mob, led by your dad, needed to eat right away, because it was halftime," I said.

"I'm so disappointed," Liz said. "I rushed like crazy to be here."

Henry said, "Don't be silly. The food's not that good. I could shingle the roof with this dry turkey. It's the company that counts, Liz. Good to see you and the girls."

Dr. Emma said, "Liz, things were a little hectic. Nick tried to slow the mob." She got two points for that.

Liz gave a round of hugs to everybody. She hadn't had a chance to see her folks since they had arrived from the West Coast the night before. "Wolfie, maybe we should have taken you up on your offer to host my family, instead of doing it here," Liz said.

I said, "Attention all rude guests, the chef is sitting at the table. I think I deserve a little more than being told my food sucks. I had my arm elbow-deep in this bird before sunup."

"Nick showed real courage today for cooking this meal. He is going outside his circle of confidence," Dr. Emma said. Another two points.

Scotty sneered.

"I love your food, Daddy," Claire said from the kids' table. I wasn't sure if she had taken a single bite, but the moral support felt good. Claire got two points for the compliment and two for being just plain cute.

Wolfie came to my rescue as well. "Turkey is not the easiest thing to do well, especially doing it the first time. Nick should be commended. He has been my student the last few months. While I would never let him work in my kitchen, I give him an A for effort." He hoisted his glass of wine and drank. Later, he would replace my cheap table wine from the backwoods of Pennsylvania with something nicer that he had brought. Wolfie recouped his negative points.

"Mom should have cooked," Scotty said.

Maude and Alden started to flick mashed potatoes at each other. Wolfie was the closest adult. "No food fights, guys. You know better, Alden. Show Maude good table manners."

In a low voice that I could still hear, Alden said, "I can't eat these. They taste like Play-Doh."

"Just dump some gravy on it," Wolfie whispered.

Alden emptied the remaining gravy onto his potatoes. A swamp formed on his plate and nearly spilled off it. He lost four points for insulting the cook.

"Daddy, I want gravy now. Alden used it up," Maude said.

"Can you say the magic words?" I said.

"Abracadabra, I want gravy." Maude giggled. Cute and clever retort got three points.

Eventually, the Lynch mob softened up. The number of acerbic comments against me temporarily waned, as Liz brought everyone up to date on news from her fellowship. None of her family seemed overly eager to see her stay on the East Coast. But if she were lucky enough to get her dream job at the practice, they could understand her desire to stay. The Lynches were traditionalists who valued achievement over happiness.

Before both dessert and the effects of tryptophan started to kick in on the couch jockeys Henry and Scotty, the doorbell rang. It was Kelly and her kids. Her lateness for dinner was partially my fault, since the turkey had cooked faster than planned, making dinner a little earlier than I had told her. However, she still would have been late had dinner started on time.

"I'm so sorry we're late. Their father wanted to talk to them on the phone," Kelly said.

Everybody politely nodded, except Scotty. "Where is he? Isn't he coming too?"

"Their father and I are recently divorced," Kelly said.

A rare event occurred: Scotty looked embarrassed. "I'm sorry. Nobody told me."

Kelly smiled. "I brought some chocolate mousse that I made."

I made a round of introductions. Liz politely smiled.

Scotty actually got up from the couch and took the dessert from her. He must have been attracted to Kelly. In my next life, I want to come back as a model. "This dessert looks amazing. Nick, do we have any food left for your friend and her kids?"

"Of course," I said. "Sit down, and I'll put together some plates for you. Do you like white or dark meat?"

Zoe and Tasha slid into the seats reserved for them. Claire held out the chairs for them—my little Miss Manners.

"The girls and I all like dark meat," Kelly said.

"Me too," Scotty said as he sat at the table. Kelly looked at him oddly.

"You have really pretty hair," Carly said from the kids' table.

"Thank you," Kelly said. "I like your holiday dress. Purple is one of my favorite colors."

"My daddy says that you're one of the prettiest people he has ever seen in New York. I think he's right," Carly said.

Dr. Emma shot daggers at her husband. Wolfie would be sleeping on the couch tonight. In short order, Scotty decided to play reporter. "So how did you meet Nick? Was he changing diapers in the park or something?" He chuckled at his own joke.

"It's a funny story, but Nick's double stroller broke right in front of my building, and I sort of came to his rescue by giving him my old one," Kelly said. "Now, our girls are best friends, and I see him at the gym almost every day."

Kelly got minus five for bringing up the wrecked stroller.

"You never told us that the stroller we gave you broke," Mimi said. "I could have gotten my money back or gotten you a new stroller. Nick, that is so wasteful."

"I didn't think about it—sorry," I said.

To no one in particular, Mimi said, "Nick doesn't think about a lot."

I hadn't seen the Lynches in nearly half a year, and you would think there would have been some built-up goodwill. Guess not.

I looked at Liz to say something, but she gave me a "you're on your own" look. She was often spineless when it came to standing up to her family.

Asshole Scotty chimed in. He was a workout fiend. "Does Nick go to a gym? He'd rather hit a buffet than go to a gym; he's so lazy."

"Scotty, haven't you noticed that Nick has lost twenty-five pounds since coming to New York?" Kelly asked him. Five points.

"Can't tell—he always wears baggy clothes," Scotty said.

"Nick has been going to the gym five days a week," Kelly said.

"We got Nick that membership to the gym, with a big block of training sessions. We were worried that he would die on Liz from a heart attack and make her a widow," Mimi said. "Are you still seeing a trainer, Nick?"

"Nick hasn't been going to the gym as much lately," Liz said. "He has a lot going on."

I added, "My trainer was having some issues and canceled several appointments, so I have to find another person." I inadvertently looked at Kelly. She seemed to blush. I could tell everybody noticed our eye contact and assumed something was not being said.

"What kind of 'issues' could a trainer have? That's pretty unprofessional for him to cancel," Scotty said.

"It's complicated. Having a trainer is like being in a relationship. You just can't jump to somebody else. I was trying to stick with him. But he's since left the gym. So now I can't start up again," I said.

Scotty said, "Nick, I love you, man, but you are prone to drama. I would've ditched the guy if he wasn't showing up. Knowing you, I'm sure there's more to the story, but we'll give you a pass." Anybody who says "I love you, man" is really trying to say in a passive-aggressive way that you suck.

"Nick is my hero," Wolfie said. "He's dynamite with the kids and keeps the home fires burning for Liz. Not many guys are willing to take the plunge and be home full-time. It takes a bit of courage." Two points.

"Nick is very sweet with the girls," Kelly said.

"And he's the president of the family association," Liz said. "He's certainly a better cook thanks to Wolfie, though today's food is not a good example of it."

Henry apparently had been listening from his position in front of the TV. "He didn't choose anything. He lost his job and had nothing else better going on. He's a slacker. I didn't want to get into it today, but we can't keep helping you kids out with money. Nick has to take care of his family. Earn some money again."

"Nick is right where he belongs, Daddy," Liz said.

"What is that supposed to mean?" Henry said.

"It means Nick has stumbled into something that's good for him and the girls. Our new situation in New York has been hard on us. Right now, our money is tight, but that will change next year when I'm in private practice. If you don't want to give us any more money, I understand. You and mom have been more than generous, and I will pay you back for the money you've lent us," Liz said. Nice speech—three points.

Henry said, "We don't care about the money, Liz. We just don't want Nick to be dragging you down. He's always been a little bit of a good-time Charlie, but now that things are tougher and you might move away from San Francisco, your family can't support you as much emotionally. We're worried about you."

"Don't worry. Nick is an old shoe, and I love him. There's nobody else I want to share my life with, or have raise my children," Liz said. It had been a long time since Liz had said something nice about me. And I knew how much it took for her to stand up to her family for me. Or was she just saying this stuff in front of her family to keep up appearances?

"Nick has to take financial responsibility for his family. Why he is running about with Miss Barbie here, playing housewife, is beyond me. We want better for you, Liz," Henry said.

"I find that comment offensive, Mr. Lynch," Kelly said.

"Look, miss, I don't know you, but you shouldn't be hanging around with someone else's husband. The whole hospital is talking about you and Nick. I think you've caused enough trouble," Henry said. Liz shot her father a look that said "how dare you reveal my confidences in public." Looks like Henry had drunk a few too many beers.

Kelly looked at me, hurt. "I didn't know that was happening. The whole hospital is gossiping about it?"

"It's nothing. Forget it," I said to Kelly.

"It's a little more than nothing, but we're done with it. Aren't we, Daddy?" Liz said.

Henry now seemed to realize his impropriety. He looked between Mimi and Liz. "Liz, I'm sorry. I shouldn't have said anything. Not here. Not now."

"Thank you for acknowledging that, Daddy." Liz was always quick to forgive her father.

"I think we're beginning to heal now," Dr. Emma said.

"I think the therapy session is over, dear," Wolfie said.

"And you're still in the doghouse." Dr. Emma patted his leg.

Mimi softened. "I've changed my thinking. Just because Nick is not getting a paycheck, that doesn't mean he is not contributing. If Liz were the one home with the girls, we wouldn't have said any of this to her."

"Henry and Mimi, I need a hug," I said.

Henry threw a pillow cushion at me. "You're something special." He returned to watching the TV.

It was obvious that Kelly had been hurt by what Henry had said. I sensed that she was upset with me for not telling her that we were the subject of hospital gossip. The balance of the evening's conversation revolved around the kids and idle chitchat. No one spoke to Kelly. After the dinner was cleaned up, she said good-bye to me and Liz in a quiet manner. I felt awful. It was embarrassing to me to have a guest spoken to that way in my home. I should have said something to Henry in her defense, but I didn't want Liz to suffer any more loss of face over the situation either.

An hour later, Scotty noticed Kelly was missing. "Nick, did your hottie friend leave already?"

24

I ALWAYS WANTED TO HAVE DINNER AT TAVERN ON THE GREEN

Tara at *La Niña Abandonada Hambre* didn't have our name in her reservation book. The place was crowded with the preholiday crush of shoppers and tourists.

"Look again," I said, "Nick Owen, party of two. I know I made the reservation. I called like two days ago, and the woman on the phone, who might have been you, said that we were very lucky that somebody had just cancelled and that you could fit us in for tonight."

Liz pulled on my arm to go.

"I'm sorry, sir. Saturday is our busiest night of the week, and all requests are taken through our reservation department. I wonder if you've made a mistake. Maybe you called another restaurant?" Tara looked over my shoulder dismissively and smiled at the next guest. The restaurant was crowded and smelled of wet carpet and Bengay lotion.

"Let's bail," Liz said.

I held up my finger. "I remember having a whole discussion with somebody, and she told me that she could set us up in the Pancho Villa room, with a window view of Central Park."

Tara was clearly annoyed. "Sir, that is not true. Specific à la carte reservations for one of our vanity-themed rooms cannot be made within forty-five days of the requested day, and you just told me that you called the other day. I'm going to have to ask you to let me attend to another client."

"I really did call. I would like to speak to the manager!" I attempted my toughest guy pose—no luck.

"The manager is not available at the moment, but if you would like to wait over to the side, or in the bar and enjoy a glass of wine with your companion, then I will certainly let the manager know about your concerns." Tara had definitely not slept through the class on assertive customer-service tactics. My alpha-male routine had failed, and I had been told to cower in the corner.

"This is a special night for my wife and me."

"We like it to be a special night for everyone at La Niña Abandonada Hambre. I know you're excited to dine with us, but, unfortunately, I've had at least a dozen people tell me the same story, or something like it, all night. You're welcome to try another restaurant or our sister restaurant, *El Diablo Olvidadizos*. I wish we could accommodate you the way you had hoped. I'm so sorry. May I help whoever is next?"

I wanted to wait for the manager, but Liz would not have it. "Let's just go to Wolfie's place. I love his food, and he always has room for us. I don't really care about going to an overpriced restaurant with underwhelming food. This place is a tourist trap. Anybody with half a taste bud isn't eating here."

I had failed Liz again. I had been tricked by a pretty magazine ad, thinking the famous Pancho Villa room could spark some of our old romance, with its bandito charm. Who could resist being in a replica of Pancho Villa's rebel hideout, in the mountains of old Mexico?

"We haven't been out together without the kids since we came to New York. This place is famous. It's been in the movies. It hosted the MTV awards," I said.

"I know you're trying to do something different, but I don't really care if it was featured in an earthquake scene from *New York Armageddon*."

"My real first choice was Tavern on the Green, but I just found out it closed." It too had served as a film location, for *Ghostbusters.*

"I find that hard to believe. You didn't know it had closed? That's so unlike you. You usually know about all that shallow pop culture stuff. Even I, who has lived under the rock of medical training for the last decade, knew that Tavern on the Green was kaput."

"Even Einstein forgot stuff."

"You ain't no Einstein." The simmering hostility had not dissipated, despite things having improved between us over the last couple of weeks.

Outside the restaurant, across Central Park West, I spotted a horse carriage. It was lightly raining and not too cold. Thank God for global warming. I hate cold weather. "There's an empty one; how about doing a loop?"

Liz rolled her eyes. "I'm not a big fan of city carriage rides. The owners don't take care of the horses properly, and the pavement isn't good for the horses' hooves."

"Don't be a wet blanket. Once around the park, and then we'll go to Wolfie's place to eat."

"I feel like I'm being bullied."

"It's not like that," I said. Thinking back, I kinda was bullying her. I called Wolfie's place as we got into the carriage, and confirmed a spot for us. The hostess knew me well. Knowing that a good meal at a place she liked was forthcoming, Liz relaxed a little and got into the spirit.

The carriage driver was decked out in a faded nineteenth-century livery costume. He tipped his top hat as he closed the door behind us. "Be sure to pull the riding blanket up nice and tight, because, outside the cover of the trees, it's raining a bit. I've got the top up, but it won't protect your legs totally."

The blanket was made of thick, scratchy wool, and it reeked. One of the wooden carriage wheels was either warped or out of alignment, because we seemed to wobble as we moved forward. Not the enchanted ride I had expected. I whispered to Liz, "Are we having fun yet?"

We both giggled when Liz replied, "This blanket smells like horse piss."

The carriage driver offered to sell me a single rose for eight dollars, for "the beautiful goddess in my life." The rose was tiny and a little wilted. I declined, and we pulled the blanket over ourselves to hide our laughter from him. How many people buy an eight-dollar rose, just because of a line like that? I guess somebody does, since he keeps on asking.

When he started doing his faux version of the history of the park, telling us how "all the pretty women and stately men would come to picnic on the Great Lawn and listen to music on Sundays," we struggled to suppress our laughter. It felt good just to be stupid.

"Where can we find the Sheriff of Nottingham? Because I see Robin Hood in yonder dense wood," I said.

The carriage rolled past Wollman Rink. We caught views of people skating beneath the apartment towers of Central Park South. "We should bring the girls here and teach them to skate," Liz said.

"That'll be loads of fun. Claire crying she can't do it, and Maude making fun of her."

"I love skating."

"Since when, California girl?"

"Believe it or not, I had a life before you. I got lessons when I was about ten. Mom drove Scotty and me over to Santa Rosa."

"I see Scotty as more of an ATV kinda guy than a figure skater in tight spandex."

She laughed. "If he could drive an ATV on ice, he would be in heaven."

"Excuse me, sir," our driver said. "Would you mind if I made an emergency stop?"

"What does that mean?" I said.

The driver seemed embarrassed. "I ate something I shouldn't have from a food truck, and I think it's trying to fight its way out of me in a hurry."

"Can't it wait, dude? Aren't we almost done?" I said.

He wobbled his head quickly to indicate that time was running out.

"Of course," Liz said. "If you're in pain—we'll wait here."

"Thank you, madam. But I need for one of you to hold these while I'm away."

Reluctantly, I alit from the carriage and took the reins from him. The last time I had interacted with a large animal it had dragged me across a living room.

"Do any of you have any tissues?"

I rolled my eyes. Liz dug through her purse and pulled out a fistful of tissues. He disappeared into the wooded underbrush.

"What now?" I said. "Are we having fun, milady?"

The flash on Liz's iPhone went off. "I think this should be one of the pictures in our holiday card this year. Try another pose."

I bowed and swung my hand in a stately manner, à la Little Lord Fauntleroy. Liz laughed and took another picture, but the sweep of my hand jerked the reins. The horse moved forward.

"Horse, please stop," I shouted. But it still moved forward in a slow methodic step, taking Liz in the carriage.

"Pull back on the reins."

"I'm trying," I said, pulling hard. "But I think it just wants to go home, and it's not going to heed me."

"Off to the races." Liz giggled.

I shouted into the woods. "Mr. Driver, your horse is getting away. Can you hurry up?"

Liz had started filming this debacle on her iPhone. "Honey, I don't think this is a good time to be playing Steven Spielberg. I'm getting worried."

Liz said, "This ride is way more fun than I thought it would be. Quick, jump in the driver's seat. We're going to post this sucker on YouTube."

"Glad somebody's having fun." I pulled myself up into the slow-moving carriage.

I snapped the reins, trying to make the horse stop. Instead of stopping, the horse interpreted my action as a green light to move into a trot. "Help, Mr. Driver! Help, somebody, help!"

"Once around the park, James," Liz said. She settled back into her seat. "We'll stop at the end. It probably thinks you're the driver, since its wearing blinders. Turn around and smile."

I went with the flow, waved into the camera, and wished Claire and Maude well as I blew them a kiss.

It felt like the old times again with Liz. I had forgotten what a daredevil she could be.

As with most things, Liz was correct, and the horse stopped at the end of the lower loop. We waited a few minutes until the driver came running over a knoll that surrounded the park's nearby pond. He was out of breath and very apologetic.

"I'm so sorry. This has never happened before." I should hope not.

"Piece of advice," I said. "No more food trucks."

Despite my best effort at trying to convince him that we deserved a free ride, he shockingly would not budge. He shook his head and said that accidents happen, but that he should not be made to suffer. From my perspective, this was an untenable position, since I was the one who had suffered. He, at least, had gotten to relieve his bowels.

I then threatened to call the police, but Liz chose mercy. She whispered into my ear, "This guy is a crook, but the fifty bucks will make a difference in whether the horse gets to eat today."

■ ■ ■

We found a taxi to take us down to the Meatpacking District (not an easy feat in the rain). Usually, we would take the subway to save a little money, but it was a date night. Also, Liz had been moonlighting a bit at another hospital, so we had a little extra money this month. L'Usine de Nourriture was crowded. Wolfie and his team were hard at work in the center of the restaurant, where the kitchen was located. The open kitchen was surrounded by a large wraparound butcher-block counter.

When he saw us, Wolfie smiled. "You hurt my feelings wanting to go to La Niña Abandonada Hambre. I guess you didn't feel their love too much, huh? What a shitty name—The Hungry Waif. And their sister restaurant, the Forgetful Devil, is a raw vegan place that is marginally better than a supermarket salad bar. What were you thinking?"

"You're always telling me to go where you're loved the most," I said.

"You took long enough to realize it," Wolfie said. "I insist that dinner is on me. It's not often that you two crazy kids get out of your cage. Number one rule tonight is to not talk about either Claire or Maude." Wolfie grinned. "I'll leave you two to rekindle the dying embers of your marriage." He rejoined the blur of motion that was his kitchen staff.

"Are we dying embers, Liz?" I smiled.

"Let's not get into stuff tonight." Her response was an unexpected buzzkill.

"I thought we were getting better. I've been doing more, trying to remember all the things I'm supposed to do."

"I'm not your taskmaster. I'm your wife. You make your life seem like an unwelcome obligation."

I had fallen into the deep end of the relationship pool by surprise. I was treading water in the middle of a conversation, with no visible escape. No way to win. I had no idea what to say to make Liz happy. Should I joke my way out of it? I had been down that road and burned often enough to know that it would not be a smart move. Liz was being serious—relationship serious. I paused. No adequate response came to mind. I panicked, knowing that my silence could and would be used against me.

"I don't know what to say. I don't want to piss you off with a stupid response. I thought you wanted me to grow up and be more of a partner?"

"That's part of it."

Liz was not going to make things easy by giving me the answer to the test. What was missing? What didn't I understand?

"I want to think about us, and I want to get back to you and talk some more," I said.

I was glad that I had been watching Dr. Phil of late.

She nodded, which I inferred to mean "smart boy."

25

UNDER THE MISTLETOE

I had an opportunity to kiss Supermom under the mistletoe.

The holiday Christmas party almost got ruined, because the Santa that I had hired failed to show. On the phone, I asked the actor why he hadn't shown up yet. "The party starts in about twenty minutes. Where are you?"

"You guys called me and cancelled a few hours ago," he said.

"Who called you? Did they give you a name?"

"Lisa Fratelli. She told me there was water damage or something in your party room, and you had to cancel."

"I was the one who hired you. Why would you listen to somebody else?"

"She had all the details. I don't wanna get involved. The company is going to give you a bill anyway for canceling on short notice," he said.

"We're not going to pay if you don't come," I said.

"I don't care what you do with the bill. I gotta go to another gig that was just booked at the last minute." He hung up.

I didn't need three guesses to know who the saboteur was. I had never heard of a person named Lisa Fratelli. It was almost laughable that Supermom would stoop to a level where she felt that she had to undermine the things I did. Had I done anything that bad to merit having an archrival? The situation with Supermom was turning into a really bad cable movie. Who actually does things like that? How could someone really think it worth his or her while to do something so juvenile?

I remembered when Maude had found that old Santa Claus costume. It looked like hiding the costume back then hadn't save me from having to wear it after all. It was too late to find somebody else to play the role.

When I arrived at the storage room, located on the top floor of our building, I failed to notice that Mitch and Supermom were talking in the exercise room. It was only after I located the worn Santa suit again that the shouting pierced my consciousness. They were in a heated argument, or, rather, Mitch was venting and Supermom was meekly responding. I reflexively froze, not wanting to make my presence known, before I passed by the open door. A few months ago, it had been Kelly and I in the exercise room, having a discussion, and Supermom had caught us. Did the exercise room possess some crazy mojo that drew people there to have private meetings?

It was obvious that Mitch had hit the eggnog a little early. His arms were wildly animated, and his cheeks were flushed. "The school told me that you didn't send in the paper work on time."

"Not true. I mailed the application weeks in advance. They're just not telling you the truth," Supermom said.

"Why would they lie?"

"I could tell from his interview that the admissions director didn't want our son at their school. Mitch Jr. was unfocused and couldn't sit still. He's not a match with that uptight, stuffy school. If you don't fit the mold at a private school, they don't want you. They just told you that we missed the application deadline so they can keep their rejection simple and clean," Supermom said.

"Why wouldn't they want Mitch Jr.? My father went there. I went there. My family has given them plenty of donations over the years, attending all their stupid fundraisers."

"Mitch Jr. is not as smart as we had hoped, and he's a little hyperactive. I don't think that school would have been a good place for him. We'll find someplace else that's better for him."

Mitch didn't like that idea. "Don't try and feed me that touchy-feely crap, that he has attention deficit disorder. The boy needs discipline. You're too easy on him, always have been—too much coddling. The Higgins School is a gateway to better things. I'll not accept this result."

"You're going to have to. Tomorrow I'll start looking at other schools for him," Supermom said.

"No! I want you to get your ass down to the Higgins School and make this right. Do whatever you have to do to fix it. All you have to do is take care of the kids. You don't work. What do you do all day? You're spending way too much time doing nonsense stuff for the family association, and you aren't even the president anymore. You lost to that flake asshole, Nick Owen. I depended on you to get our son into the Higgins School, and you blew it," Mitch said.

"We should find a place which is good for Mitch Jr. If we force him into Higgins, we're only going to revisit these issues later, when it truly is too late."

"You wanted to stay home with the kids and not work, and I let you. Should I consider getting a nanny to replace you? Right now, with the game on the line, you're blowing it. Mitch Jr. needs to be in that school. I'm not going to tell my father that my son is breaking the legacy. Are you going to tell your parents that their first grandchild has ADD and can only get into a retard school?"

I expected the Supermom that I knew to push back and confront him. He was out of control, and, in my opinion, a borderline psychopath. Instead, as if this dysfunctional drama had already been played through on many other occasions with the same result, Supermom nodded. "I'll go tomorrow to Higgins, and beg if I have to."

Mitch appeared satisfied. "This day has been a train wreck. First, I hear that the incompetent Liz Owen got my job out on Long Island, and then I get a call about this Higgins bullshit." After a pause, he said, "I'm going to get that practice to reconsider their decision to hire her. John Warner is going to put another call into them on my behalf. Bad stuff like this just does not happen to people like us."

There was no mistake. John Warner had told Liz that he had given a confidential recommendation on her behalf for the position. Mitch found himself out in the cold on this one. He eventually found another lucrative surgical practice in Manhattan, and he probably considers himself to have a wonderful life, if you define a wonderful life as having a lot of possessions and a family that fears you. Eventually, Mitch Jr. did get into the Higgins School. At what cost, I never did find out.

Mitch said a few other gratuitously nasty things to Supermom before stomping off though a door on the other side of the room. She didn't cry as I would have expected. Instead, she took a deep breath and left a minute or so after Mitch, by the door nearest to me and the party room. Behind her on the floor was a sprig of mistletoe. My guess was that she had been looking to playfully give Mitch a kiss after his workout. Instead, she had been confronted with his angry outburst. There was no way that she didn't notice me as she passed by the storage room. Supermom said nothing and did not make eye contact with me.

■ ■ ■

As one would expect, being in a Santa Claus suit is not a lot of fun. It's hot, the fabric doesn't breathe, and the costume wig and beard make your face itch. Kelly helped me put on the Santa suit. She had come looking for me near the party room and had found me struggling in the exercise room with the costume and its fat padding. She had brought her kids to the Christmas party. Things had been different between us since Thanksgiving. She was less ebullient, less forthcoming with her usual charm, and less confiding of her insecurities. We hadn't really talked about what my father-in-law had said about her. What could I say about it? Kelly's role in my life now seemed more like a habit—we were just used to hanging out with each other during the day. It was a little weird to continue things as they were.

"I thought you hired a Santa," Kelly said.

"I did, but he bailed, so now I get to be good ol' St. Nick." I told her about my suspicion that Supermom had canceled the Santa actor. The acrimony between Supermom and I had gotten out of hand.

"You're too sweet a man. Not many guys would put up with all the crap you do," Kelly said.

"What do you mean?" I said.

"Everybody hassles you one way or another, because you decided to stay home with the kids."

"You're exaggerating."

"Am I? Why are you in a Santa suit right now? Why are your in-laws not as nice as they should be to you? Why is Liz always a little bit angry with you? You're a sweet guy, and nobody seems to be getting it. You've become a better husband and father than most guys—believe me."

"Not so sure about the better husband part, but I'm working on it." I still hadn't gotten back to Liz about the heavy relationship stuff we had talked about a week earlier.

"Liz doesn't appreciate you." While that was nice to hear, it was not entirely true. I didn't want to get into the fact that I was suffering from Peter Pan syndrome.

We finished putting the big red suit on me, complete with stuffing in the belly. I grabbed the satchel of candy canes that I had bought (to give to the actor to hand out). "Do you want to tell them that Santa is ready? Maybe have somebody introduce me?"

"You look adorable, St. Nick," Kelly said. She bent down to pick up the mistletoe sprig that Supermom had left behind.

"We should hang that up. The kids might get a kick out of giving each other kisses," I said.

"I bet some of the adults would get a kick out of it as well." She gave me the same look that awkward teens possess at the end of a first date, when saying good-bye.

Kelly approached and touched my shoulder with her left hand, while holding the mistletoe above her head with her right. "How about a little Christmas cheer?"

At that close of a distance, I could smell the wonderful, faint scent of her lavender body spray. She was the prettiest woman who had ever wanted to kiss me. Kelly was a powerful temptation, like a plate of chocolate mousse or a bag of Cheetos. But Liz and the girls were my *raison d'etre*. That is a fancy French word that Liz had whispered in my ear once, a very long time ago, when we were undergraduates in college. It means "reason for being."

"I don't think practicing some old pagan custom of kissing under the mistletoe is going to do wonders for my marriage. I think you've misconstrued the friction between me and Liz as something more than just a speed bump in our marriage. Liz is my wife, and love."

"I know the reality, but sometimes it's fun to pretend, even if just for a moment," Kelly said.

"I'm not even your type—not even close. You're drawn to the bully types."

She laughed. "You're a marshmallow, and I wanted to kiss you just once. I know things wouldn't last between us—sometimes it's fun to have fun."

"Let's forget about this and just go back to being buddies," I said. But I knew that this emotional-friend dynamic had run its course. I should be emotionally connected with Liz, not with somebody I had met by accident on the street corner one afternoon.

She wrinkled her nose. "It's too weird. I'm joining another gym. I don't know that we'll see each other much anymore, Nicky," Kelly said. She handed the mistletoe to me.

"You don't have go to another gym. Our kids have so much fun together. We can be adults and forget this crazy notion of being emotional friends. Let's just hang like dudes." It was a weak argument I was making.

Kelly paused before she spoke. "Absolutely—let's give it a try."

After the Christmas party, Kelly did join another gym, and I really didn't see her that much, except chance encounters in the park from time to time. Our infrequent conversations were polite but never the same. I stopped inviting her to family association parties. Eventually, when Liz completed her fellowship and we moved out of the city, Kelly became one of those numerous locational friends that one makes, connects with, and then drifts away from, as soon as the circumstantial link between you ceases to exist. I sometimes wonder what it would have been like to kiss her, but I certainly have no regrets that I didn't.

■ ■ ■

"Daddy, is that you?" Claire said. She pulled at my fake white beard and removed the Santa hat from my head. She promptly placed it onto her head and giggled. It was her turn to sit on Santa's lap during the Christmas party. We had all gathered in the main playroom downstairs in our building.

I whispered, "Don't tell anybody it's me. All the other little kids think I'm the real deal."

"Can you give my wish list to Santa?" Claire said.

"Did Maude tell you anything about Santa?"

"Maude told everything." She scratched her head vigorously with both hands.

"What did she say?" I took the Santa hat back and pulled it over my chrome-dome head.

"She said that Santa can't go everywhere in one night, so he needs big people like you to help out."

"So you think I'm helping out Santa today?"

"Yes. Can you tell Santa I need a big dollhouse?" She kissed my cheek and slid off my lap.

"I'll pass it along to him, sweetheart."

The next child to come into my lap was Sofia, daughter of Nifty-Fifty Wife. Nifty-Fifty Wife winked at me. "Tell Santa what you would like to get this year."

Sofia did not react well to me. She pulled away from her mother and cried loudly. The sight of a strange man in a big red suit freaked her out— smart kid. I put the Santa hat on her head, hoping it would amuse her like it had Claire. She threw it to the floor.

"No worries, Sofia. You can have your Mommy help you write a let- ter, telling St. Nick what you want for Christmas," I said. "Here's a candy cane."

Nifty-Fifty Wife said, "I'm so full of embarrassment. Sofia no act this way in the most public of places."

"You shouldn't be embarrassed about anything ever. She's a great kid."

"Thank you. You are very generous. Your words are kind."

"Any more problems with mice?"

"I don't know what you said to the building people, but no more mice, gracias," Nifty-Fifty Wife said. She removed the hat from the floor, and handed it to me.

Good Heart's daughter had a very long list of things that she wanted from Santa. "I will need extra reindeer to help me pull the sleigh Christmas Eve, Sammie."

"We live in a big building, Santa. You can park the reindeers on the roof," she said.

"Will you leave out some extra cookies for the reindeer?" I said.

"Mommy says that too many sweets are bad for you. Do they like carrots?" Sammie said.

"Reindeer need sugar to fly. Tell your Mommy that organic food is not very healthy for magical creatures."

Sammie nodded. Good Heart overheard me and rolled her eyes.

Mitch Jr. just wanted a bike. He was subdued. "What's wrong?"

"Santa, Daddy is very mad at me. I don't think I deserve toys this year."

"Why is he angry?" I said.

"Because the man at the school didn't like me."

Supermom interrupted. "That's not true, Mitch Jr. The man was having a bad day. Mommy will make everything better tomorrow. Don't be sad for Santa." She asked him to smile for the camera.

I said, "The only thing wrong that you can do is to not be true to yourself. Go have fun, and don't let the adults bring you down."

Mitch Jr. gave me a queer look before he grabbed a fistful of candy canes from my satchel and slid off my lap. I was going to tell him one candy cane per kid but thought better of it.

Supermom said, "Should we call you Buddha-Santa now? Don't fill his head with all your California-dreaming nonsense."

So much for feeling sorry for her about her dysfunctional marital relations. Mitch and Supermom were the opposite of the sitcom couple Mike and Carol Brady. If they had their own TV show, it would be called *State of Denial: A Love Story*. I didn't understand them and had now reached the point where it didn't matter much to me if I did. I realized it was time for

me to disconnect from her negative energy. Let the shark be the shark—
it was time for me to get out of the water and enjoy life on the beach. I
had reached the end of my patience with the drama I was having with
Supermom.

Lion Tamer's pack of kids was running loose and causing their usual
level of mayhem. None of them came to ask Santa for anything. Her older
twins pulled off the tree ornaments and threw them at younger kids. Most
of the adults clucked at them and shot stern looks at Lion Tamer. She
seemed not to notice their dismay and remained in the corner of the playroom, talking to a few of her international friends in the family association.

I asked her twins, David and Saul, to please stop destroying the place.

"We don't believe in Santa Claus," Saul said.

"Neither do I—but it can't be right to ruin everyone else's day by dis-
respecting their holiday tree," I said.

"We're only playing a game," Saul said.

"Do you think the monster in your closet would approve?"

Saul seemed amused.

"Does this mean you'll stop?" I said.

Without a word to me, they picked up a few of the thrown ornaments
and sloppily put them back on the tree. Lion Tamer's twins really understood her dark sense of humor.

■ ■ ■

After playing Santa, I came down from my snow-dusted candy cane throne.
I ripped off the white beard and red jacket, including the fat stuffing. I was
sweating, and I grabbed a water bottle to guzzle. It felt good to end the first
part of my presidency, and the calendar year, on a good note. Everybody
seemed to be having fun. The party was a hit. It was worth all the hard
work I had put in to organize the activities and games. Oddly, Supermom
had done very little to help, not even injecting acerbic comments about my
ideas for party preparations. Other people had noted her lack of involvement to me. I came to believe that she wanted the holiday party to fail in
order to make me look incompetent to the family association.

Supermom was working the room, flashing smiles, laughing, and creating the impression that she was the one responsible for the holiday cheer. My annoyance turned to pity for her—and then did a left turn and became a sophomoric wish just to mess with her as often as I could. I was done with the meager hope that she would somehow come to accept me. After all, I needed to follow Wolfie's wisdom, which was to only spend time with the people who are happy to be with you.

I announced that I had something to say. I called Supermom to stand with me by the playroom pirate ship, which served as an indoor jungle gym. By odd chance, we were standing under a sprig of mistletoe, which dangled from a string. The adults turned to face us, our children still loudly playing in the background, oblivious to their parents. Mitch was not around; he was probably sulking back up in his apartment after his workout, sipping on beer and watching sports.

"I quit." Sometimes it's nice to skip the boring, polite preamble, in which everybody is individually thanked and appreciated, blah, blah, blah. "I ran for president of the family association, because I wanted to change things up. And because of all of you, things are better now. Everybody's kicking around ideas, and the kids are having more fun than ever. There's no turning back now."

Supermom's eyes had begun to gleam as soon as she had heard the words "I quit" from my lips. She nodded her head to the crowd, waiting for me to finish announcing the end of the Nick Owen family association administration. I knew she was salivating to enter the power vacuum and reinsert herself back into the presidency. No doubt she was already crafting the words she was about say in that big Harvard brain of hers.

It was time to wrap it up. Time for me to do the Lucy trick, pulling the football as Charlie Brown prepares to kick it.

"I'm quitting, not as president, but as the person who dresses up in costumes for the holiday parties. I'm nominating my vice president to be the lead organizer of the spring festival, and the one who dresses up as the Easter Bunny. I think she would do an amazing job. I don't think I would look as good in big, fluffy ears. And, my butt is too big for a button tail."

No one seemed to care. There was silence, followed by silence—until, of course, Supermom was the first to speak. Her suppressed anger blocked her diplomacy software. "I'm not surprised that you're quitting, and leaving our biggest fundraiser in disarray. I always knew that you were a slacker."

Lion Tamer shouted, "Do your job as vice president. Just lead the spring party; you did very little for this one. Nick made this place a home for me and my family. You only push out rules and rules, little Miss Perfect."

Lion Tamer raised her hand in a fist. I hoped a riot would not break out. But the response from everybody was muted, except from her twins David and Saul who seemed agitated that their mother was upset. I guess most people were used to not really understanding what Lion Tamer was talking about half the time anyway. And, as to Supermom's comment, the family association was already used to Supermom publically ragging on me—it didn't even register as out of the ordinary.

I continued, not addressing Supermom's recent comment. "On another piece of business, I think we should disband the Child Development Committee (CDC) that has been so wonderfully led by our former president, since it has met its goals to the fullest. Instead, I think that committee should take direct control and responsibility for the deep cleaning of the playroom and for its repainting, since the hospital management has said that it would be only responsible for cleaning the kitchen, bathroom, and carpet. I, like you, am very worried about the hygiene of our toys, especially going into the flu season."

That seemed to get everyone's attention. Everybody nodded approval. Some people clapped. For obvious reasons, the medical community is germophobic, especially for their kids. I figured everybody knew that I was the one for a good time and that Supermom was the one diligent enough to literally take care of the dirty stuff. Happy scrubbing, Supermom. Have fun painting.

The best of leaders delegate, and I had a few more projects in mind for Supermom.

A rare thing happened. Stammering, Supermom said, "I'm flattered that everyone believes I can tackle the cleaning job, but it's really the responsibility of the hospital."

Supermom was drowned out by cheers for her to get it done quickly. A few people jeered that the hospital was useless for this kind of stuff and that we had to take it upon ourselves to keep the place clean for our kids. Checkmate.

"Don't be modest," I said. "Let's give her three cheers. Thanks for doing the heavy lifting."

After the cheering subsided and Supermom was silenced, Nifty-Fifty Wife jumped into the mix, despite her husband narrowing his eyes to her. "As well, three cheers for Nick. I think he is like one of the moms."

I remembered Kelly saying the same thing to me on the subway ride back from Coney Island, but this time I kind of liked the sound of it. It no longer felt like an insult to my masculinity. "Does this mean I finally get invited to girls' nights and all the wine-and-cheese parties?" I said.

Good Heart said, "You are definitely welcome to any playdate with me, anytime."

Sporadic clapping flowed through the crowd. "The girls and I are up for a playdate anytime, anywhere, with anybody—just call. Thank you." I pulled the Santa hat off my head and placed it on Supermom's head

Good Heart's husband, Daniel, chimed in. "You kids should kiss under the mistletoe and make up." Chuckles scattered across the party.

I looked up at the mistletoe. "No more adult punch for you; that's an executive order."

"I'd rather kiss a leper," Supermom said. Hooting rang out, and the party continued.

As Supermom turned from me to leave, I said, "I think we should kick Lisa Fratelli out of the family association."

"Who?" Supermom said.

"Didn't Lisa Fratelli cancel the Santa actor?"

"Who is Lisa Fratelli?" Supermom said.

"I know you were the one who canceled the Santa actor, giving the fake name Lisa Fratelli."

"Do you really think I would do something like that and ruin the party for the kids?" Supermom said.

She took the Santa hat from her head and gave it to Mitch Jr., who was begging to wear it.

I didn't answer. Had the Santa actor lied to me so that he could get more money going to another gig at the last moment? Or was Supermom just that good at being a liar. I never found out.

Supermom walked away, shaking her head.

Liz now stood next to me. She kissed me on the cheek. "You're a mess."

After two other chances under the mistletoe, I had finally gotten a kiss from somebody I loved.

"Let's have another date? Maybe a Broadway show?"

"I'd like that, but only if you go and stand in line and get twofers. I haven't started my new job yet."

Mitch Jr. was the first child to realize that I was at the party still half dressed as Santa. He looked up at me. "You're not Santa. Where's Santa?"

"Please don't tell anybody, Mitch Jr.," I said. "Let me just get out of my costume before anybody finds out."

Mitch Jr. started to cry. "How could you be Santa? Why is Santa living in my building? Where do the elves live?" He called for Supermom.

David and Saul were drawn to the commotion. They held fistfuls of mini chocolate cupcakes. Their faces were smeared with icing. "News flash, Mitch Jr.—there's no Santa Claus." They started laughing.

Word spread quickly among the little kids that something was amiss. Was Santa not real? The whole room became aware that I wasn't in character anymore. Many of the adults laughed it off as yet another goofy thing that I had messed up. The parents of the young kids found ways to distract their children from the unfolding scene. "Santa is real, honey. Mr. Owen is just helping out today."

Supermom scooped up her crying son. She pointed a finger at me. "You're a very bad person. Why would you ruin Christmas?"

I was at a loss for words.

Suddenly, David and Saul together yelled, "Food fight."

Instinctively, I pulled Liz down to the floor with me as the mini chocolate cupcakes, which had been aimed for me, hit Supermom instead.

It took about four hours to clean up the mess that ensued. For most of the people, and all of the kids, it was their first food fight.

26

HONK IF YOU LIKE LICE

In the fourteenth century, the bubonic plague killed a third of Europe, disrupted kingdoms, and caused war, crime, and general mayhem. It was spread by the bite of fleas that traveled about on the backs of rats. The family association had its own plague. No one died, but the lice infestation felt medieval. The initial carrier of the lice was a big, floppy red Santa Claus hat.

Almost immediately, everyone knew that the hat was the root cause. Supermom made it clear that she contracted lice when I quit wanting to be the Easter Bunny and placed the hat on her head. Among the kids, the chain of infection was easy to follow, even though we could not deduce who patient zero had been. Claire was the first publicly known case—and the first to have the treatments done to remove the bugs. She gave lice to Maude, Sofia, and Mitch Jr., who gave it to the whole gang of kids they played with every day in the playroom. The kids spread it among the adults, at least those adults with an appreciable amount of hair. Lice love the warmth of the scalp. They nest among thick hair follicles, sucking blood. I was spared, never so glad that I had lost my locks prematurely.

As no surprise, Lion Tamer emerged as a leader, to help teach us how to remove the lice effectively. She had the resolve to handle most anything—she had served her mandatory time in the Israeli military. My time in the Cub Scouts tying pretty knots didn't count for much. We bathed the victims' heads in olive oil, waited, applied a mixture of baking soda and conditioner, and then we picked out the nits with a metal comb. We gathered in groups, akin to a barbershop, and applied the treatments once a day. It was good bonding time; no one of importance to me held a grudge about the Santa hat. Missing from our circle was Supermom. She chose to hire a professional nitpicker, who came to her apartment for her kids and herself. Part of the collateral benefit of the lice was that I never again spoke to Mitch Sr. or received future holiday cards.

Lion Tamer advised that we give crew cuts to the boys and set them loose. For the woman and girls, she developed a daily combing regiment, which divided the head into regions, which were to be combed in four directions. We named the comb strokes: shaggy dog, slicked back, lefty louse, and righteous reach. We spread a tarp out in the playroom to capture the sprays of the concoction that we lathered into hair. It took hours each day to comb the nits, and the kids just cried and wailed, as we tugged at their hair. As for the adults, I was responsible to comb out the nits for Good Heart, Nifty-Fifty Wife, and Lion Tamer. None of their husbands wanted to be involved in such drudgery.

Claire and Maude were troopers about the lice. They sat somewhat calmly for every treatment, even the ones in which I bungled the use of the metal lice comb and accidently tore out chucks of their hair. Perhaps they thought I might give them crew cuts, if I got too frustrated. I really regretted that night when I had cut their hair—bad parent move. Fighting with lice was all consuming for the better part of ten days, the length of the louse's life cycle, but at least it forced me to wash all the sheets and towels on a timely basis, and to clean our apartment.

I grew to respect the enemy. Lice are quite good at what they do, which is to suck blood. They can't jump or fly, but they are stealthy, keeping a low profile as they walk between adjacent heads. Flies and bees have it all wrong. They come swirling through the air, buzzing an announcement of their approach. You have plenty of warning before snapping at them with a swatter. Lice are millimeter small. When you rummage for them, they scamper back into the deep hair, behind the ears and neck. A louse is the ninja of the insect kingdom.

Lice play the numbers game. They lay up to eight eggs a day before dying in a month. The offspring hatch in about a week or so, and they repeat the cycle. So if the lice are around for just a few weeks, you are way behind, before the symptoms of an itchy head really make you notice. Miss one egg, and you are back to the races all over again. Fighting lice effectively requires discipline, patience, and a whole lot of time for nit picking. Lion Tamer grabbed the metal nit comb from my hand during one of our group nit-picking sessions. "You're not bringing the comb close enough to the scalp. This is where the eggs live." She nudged me aside and showed me the proper way.

I took the comb back and brought it down firmly into Good Heart's hair, parallel to the scalp.

Good Heart yelled and took a swipe at me with her arm. I guess even Good Heart had limits on amiability. "You're drawing blood. What's the matter with you?"

I logged my hundredth apology for the day. "We're almost done. I've only found six nits so far."

Our kids were all done. They played in the far corner of the playroom, doing their best to avoid capturing the attention of any parents. They were spent from the lice ablutions.

"And I think you've taken out about ten times as many hairs," Good Heart said.

"Nick is good man," Nifty Fifty Wife said. "Matías is a more traditional man. He would not be picking lice from Sofia. Not his job, he would say."

"Matías is a Daddy 1.0," I said. "The first model—the man makes the bread, and the wife takes care of the kids." I recalled Miles Brenton's comment to me last fall in the men's room of the Asphalt Green complex. He had said I was a Daddy 2.0, a guy willing to split the duties of child rearing fifty-fifty.

Lion Tamer said, "Avid is like a Daddy 2.0, when he's not working so hard. He likes to be with our kids and helps me. Very good man as well."

"Actually," Good Heart said, "if you want to get technical, Nick's really a Daddy 3.0, since Liz makes all the bread, and he does all the kid stuff."

I laughed. "Since you're cataloging people, what is Daniel's Daddy version?"

"My husband's only a Daddy 1.5. Does anybody know where I can get him upgraded on the cheap?" Good Heart said.

"When you find that place," Nifty-Fifty Wife said, "can you find out if you can take a husband straight from Daddy 1.0 to Daddy 3.0?"

We laughed, and I found one more nit in Good Heart's hair. "Seven."

■ ■ ■

Later that week, I got Broadway tickets to a show called *Wish You Were Here*. It was a revival of a 1950s musical that takes place at Camp Karefree, a mountain retreat for adults. The review in the paper said it was a "cross between *Dirty Dancing* and *Melrose Place*." It would have been perfect for Liz—lots of kissing, singing, and dancing. But we didn't go, because Liz walked through the apartment door an hour before the show and announced that she had lice. One of the nurses on the floor had seen her scratch her head repeatedly and had offered to inspect her scalp. I had to apply the treatments to her before she was allowed back to the hospital the next day.

I sent our babysitter, Wanda, home and went to work on the lice invasion force that had beset Liz. The kids were asleep already, so they didn't see me douse their mother's hair with olive oil, in order to asphyxiate the bloodsucking beasts. While the olive oil soaked into her scalp and hair, hopefully depriving the bugs of their oxygen, I made Liz a quick egg-white omelet with cheese. It was accompanied by a slice of wheat toast, spread with her favorite strawberry preserves.

She glumly pushed the food into her mouth. "I can't seem to catch a break. I was so looking forward to it."

I paused. "How about I download the songs from the musical soundtrack and we listen to it while I pick your nasty nits? Not the same as going, but better than nothing. We can imagine our own Broadway extravaganza." I did a little mock tap dance.

She smiled at me. Happy Liz has a smile that always gives my stomach butterflies.

From the newspaper review, I knew the plot of the musical. I shared it with Liz as I went online to get the soundtrack. A young woman named Teddy Stern takes a getaway holiday with her friend, Fay Fromkin, to think about whether she wants to marry Herman Fabricant, a man she doesn't love. As expected, the quirky characters bounce around the camp doing all sorts of romantic hijinks to each other, until true love blooms. In the end, Teddy accepts the marriage proposal of Chick Miller, who is a waiter/dancer for the resort. He also happens to be a law student—of course. Their big romantic dance scene—a showstopper—happens beneath the torchlight fires and is choreographed to the song "Tripping the Light Fantastic."

In a few minutes, the opening big-band sound of the overture began to play over our sound system's speakers, and Liz seemed to lose some of the stress of the day. The sound quality of the sixty-year-old RCA recording was not high-fidelity. Forty minutes later, I washed out the olive oil and applied a pasty mixture of conditioner and baking soda to her slick blond hair. I began to pull the metal lice comb through small clusters of her hair, careful to separate the raked clean hair from the contaminated hair. By this time, Liz was sipping on some white wine I had poured her, and, oddly, she seemed relaxed. Her eyes were closed; the music continued playing in the background. My skill at lice combing without ripping out hair had vastly improved over the last several days.

In the soundtrack, we reached a comical song entitled "Don Jose (of Far Rockaway)." It was the big number for Itchy, the camp's social director, and a love interest for Teddy's friend Fay. Itchy, in a thick North Jersey accent, crooned that he was better than any Casanova, and that he was "the man that no woman could resist…till I kiss you, oh, you'd never been kissed." Liz giggled. She was a sucker for romantic comedies.

"Passions flame when girls hear my name," Itchy continued.

In tune with the music, I joined him in iambic pentameter: "Nick the househubby…a man most chubby."

In response, Liz sang, "You're a teddy bear…who minds Maude and Claire."

"I'm married to their mother…who is like no other."

"You sing out of tune…and you are a loon."

I excused myself for a moment, and returned from the kitchen with the dozen roses I had hoped to give her before going to the show. "I should've been giving you flowers at least once a week for all the things I've messed up lately."

"It doesn't seem to me that you're messing things up now."

Rather than speak, I kissed her. I wrapped my arms around her and hugged her tightly for the first time in a long while. I didn't care much that her long hair was covered in a thick mixture of conditioner and baking soda, which slimed me. I didn't care that she was wearing medical scrubs that smelled from hospital antiseptic and dried sweat. Liz had that effect on me still. I didn't care anymore that I was not in California. It no longer seemed important to be eating pizza and writing code with my bros, for some shoestring start-up company. I cared that I was with my wife and kids. I wanted to stop imagining what I thought things ought to be. We had love.

"What's with all the romance tonight?" Liz said. She stroked my cheek.

"I've realized something."

She sighed. "Is this related to that big talk we are supposed to have at some point?"

I nodded. "I want romance again. You're the great love of my life, and I want to show you every day how much I love you."

Her face fell into a soft smile. For a moment, I thought she was going to cry. "That was not what I thought we were going to be talking about, but frankly I like your idea much better." Liz was a hopeless romantic at heart. She had a stack of romance novels hidden under our bed to prove it.

We kissed a little longer this time.

I took Liz's hand. "I know we've talked about it already, but I'm really glad that you're joining this practice. I know that you're still going to have long hours, but I'm really excited for us. You've worked hard for this opportunity. Being back in San Francisco doesn't seem as important anymore. Staying here in New York is the right thing for you—for us—and the kids."

"Are you still looking for a job in New York?"

"I like being home. I didn't think I would, but I feel good now that I can be here all the time for the kids. I like writing code, but I don't miss all the politics and stress of the workplace. I was thinking that maybe once the kids are in school full-time, I could do my thing in the whole 'freeware space.'"

"What's freeware?" Liz said

"That's where people from around the world write free software, so others don't have to buy programs from money-hungry companies. An example of freeware is the Linux operating system."

"How can you make money at that?"

"You don't, and that's the beauty. Everybody is equal in the digital world," I said.

"But isn't that going to be a problem, if you don't get a salary?"

"How is that a problem? I'm lucky enough to have married a rich doctor. I don't have to be the big breadwinner anymore." I spun her around in a ballroom-dance move.

Liz clutched me, à la tango style. "Here's to the women's revolution, I guess. You certainly are 'Livin' La Vida Loca.'"

"Shame on you—was that a vapid pop culture reference? I must be rubbing off on you."

Liz kissed me again. "You're the love of my life; I should hope so."

The *Wish You Were Here* soundtrack had reached its big finale. The entire cast sang, as the two love birds, Teddy and Chick, danced across the campground. The encore of "Tripping the Light Fantastic" kicked in, and Liz and I did our own mock dance about the living room. We giggled, until I tried to swing and dip her like they do on the dance shows. Instead of executing a flawless move that would have won me rave reviews from a television audience, I lost my balance, and we went crashing into a bookcase.

As I struggled to help Liz up from the pile of books that had fallen around her, it was unclear if the deafening crash or our tear-streaked laughter had prompted Maude to open her bedroom door. "I can't sleep. There was a loud bang."

"Everything's all right, sweetheart," Liz said. "Go back to sleep. Mommy and Daddy just tripped, not too fantastically."

Maude noticed that Liz's hair was a tangled mess from the application of conditioner and baking soda. "Is Daddy going to cut your hair too? Run, Mommy."

"Mommy has lice, sweetheart. Daddy was trying to get the bugs out like he did for you and Claire."

Maude nodded. My cell phone rang, and I answered. It was ten o'clock at night.

"Is Liz all right?" My mother-in-law was on the other end. "She didn't call us on her way home, and her father got worried." Actually, Mimi was the one who worried when Liz didn't make her daily call to her parents.

"Liz's had one of those days. Can she call you back? We're trying to get Maude back to sleep."

"What do you mean she 'had one of those days'? Is something wrong? Why is Maude up so late? Aren't you putting her to bed at an appropriate time each night?"

I interrupted. "Mimi, Liz will call you back. She has lice, and she just fell hard into a bookcase, so now is not a good time."

"Nick, what are you doing? Things seem so out of control..."

"Mimi, you're breaking up a little. I'm only getting every other word." I snapped the phone off. I loved the "bad connection and dropped call" excuse.

"I wanted to say hi to Grandma," Maude said.

"You can call her tomorrow. Let's go to sleep," I said.

"Can we do a group family hug?" Maude said.

Liz reached her arms out.

Maude screamed loudly for her sister.

I shushed her. "You don't have to wake up Claire Bear."

"It wouldn't be a family hug then," Maude said.

Claire appeared, blinking her eyes in the light of the living room. "Is it time for school?"

"Group hug!" Maude said.

We all gathered in a huddle and squeezed out our mutual love. I smelled a plethora of things at once: sweat, laundry detergent, baby shampoo, fruity conditioner, baking soda, dried pee in a pull-up, and hospital disinfectant. It was the aroma of my life.

Liz and I gathered up the kids and carried them into their bedroom.

My cell phone rang again. Mimi was not very patient. This time I had the sense not to pick up.

The *Wish You Were Here* soundtrack recycled again to the overture.

39055985R00142

Made in the USA
Middletown, DE
03 January 2017